I WAS A STRANGER

I WAS A STRANGER

By

GENERAL SIR JOHN HACKETT

1978

CHATTO & WINDUS

LONDON

Published by
Chatto & Windus Ltd
40 William IV Street
London WC2N 4DF

✳

Clarke, Irwin & Co. Ltd.
Toronto

First published October 1977
Second impression October 1977
Third impression January 1978
Fourth impression June 1978

British Library Cataloguing in Publication Data
Hackett, Sir John, b. 1910
  I was a stranger
  1. Great Britain. Army. Airborne Division,
     1st
  2. Soldiers—Great Britain—Biography
  3. Escapes
  4. World War, 1939–1945—Personal
     narratives, British
  I. Title
  940.54'21'0924   D805.N/
  ISBN 0-7011-2211-0

Printed and bound in Great Britain by
REDWOOD BURN LIMITED
Trowbridge & Esher

AUTHOR'S NOTE

THIS is the story of something that took place in Holland after the battle which the English call the Battle of Arnhem and the Dutch the Battle of Arnhem–Oosterbeek.

It is not the story of that battle, which was no more than the occasion of the events related here. Nor do I see it as my own story. I have set down, as far as I understood it, what happened. I was myself concerned in what happened, most intimately, but do not find it particularly important that any part of all this happened to me.

In the summer of 1945 I sat down and wrote nearly the whole of this narrative while impressions were still sharp in my mind. It was not, however, until the summer of 1950 that I was able to finish it. Twenty-five years later I brought out again what was then written. I now offer a shortened version of it for publication, at least in part because there has been recent published reference to some of these events which has, at best, been incomplete.

December 1976   J.W.H.

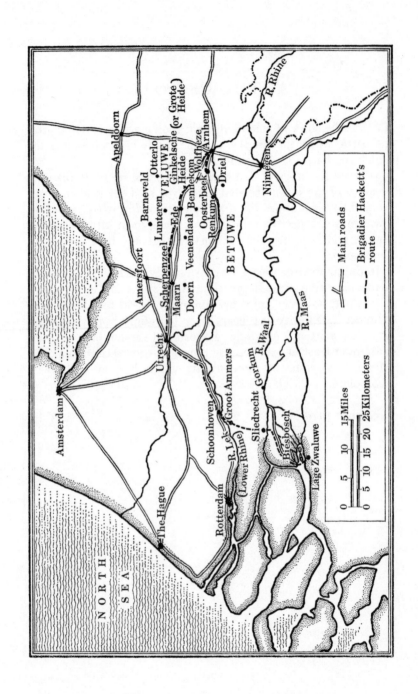

PROLOGUE

RATHER more than thirty years ago now, in the summer of 1944, when the impetus of allied armies surging eastwards from Normandy had petered out in the Low Countries, a bold plan was made by which it was hoped to bring the war in Europe to an early end. The intention was to lay an airborne carpet northwards across three river lines at once and then wheel the following armour and infantry righthanded down into the Ruhr. An airborne corps of three divisions, two American and one British, set out in mid-September of that year, in the biggest airborne operation ever attempted, to put this plan into operation. The two southernmost crossings were successfully consolidated. The most northerly and the most hazardous, where the British 1st Airborne Division with the Polish parachute brigade was set down near Arnhem on the Lower Rhine, was not.

Under my command in the operation was the 4th Parachute Brigade. I had raised this formation in the Middle East, taken it into battle in Italy, lived with it and in great part for it during nearly two years of war and was now to see it destroyed. I had been its midwife and was now to be its sexton.

The heavier allied forces which were to follow us up into the Arnhem bridgehead overland were held by the enemy and could not reach us, while our own weapons, as happens with airborne forces, were too light to withstand for long those which could be brought by land against us. The ammunition, food and other things we had carried in with us, enough for two days' fighting, had, with very little added in resupply by air, to last for eight. In the absence of reinforcement the issue could not long remain in doubt and in the end the remnant of the 1st Airborne Division was withdrawn across the river, two thousand men out of ten, leaving the badly wounded with the enemy. Of my own brigade, about a thousand strong in parachute infantry when we dropped, not many more than a hundred came out and I was not among them.

On the morning of 24th September, the day before the evacuation, a shell splinter had hit me in the stomach and caused severe internal injuries. Another had pierced my thigh.

9

1

THE blow came before the sound of the burst. I dropped on my knees, sick, bewildered and unhappy. It had not been a tree-burst like so many of them, detonating in the branches overhead. This violent thing had happened there on the ground, a few yards in front of me. Was it a mortar bomb or a shell? Had there been a whine before it? Had there been one of them, or two?

Anyway, whatever it had been there were probably more on the way. I crawled on my hands and knees to a shallow slit trench a few feet from me. I had taken refuge in this before and now tumbled into it once again, flattening myself against its side and thrusting a grateful face into cool sandy earth. The ground rang and shook as the rest of the concentration came down, spasmodic bursts in quick untidy groups. Then it was over.

I felt sick and shaken. I told myself not to worry: that would only be shock. What I had to find out was what was really wrong. There seemed to be a good deal of blood about, apparently coming from somewhere above my left knee. I carefully bent the leg: it was not broken. This was almost a disappointment, since I felt so confused and sick.

I shouted. There was another cry from the next pit. That would be the trooper from the Airborne Reconnaissance Squadron, Fred Gough's people, the man who had come back with me after my own visit to the Squadron, to guide the newly arrived party of Poles to where I wanted them, which was in that part of the Brigade sector.

'How is it with you?' I shouted.

He shouted back 'My leg is broken.'

I wriggled my own injured leg about. It worked. Something would now have to be done about his.

There was a dull, singing little pain in my middle, as though someone had punched me hard in the solar plexus. Perhaps the nose cap of whatever it was that had burst had bounced up and hit me there.

I looked around the safe and friendly little trench, reluctant to leave it for the chill, hostile world outside. Against one corner stood a branch, roughly trimmed as a stick with a forked top. I took it up.

Outside the trench the concentration, which had seemed to be directed especially at our two selves, was over. The shells were still falling somewhere, as usual. I knew from the last few days of moving about the remnants of my brigade, which was holding the Eastern half of the Oosterbeek perimeter, how they seemed to follow you around wherever you went.

Divisional Headquarters in the Hotel Hartenstein was less than a hundred yards away. There was some sort of a medical aid post, I knew, in the cellars. I took the stick I had found and crawled wearily out of the trench.

'All right,' I shouted to the man. 'I'll get help.'

It was queer to be walking again under the sad grey sky, over the well-known turf, with the torn limbs of the trees upon it, the wrecked jeeps and the occasional blood-soaked blanket. Bits of equipment were scattered around and here and there were men, some walking about, some digging, some just lying. This was only a resumption of my journey, interrupted a few minutes back, but there was now a dreamlike quality upon it, as though I had passed out of one world into another. I felt very odd and was irritated that the feeling was not passing off. Perhaps it would soon. We were all rather tired.

I had come into this hotel, which was the Headquarters of the 1st Airborne Division, many times before.

To begin with, when what was left of the 4th Parachute Brigade after two days of close fighting in the woods had joined the Air Landing Brigade and Divisional Troops in the Oosterbeek position, I had used the main steps and the hotel's front door. The concentrated artillery bombardment of the last few days had not then begun. After that, when the upper floors had been evacuated, I used the side steps leading down to the cellars. I now went down these again, past the huddled shapes of orderlies and clerks, worn out and sleeping in the little time of rest allowed them.

The door to the Aid Post was the first out of the concrete passage on the left. Inside there was a young medical officer, harassed but efficient, trying to deal with many more casualties than his resources allowed. There was blood and torn clothing on the floor. Men were strewn about with that air of settled resignation upon them which you see on the wounded once the army medical people have taken them in charge. Their future is now no longer in their own hands. They know there is no more for them to do — except keep quiet.

Someone offered me a chair but I told him about the trooper. The medical officer at once set about organizing a stretcher party: I think he took it out himself. The shelling around us had begun again by then.

'What's wrong?' they said to me.

'Leg,' said I, 'but not broken'.

I took off my webbing equipment and put it by and sat down on a chair. Scissors ripped off my battledress trousers, now soaked in blood, and I could see the holes where a smallish piece of metal seemed to have gone through the left thigh. It had missed the bone. They gave me a cup of tea and put on a first field dressing and then, as I still felt sick and queer, sat me down on the floor with an injection of morphia. My stomach ached badly from the blow it had had. Just to put my head back increased the fierce pain there.

I sat between two N.C.O.s or private soldiers, wedged tight. Our legs were stretched out and our backs were leaning against what seemed to be a bedstead. There was nothing any of us could do except to try not to disturb the others when he moved.

I was worried about my command. When the thing burst I had been walking back with the man from the Reconnaissance Squadron to the few small trenches holding the remnants of my brigade headquarters. These were hardly more than three hundred yards from the Headquarters of the Division. We had set up in them the day before when the Brigade Headquarters house, which, according to the sign outside it, was once a little private technical school, had ceased to be in the front line of the brigade sector, where it had been for some days, and had now found itself instead, in a situation possibly unusual for a brigade headquarters, out beyond it.

The Germans had come to me there in an armoured personnel carrier under a Red Cross flag. They said they found themselves obliged to put down a mortar concentration on the disputed ground at the crossing on the Utrecht–Arnhem road, which was just in front. This was where our main dressing station was located, divided between two hotels, the Schoonord and the Vreewijk, one on each corner of the main road on the Arnhem side of the crossing. There must have been three hundred or more of our wounded in them, which the Germans knew well. Unless we moved all troops eight hundred yards further back from the crossroads, the German officer said, they would have to put the concentration down just there. After several exchanges I agreed to move back my forward positions (a fine name that was, for a handful of stouthearted men in holes in the ground!) just two hundred yards and back we had to come. That left brigade headquarters out in front. It could stay out there, what was left of it, and the men still there could go on fighting it out from the house. This stood on a useful bit of ground. I took out one or two clerks and signallers and dug them in a hundred yards further back. There had to be some sort of a communication centre as a tactical headquarters, though it was unusual in normal staff procedures for a Tac H.Q. to be set up in rear of Main.

We were all friends in the brigade headquarters. In Egypt, Palestine, Tunisia and Italy we had found out about each other. I do not think any one of us would have chosen to be anywhere else when we jumped in, or in any other company.

Few of us were left now. Bruce Dawson, the Brigade Major, had been killed by a bullet, fighting at close quarters in the woods near Wolfheze, on the third day of the brigade's battle — 20th September. George Blundell, the Intelligence Officer, had been shot dead almost at the same time. Bobby Temple, G.S.O. 3, had had his arm broken by another bullet, also on that morning. He was still with us, in pain and trying to do far more to help out than was fair. Bill Kennett, who ran our signals, had been captured in the woods trying to keep his wireless sets going. Dick Bonham Carter, that kindest of doctors whose business in peace was healing children, had stayed there with his wounded and been taken too. Jimmy James, an old member of the brigade staff who had managed to get back to us on attachment for the battle, had also, I believed, been killed. When we got the remnant of the brigade into the haven of peace (as it seemed to us on that third night, by comparison with where we had been) of the main divisional position I had been ordered by General Roy Urquhart, the Divisional Commander, to organize the defence of the Eastern sector, while Pip Hicks, the sound and sensible Infantry Brigadier fifteen years my senior who was commanding the airlanding brigade, held the Western. The southern flank of each was on the Rhine.

The Divisional Commander had added to the remainder of my brigade such other troops as he could find. They included what was left of the First Airborne Reconnaissance Squadron, a fine unit though now without its splendid commander, Major Fred Gough; some good men out of the glider pilots, all sergeants, trained to operate as infantry soldiers of the highest quality once they had landed their gliders; Boy Wilson's Independent Parachute Company, picked troops, who had marked our dropping zones when we came in; and a handful of men from the Royal Army Service Corps, who had jumped in with a resupply mission as though from another planet, clean and tidy and full of English breakfast. In their very first battle as infantry they demonstrated the soundness of the 1st Airborne Division's policy of making every member of it a fighting man. All these, with the remnants of my own three battalions, the 10th, 156th and 11th, now no more than about forty, sixty and seventy strong respectively, and a handful of South Staffords stoutly led by Major Robert Cain, gave us a total strength under 4th Para Brigade command of some five hundred, more or less, to defend the two thousand-odd yards of our share of the perimeter. That included what in my own view were possibly the best fighting men of the lot, the remains of brigade headquarters with its Defence Platoon, the Brigadier's own little private army, and the Signal Section. What was left of them were now holding the brigade headquarters house, the Technische Handels School, out in front.

To act as Brigade Major in Bruce Dawson's place I had asked for 'Tiny' Madden. He was what was described as 'G.S.O. 2 Air' at Division, a staff officer whose primary task, now that the Division had been brought by air into the battle, had largely come to an end. He was an old Desert Rat, like me, whose regiment of Royal Horse Artillery (they were still called that, though they had lost their horses) I had known well in the 7th Armoured Division in the desert and held in high regard. Tiny, a charming, efficient and cheerful person, was always very much at home in 4th Para Brigade, with its Middle Eastern background, and was greatly liked. He was allowed by Division to come to me as Brigade Major and did so with alacrity, bringing his scanty kit the few hundred yards from the Division's headquarters to my own and coming out with me at once to look around our sector. For the few hours he was with the brigade he was a fulfilled and happy man. A mortar bomb killed him the same morning as we were standing on the lawn of that brave and compassionate woman, Kate ter Horst, whose house hard by was full of airborne wounded. When the bomb fell we were discussing how to organize a stronger force for Londsdale, who was holding the ground near there round Oosterbeek Church. That was two days ago. Since then there had been very few of the brigade headquarters staff left. There was Jasper Booty, the Staff Captain, smiling and unshakeable, Colin Harkess, the Brigade Supply Officer, a cocky and courageous little Scot, and Staff Sergeant Pearson, whose proper office was chief clerk on brigade headquarters but who, from the time

15

it was formed in Egypt round about Christmas 1942, had always been a sort of nanny to the lot of us. That, with Bobby Temple, doing as much as he could with a broken arm, was all.

The night before, in another cellar of the same building where I was now, the Divisional Commander had told me to take under command about two hundred men of Sosabowski's Polish Parachute Brigade, ferried across the Rhine after their drop on the south bank. I had been setting about putting them into the defensive layout when my own mishap occurred.

All this was in the past now. A curtain had come down. Lying in the cellar, I was wondering how things were in the 4th Parachute Brigade and reflecting that something had now to be done about these Poles too, when the Divisional Commander, Roy Urquhart, came in. He knelt down beside me, his usual confident and kindly self. With him was Iain Murray, the Lieutenant Colonel commanding a Wing of the Glider Pilot Regiment. I told them my leg was hurt and that a nose-cap or splinter or something had hit me in the body but seemed somehow to have been kept out by my equipment. I was pillowed on a little fleecy cloud of morphia at the time. I wanted to hand over my charge sensibly and lucidly but felt I was making rather a hash of it.

Murray was to take my sector over, which relieved me greatly, for I had no one to hand it to. All three lieutenant colonels in the brigade were now casualties and there was only one battalion second-in-command. That was Major Dickie Lonsdale of 11th Para Battalion, whose C.O., Lieutenant Colonel George Lea, was missing. Dickie was doing so well with his mixed command at the southern end of the sector, where it came down to the river bank, that the General agreed to take his force out of the brigade and keep it on as a separate command directly under Division.

There was little enough, as Roy Urquhart probably knew better than anyone else, for me to hand over. I had myself walked or crawled round as many of the positions as I could, encouraging the men in them to sit tight and hit back when they were able, sending out to where it was most wanted what very little food and ammunition even Colin Harkess could find and trying, in general, to keep the enemy out of the brigade position. It was no Hindenburg line we were defending but we were all right. I remembered Jasper Booty, two days before, perched on the side of the slit trench in which I was sitting in the back garden of the technical school, while shells were exploding nearby. He was twirling around his finger the red beret with the bullet hole in it and grinning cheerfully.

'These Germans!' he shouted above the din 'their trouble is they don't know what to do!'

Roy Urquhart, with certainly more on his mind than his manner ever showed, wasted no time there in the cellar. After I had told Iain Murray all I could he was taken off, leaving me feeling a poor fish to have packed up for what seemed so little. I felt more confused and sick than ever. Time seemed to be standing still.

Graeme Warrack came in, the big, gentle man who was the senior medical officer in the Division. We were good friends. I had often teased him about the so-called medical comforts (including brandy and even, it was rumoured, champagne) which were said to be at his disposal but which he never made available to his friends. Here, I told him now, was our big chance. He had every excuse to give me a generous tot of brandy with no trouble at all to a good Scots conscience. He vowed if there was a drop of the stuff anywhere I should have it and off he went, only to come back soon to tell me sadly there was none. Knowing how bare the cupboard was all round I should have been surprised if he had found any.

My mind is not at all clear about all that happened while I lay on the stone floor of the cellar. I remember a visit from Padre Harlow, Senior Chaplain to the Division and an old friend from earlier days in the war, in Syria; I was, as always, glad to see him.

I remember too when some time later they brought in my own Staff-Sergeant Pearson. A tree-burst had got him and there were splinter wounds in his back and shoulder. He was cheerful enough to begin with and sat up while they dressed his injuries. Later I saw him leaning back with his eyes closed and was shocked and grieved to see how tired he was, this man for whom I had so deep a liking and regard.

It was early afternoon now: I must have been in the cellar for about four hours. During this time the shelling and mortaring had not stopped. Often the building shook to a direct hit and glass could be heard splintering upstairs while plaster fell upon us in the cellar. I knew nothing of how the battle was going but did not see why there should have been much change from its pattern of the past few days. Then, from certain whisperings between the Medical Officer and two staff officers, it was clear to me that something else was afoot, something that concerned us, lying there in the cellar. A glance or two of compassion from the younger of the staff officers told me all I wanted to know. The wounded were to be handed over to the enemy's care. I was a little irritated that they should try to conceal it. Perhaps I knew as well as anyone that the dressing-stations in the Schoonord and the Vreewijk hotels, once in no-man's land, were now firmly held by the Germans. It was now clearly impossible to evacuate casualties anywhere but into German hands. If they wanted to break the news to me gently, and at the last moment, let them. I could not help enjoying, when it came, the solemn but determined embarrassment of the young officer who had to tell me. He was so like anyone's mother with the castor oil.

The Medical Officer, for whom my admiration by then was unbounded, told me that a jeep would take a load of us through our own and the enemies' lines to St. Elizabeth's Hospital in Arnhem town. Some of those to go were badly hurt and stretcher bearers were few: would I mind considering myself walking wounded as far as the jeep? I was a little ashamed that he should feel obliged to ask me this so civilly and agreed at once. They helped me to my feet and I walked up the cellar stairs again, out into the mournful grey of the late September afternoon. A jeep marked with red crosses stood in the drive only a few yards from the slit trench in which I had lain that morning. There were stretchers on the jeep but the driver was missing. Shells were bursting round us as the Medical Officer charged off in a blaze of anger to find him. I stood by the jeep and waited, without trousers, shivering with cold. Just then a shell burst with a huge rending clang in a tree immediately behind and it seemed to me, in the hazy detached state I was in, not at all remarkable when a long black hard-looking thing of indeterminate shape whirred swiftly down over my right shoulder and disappeared into the ground beside the jeep's front wheel. I was interested to have seen so big a shell-splinter in flight so plainly, and thought how fast it must have been going to vanish thus completely into the ground, leaving a clean outline of its shape upon the surface.

At last the driver came. I climbed into the jeep and sat beside him. He did not seem quite to know what to do, while shells went on exploding around us. I helped him to start the jeep by pulling out the choke and we drove off, out through the hotel gate and down right-handed onto the main Arnhem road. Almost at once we were passing the old 4th Brigade Headquarters house, still with the sign up—T.H.S. for Technische Handels School in big letters. Nothing was moving there now.

18

We were on the piece of road where Colin had frightened the quarter-master so unkindly by telling him, quite truthfully, as he drove him down it, how it was usually swept with machine-gun fire. I remembered how Pearson had given me a kindly reproof for driving in and out so often in our one borrowed jeep: this might attract the attention of the enemy who in this confused situation were not more than a few hundred yards away.

We were now passing the houses at the northern end of the brigade sector where C Company of 156 were holding on. There were probably not more than thirty of them now, under Geoff Powell's command. With a few more from other companies this was all that remained of the battalion. Over there on the left was where a handful of glider pilots were still fighting hard. In the ravaged buildings to the right the remnants of Boy Wilson's Independent Company were putting up a fine performance. We were now coming to the crossroads where the two battered hotels, the Schoonord and the Vreewijk, had housed the main dressing station, where ragged Red Cross flags still hung and there were hundreds of our wounded. The confused uproar of the battle grew louder as we drove on into it under our own Red Cross. I could now see around me German troops in action behind cover.

By the Vreewijk Hotel the driver slowed down and made as though to turn in.

'Where are you going?' I said.

'In here,' said he.

'Why?'

'Well, this is where they usually go.'

'Didn't they tell you to go to this Elizabeth Hospital in the town?'

'This the M.D.S.,' he said. 'This is where we usually put them.'

'You drive on to that Elizabeth Hospital,' said I, 'or I'll break your bloody neck.'

I do not think I could have broken an egg.

On we went. There were the houses beyond the M.D.S. to the east, where the remnant of 10th Battalion, thirty or forty strong, had put up as hard a fight as any around the perimeter: where that best of young officers Peter Saunders had been killed, and Ken Smyth, the Colonel, was badly wounded for the second time and Peter Warre was gravely wounded too, and taken prisoner. With no officers left the handful of 10th Bn. men remaining, bewildered and leaderless, had begun to drift back. They were soon led up again to fight on in the same

19

houses, now crumbling one by one to the fire of self-propelled guns. Flashes of recollection came as we drove. This was where Sergeant Bentley had gone back to bring his 3-inch mortar out. Other troops had relieved them and taken his mortar over. They had then themselves been driven from the house and left Bentley's mortar behind. Bentley and the mortar had come in on the same parachute and came now to get it back.

There still lay the upturned lorry which had driven full of straying Germans right through the divisional position from behind us, following (by accident I think) a Red Cross jeep and so not-fired on, to blow up on 10th Battalion's mines just before reaching the safety of their own friends. We had watched that happen and no one got out.

Now the jeep was travelling among German soldiers standing in the open, plainly to be seen in their grey-green uniforms. Helmeted heads were peering out of houses here and there; German military vehicles stood around. By the roadside one of those accursed self-propelled guns, our greatest bane, was moving into position. It was like seeing wild animals outside their cages.

We were on cobbles now, moving fast and roughly. Every bump gave me acute discomfort. I was bitterly cold and my teeth chattered. All the same there was some comfort in what I saw, grim though it was. Torn vehicles, German bodies, great craters in the road, shattered houses just behind the German forward position showed where some great gunners of the Second Army's medium artillery, of the 64th Regiment I think, had put down their shells. I remembered the encouragement we had taken from the sound of those concentrations screaming overhead; the temperate skill with which the Divisional Commander of Royal Artillery, Robert Loder Symonds, another old friend from the desert, had got them on target at maximum range; and the speed with which the British guns, ten miles and more away, had responded.

On we went, jolting painfully. By the roadside I saw half a body, just naked buttocks and the legs joined on and no more of it than that. There was no comfort here. It was like being in a strange and terrible nightmare from which you longed to wake and could not.

Now we were coming into the town. Did the driver know the hospital, I asked? He had been there, he said: it was up to the left somewhere. We turned up. German S.S. troops were moving in and out of houses looting. I felt a deep and personal hatred for every one of them.

We were stopped by an under-officer of sorts. I spoke my halting German: we wanted St. Elizabeth's Hospital. The young man turned to me. He was big and blond and I found him enormously unpleasant. Everything about him was cocksure and beastly, his nose, his mouth, his tunic, his manner.

Was I an officer? I was.

'Come over here boys and have a look,' he called out to the others, 'here's an officer!'

They ran their thick fingers over my one remaining shoulder strap. The badges of rank on it, the crown and three stars of a brigadier, clearly meant nothing to them. Well, well, an officer. And wounded, eh? Yes, we wanted to get to this hospital. Slowly the under-officer pushed the British driver out and got in himself. A bigger and even more beastly blond winked at him and jerked his thumb first at the jeep and then back at himself. I could not remember a gesture I had ever found more hateful. The cocksure beast nodded, started the jeep and drove off.

But he did drive us to the hospital, up an incline to a small rounded enclosure which was formed by twin curved ramps rising to the main entrance on the first floor, with a door into the ground floor below it. There were civilian men and women there, wearing Red Cross armbands, some with white-painted steel helmets. In the background were hospital nurses and nuns. The men with Red Crosses lifted off the laden stretchers. They brought another for me, when I stepped out of the jeep, and I lay on it very uncomfortably with my head back flat and the bruised muscles of my stomach aching, thinking how odd it was to drive up to a hospital sitting in a jeep and then lie down on a stretcher to be carried inside.

There were no shells bursting here. There seemed no noise at all, just then, and none of these people had the look on them of being in a battle, like those I had left in Oosterbeek. This was another world.

We were laid out in a row—a dozen stretchers, perhaps twenty—in a stone hall. I was miserably cold. Someone gently raised my head and put a haversack beneath it and a man brought me a blanket. They gave me a cup of thin soup.

The light was failing now. One by one the stretchers were carried off down a dark passage. Mine was nearly the last but not quite. Staff Sergeant Pearson was after me. Soon we were carried in to where there was a light, Pearson and I together, and a pleasant-looking R.A.M.C. doctor in a white coat, whom I knew but could not just then name, was examining people on

21

a table, filling in cards and passing them on. Pearson was last. We lay side by side on the floor and I looked at him lying silent there, his eyes closed and his face grey and drawn. I earnestly hoped it would be well with him. I wondered whether the pleasant-looking doctor ought not to look at him first, made a half protest, let it go and climbed up to lie on the table. The man in the white coat looked at me and I did not much like the thoughtful look in his eye. I told him of my leg, and the blow in the solar plexus which had made my abdominal muscles so weak and sore.

He opened my smock and then the battledress jacket and shirt, looking rather intent.

'There's a hole here,' he said, half to me, I thought, half to himself. 'Is there another one?'

I didn't think so. He ran his hands over my stomach and found a brilliant star-shaped pain. I may have made a noise. Then I looked at his face and had a real fright. He was beginning to bustle about and there was a sudden note of urgency in the air. Very soon I was being carted off on a stretcher by two bearers and found myself under a bright flat light with someone standing there, shrouded to the eyes in white, with other dim white figures near him. A mask came down upon my face, with something heavenly dropping on it. I breathed in deeply and most gratefully. With the best possible will in the world I slipped under the anaesthetic into unconsciousness.

2

It seemed to be some sort of a passage, dim and gloomy. I was in a hard little bed propped up in a sitting position. As more of the sensible world came to my attention I was aware of a good deal of constriction round my middle, something interfering with the free movement of my left leg and a stone waterbottle warm against my feet. A thing that looked like a hat-stand stood beside the bed with a can hung on it, from which a tube disappeared under the bedclothes. There was an unusual hard sort of feeling at my right ankle and a general wetness at the foot of the bed.

A soldier in battle dress with a pleasant face stood looking down.

'How is it?' he said.

'Feet wet,' said I.

He whipped back the bedclothes and fiddled with the hard feeling in my ankle.

'Sprung a leak,' said he, adjusting something.

'Who are you?' I asked.

'They call me the plumber,' he said. 'I look after the hydraulics.' He tidied up the end of the bed and went away.

I felt no sickness at all and, remembering what it felt like to vomit after an anaesthetic, was content and grateful. Something warned me that in the present situation vomiting would not be pleasant. My fingers found a mass of wadding around chest and stomach but very soon stopped exploring. All that was clearly better left alone.

There were other people moving about beyond the screens round my bed. Where these were open at the foot women could be seen whispering amongst themselves. Some seemed to be nuns, others nurses. The light was very poor.

Someone in a white smock appeared, a man with a dark ugly clever face and large intelligent eyes. I knew that he was one of ours, from the Airborne Division, but could not remember his name. Anyway, this was clearly the boss. He spoke to the women in Dutch about the hydraulics and showed them what to do. He said what sounded like 'Krag dit' once or twice and I wondered what it meant.

He said to me, 'How are you feeling?'

I said, 'All right.'

He looked at me in a reflective sort of way and went off.

A kind, half-remembered face I had seen before they operated on me appeared again. I knew who this was now—Shorty Longland, a surgeon in one of the Parachute Field Ambulances, not 133, my own, but some other.

'Well,' he said. 'We've patched everything up. You ought to be all right now. They'll look after you. Lipmann Kessel did it. Quite a job.' He seemed to be going away somewhere and said goodbye.

I remembered now that Lipmann Kessel was the man I had just seen, the man with the dark, intelligent face. He was another parachuting surgeon, a South African.

I had some more morphia. It was lovely, like parachuting in still air while you can still enjoy the ride, after the slipstream has gone by and the canopy has developed, before the ground begins to come up at you and you have to think about landing. The difference was that you were now buoyed up on this morphia cloud from below and not suspended by a harness from above; but the feeling was the same, of floating in total and timeless detachment, in infinite space.

Later I was awake again, more awake. The plumber came and went. The hard feeling in my ankle turned out to be a metal tube. There seemed to be a constant group of women gossiping in whispers at the foot of my bed.

'Go away!' I shouted rudely.

They looked at me in wonder.

'Go away,' I said.

They smiled in a friendly way and went on chatting.

The stone water bottle was still there, now quite cold. I had kicked it down as far as I could with the other foot, so as not to disturb the tube in my ankle and make more work for the plumber, but nobody took it away. There was an orderly called Spencer who, I had been told, would look after me especially. He sometimes looked round the screen but not often.

'Take that bottle away,' I said, when he came after a long time to have another look. 'You're not taking this thing seriously.'

He grumbled to himself and took it out. Readjusting the screen he said loudly, 'Does anyone want the brigadier?'

I did not like Spencer.

Lipmann Kessel came again and put in another little tube, this time into a vein in my arm. He connected that up to the can on the hat-stand and undid the rubber tubing from the one in my foot. I always seemed to be hitched to something.

He told me I must drink nothing. He went further. He brought another rubber tube and poked it up my nose and down my throat. There seemed to be miles of it. He joined it up to another can, one with glass sides, through which I could see the bile, or whatever it was, filmy and yellow, being sucked up into water inside. The tube stayed there two days, or it could even have been three. It seemed a lifetime.

I smelt very badly. In the past four or five years there had been too many times to count when I had been filthy beyond words and this was the third time during the war that wounds in battle had brought me, after varying vicissitude, into a hospital. But I had never before smelt as badly as this. It did not occur to me just then to say anything about it. The people in the hospital had plenty to do and what they were doing for me was bound, by and large, to be right.

Through a door leading into my passage appeared the tall angular figure of Gerald Lathbury, the other parachuting brigadier in the Division, Commander of the 1st Parachute Brigade. It pleased me enormously to see him, for there was a warm and special friendship between us. He had a fine sense of the ridiculous, with an appearance that suggested arrogance. This was misleading. Those who got to know him well found (often to their surprise) that this highly intelligent and cour- rageous professional soldier was also a compassionate and modest man. He and I used to laugh at the same things and I always greatly enjoyed his company.

Gerald had had a little splinter in the back, he said, not much in the way of a wound but very annoying. We were pleased to see each other but had no more than a minute or two together. He could not stay long, he said, he was off. Though the hospital was in German hands it was not at all well guarded. He had been shown a chance of getting out and lying up somewhere and he was going to take it.

When he had gone I listened to the guns. Everyone was still hoping for an advance by the British Second Army and the arrival of 30 Corps, which in the original plan was expected to be up with us in two days, with the Guards Armoured Division in the van. Second Army guns were banging away and the German guns too.

There was a good deal of noise going on just then. In addition to the gunfire our own aircraft (Typhoons, I think) were hammering German armour in and around the town. All civilians except for a very few on essential services had been evacuated from Arnhem and all patients who could possibly be moved from St. Elizabeth's Hospital were also being taken away. There were only thirty or forty of us left now. I was told that we too would be moved soon. It was the 16th Parachute Field Ambulance, I learned, out of the First Brigade, which had moved into this hospital on 17th September, the very first day of the battle, with a surgical team which included Lipmann Kessel and Shorty Longland. There were also nursing orderlies and other staff. These had been working with the Dutch hospital people ever since, but the British were now being moved on, whenever this could be done, to prisoner-of-war camps. Longland had already gone, taken off at short notice with a convoy of patients. Kessel was now the only British surgeon left.

I think it was on the night after they had brought me in that I heard, dozing in my bed in the passage, the encouraging sound of a real barrage in the direction of Oosterbeek. I hoped that this might be at last the move of 30 Corps over the river and into our bridgehead. It was, instead, the covering fire for the evacuation of what was left of the First Airborne Division out of it. That was on 25th September, just eight days after the first airborne landings.

I slept, on and off, but could not eat or drink and was bored with the thing down my throat. Wanting something to drink was a long drawn out agony. Lipmann Kessel allowed me to rinse my mouth out once an hour with water. If I swallowed a teaspoonful no harm would be done — the tube would look after that — but no more. I kept beside me a little of the thin, milkless, almost sugarless tea the hospital provided and every couple of hours or so washed my mouth out with a drop of that. The astringent feeling was delicious. What I craved for was the prickly feel of brandy in my mouth but there was none.

A tall young Dutchman with a Red Cross armband looked around my screen and asked in English if I wanted anything.

'Yes,' I said, 'Cognac.'

A little later the same afternoon he came back, proudly holding up a medicine bottle with a few tablespoonfuls of brandy in it. I took the bottle and had a tiny swig. It was heaven! The Dutchman held out his hand for the bottle but I clung to it and would not give it back. He said it was all he had. It was very precious. I said it was the whole world to me and pleaded desperately to be allowed to keep it. He laughed and let me have what there was left. It became my treasure, the whole heart and centre of my little existence.

Every two or three hours I would suck in a little drop. I would say to myself, 'At the end of the next hour you may have another.' Then I would try not to look at the minute hand of the watch I still wore, creeping with deliberate and appalling slowness round the face. Twenty minutes more: this is unbearable. Half a lifetime later there would still be fifteen minutes to go and finally, an old, old man, I would watch the minute hand drag itself unwillingly to twelve.

I would then feel a great sense of peace and say: 'Good! If you're in such capital shape you can go on without it for ten minutes more.' Then I would fly into a rage and shout at myself that it wasn't fair. I would argue the point a great deal and finally, after heated discussion, agree on a compromise and slowly and lovingly drink my next little drop after only seven minutes more instead of ten.

I did not doubt for one moment that I would get well. The possibility of any other issue to the predicament in which I found myself never even crossed my mind.

Lipmann Kessel was pleased but seemed to take it all quite quietly for granted. There was no fuss on his part, no expression of relief. He told me that they had fished out a splinter a couple of inches square which had cut twelve perforations and two sections in the lower intestine. Walking, tea and soup, he mildly observed, had not been exactly the best sort of treatment for that complaint. Apart from the outstandingly brilliant piece of surgery he must have done, Kessel's attitude to me after the operation was as helpful as it could have possibly been. He never even hinted that there could be any other possible outcome than complete recovery. My confidence in him was complete.

I later discovered that a surgeon of the S.S. had advised him not waste his time on the operation he was about to do on me. 'In our service we say "Kopfschuss Bauchschuss spritzen",' the S.S. man had said – if it's a head or stomach wound give him an injection and leave it. Lipmann Kessel had insisted on going ahead and the German could not prevent him.

He told me that the field card tied to my bed upon which my injuries were recorded described me as a corporal. The Germans were taking more and more interest in the hospital every day. They still guarded the building rather loosely but German officers sometimes walked round it to see whether any more patients could be moved to the P.O.W. camp at Apeldoorn. The interest they might show in a senior officer could be embarrassing, so for the time being I was to stay a corporal.

On the third or fourth day the tubes came out of arm, ankle and throat and I set out my scheme for a Complete Personal Rehabilitation. I would be moved out of the passage into one of the smaller rooms, shaved, thoroughly cleaned, taken out of my filthy blood-soaked shirt and vest and put into a hospital smock, given some clean sheets and allowed a little more private life. They could then watch me get better.

Everything was done as I asked and a new life began. It was quieter now, in the little white room with the two other beds in it. The light streamed in through large windows just behind me, where I lay contendedly in cool clean sheets propped up on an air cushion. Not to smell any more was heaven.

The field card showed that I had now become a major. My companions in the room were a glider pilot officer called Robson with a fractured leg—he was to be moved out before long—and my poor old friend Kenneth Smyth, the Lieutenant Colonel who had been the Commanding Officer of the 10th Parachute Battalion in my brigade since we had first raised it in Egypt. He had been wounded in the arm on the third day, in the woods, and again in the stomach and spine during the tremendous fight put up by the remnants of his battalion in Oosterbeek, for the defence of the houses east of the M.D.S. He was paralysed from the waist down and lived—but only just—with tubes in his stomach. He was very low. He was to die a little later but we had been parted by then.

Quite early on I had seen a chubby, glowing face peering at me and had recognized with pleasure Danny McGowan, Roman Catholic padre to my own brigade, clean-looking, healthy and cheerful as ever. He now came to see me daily, while he carried out some of the strangest and bravest work I have ever known. Every day he used to go out from the hospital and walk over ground where the Division had fought, burying dead, registering such graves as were already marked, picking up the paybooks soldiers always carried (invaluable documents for Records), gathering in whatever was likely to be useful in the hospital from the huge quantity of miscellaneous material spilled around the countryside and doing a hundred-and-one other valuable jobs. He was always impeccably dressed in uniform as an Airborne chaplain, from the red beret on his head down to his polished black boots, clean and shining from head to foot. He went about by day quite openly, accompanied by a Dutch youth, moving freely among the German troops who were now working hard to prepare the defence of the area against the further attack expected from the British. Both wore Red Cross armbands but these were of little significance, after the traumatic events of the last two weeks, to German soldiers who saw them worn under a red beret. He was often stopped, sometimes threatened, but the astonishment, verging on disbelief, with which German troops saw a smart British Airborne captain walking freely amongst them, red beret and all, stood him in good stead. His real armour, however, was the transparent honesty of his purpose and the boldness of his approach. His command of German was poor but I knew what a determined person he was. I was almost sorry for any German who tried to obstruct him, when Danny McGowan was set on doing what he saw as his duty.

McGowan was the only English-speaking priest available to us in the hospital but he was a Roman Catholic. The strictness with which I had seen Catholic chaplains apply priorities which at best seemed dubious had before now made me restless. A predecessor of Danny's had made them quite clear. His first duty above everything else was to his Church. A general obligation to all those professing Christ came a long way second and the interests of the men in the brigade, as people, nowhere at all. I was greatly cheered when Danny came to us. His eyes may have been on the next world but he was aware that his work was in this, and that there was a war going on in it in which Christian values were at risk. It caused me no surprise to learn that in St. Elizabeth's Hospital he was bringing men together in the wards and corridors for prayer whether they were members of his own church or not. This was good, but was it, I wondered, enough? Men were dying. Some were devout Christians but were Protestants. Would he, I asked Danny, as a Christian priest deny them the sacrament of Holy Communion? He had to, he said, but it was clear that he had already given much thought to what he saw as a terrible dilemma. I pressed him. He suffered a great deal from his conscience, I know, but in the end it brought him to a decision which in all the circumstances he was certain must be right. He began to administer the sacrament to any who sought it.

There were other brave people in the hospital, among them the surgeons, for whom no praise is too high. I heard later that when an abdominal operation was interrupted by falling bombs Kessel had made the theatre staff lie down on the floor and joined them, keeping his hand with a swab in it over the patient's wound to hold the intestines in until he could go on again. Such things happened daily. There were also the Dutch nurses. They were still at work in the hospital when almost all the uniformed members of the Field Ambulance Unit had been taken off into captivity, in sufficient numbers to care for the dwindling number of patients. Some were lay women, others were nuns. All were volunteers. I never saw any sign of fear in these brave women as they went about what they were doing, undeterred by the crash of falling bombs or the noise of gunfire.

One of the nurses, whom I only knew as Isobel for I could never master her Dutch surname, had been on the point of going to an English finishing school in the Isle of Wight when war broke out. She was now just over twenty and so like a younger edition of a dear friend of mine in voice, face, walk and manner that I often used to laugh with pleasure when she came near. She and plain, patient, humorous Sister van der Sluis were the two who mostly looked after me. It was they who brought me paper and pencil for the letter I wrote to my wife and the one I began to General Urquhart and the account I was putting together of the brigade's action. I had no idea how these would ever reach their destinations but did not doubt that this would happen somehow.

Now too I began to learn from these girls a few words of Dutch. This would be useful to me when I tried to escape. I do not remember ever making a conscious decision that I would try to escape. I simply took it completely for granted that I would do so as soon as it was possible.

McGowan was my best source of help to prepare for escaping. From about the fourth day after Kessel's operation he began, at my request, to collect for me during his journeyings the things I would need. These included a pack and haversack, a clasp knife, a candle, some string and, among other things, a piece of equipment widely distributed among airborne forces known as an escape kit, of which there would certainly be a good many lying around. This contained a compass, a file, matches, a needle and thread, malted milk tablets, sticking plaster, a waterproof bag and other highly useful things, all packed in a transparent plastic case. I also wanted a couple of the yellow celanese triangles we used for recognition by our own troops.

Danny had hidden away for me my airborne smock, with the battle dress jacket, boots, silver cigarette case and other odds and ends I had jumped with and still had by me. They included the silver pencil Brigadier John Chrystall had given me after our time together on the Syrian Commission of Control, of which he had been President and I, convalescing from wounds in the Syrian campaign, had been the Secretary. This little silver pencil was important to me. It had been in my pocket in every action since 1941 and on every parachute jump. Without it I used to say I was quite unbattleworthy and I rather wanted to have it with me now against whatever might lie in the future.

Danny also found for me the sheets of the 1:50,000 maps I needed for my report. Such records as had been kept in the first few days of the brigade's battle — the headquarters had been too intimately concerned in that and too much on the move for these to be extensive — had been destroyed or scattered in the last untidy stages of the fight on the perimeter. Two brigade majors had been killed in succession and the Intelligence officer too. The G.S.O. 3 had been wounded and the Signals officer cap-- tured. The brigade commander and the chief clerk, almost the only people left who were in a position to compile a record, were towards the end too busy in the battle to be able to put anything down on paper about it and they too, Pearson and I, were casualties. I supposed that we were both now entered on the official lists as 'wounded and missing'. There would have to *be* a record of the brigade's action, all the same, if it could be put together, and this was what I was now trying to do in retrospect. The maps were easily found. The battlefield was strewn with them. Danny brought me all I needed, though he grew a little fretful when I tried to get him to describe events on them and insisted that he get the details right.

At my further request McGowan found from somewhere in the hospital a chess set. I had several games with Kessel, who was a much better player than I was, and an almost daily battle with the tall Dutch boy who had brought the cognac. I had also begun to do every day an intricate set of finger exercises which had once been taught me as an ancillary to keyboard practice on the piano. If I failed to escape and became a real prisoner-of-war it was my intention to study the piano and there was no point in not getting on with it now. The nurses, particularly the charming Isobel, used to whisper and giggle when they saw me at what they called my 'gymnastics'. It must have looked rather foolish but it all helped to make up a pattern with a purpose, leading somewhere. It gave me a routine which fitted into a plan. I knew what I was doing.

The tall Dutch boy and a sweet girl friend of his, both wearing Red Cross insignia, used to come in every day and give the soldiers whatever little comforts they could find, apples and home-made candy perhaps, with rough cigarettes which they had rolled themselves. I myself could not eat yet but I was glad to be able to smoke and took their simple cigarettes with gratitude.

I was making good progress. On the fifth or sixth day after the operation a Dutch nurse gave me a cup of thin soup. Soon I was getting three cups a day and before long tea as well. Then McGowan found on one of his expeditions a big tin of Ovaltine and Kenneth Smyth and I were given hot mixtures of it. I drank mine most gratefully.

Poor Kenneth was not doing well. Much of the time he was in a coma and even when he was fully conscious he could speak only with difficulty. We managed nonetheless, at intervals, to talk a good deal together and by the time I was promoted to tea I had had from him names and the material for citations for any decorations he wished to have recommended in his battalion. These I wrote out as best I could, with the intention of getting them into the right hands somehow or other later on. I wondered whether Kenneth would himself survive, to receive a richly deserved award for gallantry on his own account. He was almost completely helpless now and was being washed and handled like a little child. I did almost envy him once, a little. McGowan had found somewhere a bottle of splendid burgundy, Nuits St. George 1934 I think it was, and brought it down to us. I was allowed one little glass by Kessel but Kenneth might drink as much as he liked.

Every day Kessel brought me news from the outer world, heard secretly upstairs on a little military wireless set with dying batteries, the sort known as a No. 38, normally used between platoon and company headquarters. He also told me what was happening round the hospital. Allied air attacks were frequent and the hospital windows were suffering. The air effort still seemed to be mainly directed at German gun positions and dispersed tanks but our aircraft were also now attacking the main road-bridge across the Rhine which the 2nd Parachute Battalion of First Brigade had held so gallantly. Our aircraft got it in the end and broke it down: a beautiful job, I was told.

One day a Dutchman was brought to my bedside. His arm had been blown off in an air attack by our own Typhoons. He had asked to be allowed to shake hands with an Englishman.

One of the nurses, Sister de Lange, a pretty girl who was one of those helping me with my Dutch lessons, was also secretly looking after several of our men hidden outside the town. She used to go out to feed them and dress their injuries. One day she did not come. I heard that she too had been hit by one of our own bombs, and killed.

There was also a Dutch boy whom I used to see around the hospital. He had a large plain humorous face and a slight cast in one eye. He wore blue overalls and the troops called him Blue Johnny. The other one, who had brought me the cognac, they called Black Jack. I was to see more of Blue Johnny.

The Germans were pressing Kessel to get us all moved on to Apeldoorn and often a German doctor inspected the wards to see whom they could move. Kessel was polite but very firm. He said that it would be a waste of transport to move most of us, but they shifted Robson who had been lying with his leg wound in the corner bed, and I heard that Pearson had gone and that Peter Warre, very badly hurt in the shoulder, had been taken away too. There were arguments in the hospital now and then, I heard, and threatenings with hand grenades. One of our medical officers was said to have been shot dead by a drunken man of the S.S.

One day Kessel appeared with a German S.S. doctor. This was a very unpleasant-looking person, I thought, fat, fair and piglike, with little beady eyes.

'Here,' said Lippman Kessel before my bed, 'is an English major.'

The piglike person took off his glove and to my dismay held out his hand. My own line of action must clearly be to avoid notice or comment. I took the hand, which was damp and flabby, and shook it. I found this far from pleasant.

On about the eighth day after Kessel's operation I was promoted to custard, on the ninth I had a little bread and jam as well as Ovaltine and soup, and on the tenth I was given the full hospital diet with the Ovaltine as an extra. There was tea and bread and butter in the morning, a sort of stew mostly of potatoes at midday and tea and bread with a little meat in the evening. How, I wondered, could the Dutch find this food for us?

Everything in my inside now seemed to be in fine working order. I had listened for rumbles very early on and been intensely proud of them when they came. I imagined that when a bubble seemed to start at the very end and go apparently the whole way things were very good indeed. One day I broke wind: that was a triumph.

Kessel now said I should sit on the edge of the bed a little and waggle my legs to exercise the tissue round the scar. I did this. It was fine.

On the same day a man came to see me, a Dutchman wearing a Red Cross armband. He would have been about forty years old, spare of figure, with an intelligent bird-like face and a watchful eye. He told me that his name was Piet and that he knew about me.

I looked at him warily and said that there was nothing much to know: I was a major of the 1st Airborne Division, wounded as he could see, more or less a prisoner. That was all.

'Do you know Brigadier Lathbury?' he asked.

'Yes,' I replied, 'everyone knows Brigadier Lathbury.'

'I got him out of here,' said the man who called himself Piet.

We looked at each other for a long time. I knew I had to be careful. If there were a point in all this I was sure he would come to it.

I was grateful, I said at last, for all the kindness we had received from the Red Cross. That seemed safe enough.

'Never mind about that,' said Piet. 'Perhaps you heard of information coming from a Dutch civilian during the battle, about German tanks moving up?'

I had indeed heard of this. I remembered that when Roy Urquhart had got out of the predicament brought on by his visit up forward to Lathbury's brigade, when he had been pinned down for twenty fateful hours, he had come up to see me where my brigade was fighting and told me about it. That would have been on the Tuesday, the 20th. We had discounted this information somewhat but the tanks were there all right.

'Yes,' I said, 'I heard about it.'

'I brought that information,' said Piet. He gave me some of the details of it.

We looked at each other for a while again.

Then I thanked him politely for his trouble in coming to see me and there was another silence. I could only wait.

After a while he said, 'Would you know Lathbury's writing?'

I knew it very well.

'I think I might,' I said.

Out of an inside pocket he fished a wallet and unfolded from it a dirty scrap of paper written on in pencil.

The writing was all right. It was Gerald's without any doubt at all. It said that Piet was to be trusted and could help. I could talk to this man now.

'How are you mixed up in all this?' I asked. 'Who are you?'

'I am the head of the Resistance Movement here,' he said. 'They call me Piet van Arnhem.'

'What's your real name?' I asked.

'We don't use them,' he said. 'They call me Piet.'

'What's your real name?' I asked again.

He hesitated and from habit, it seemed, half looked round.

'Piet Kruyff,' he said.

We smiled at each other and I held out my hand. He took it.

'What can you do?' I asked.

'I can get you out of here,' he said.

We shook hands again and he went away.

3

THEY carried me up to the operating theatre again. The elastoplast was then taken off my stomach for the first time since the operation. All that could now be seen where the splinter had been removed was a single thin line from about the diaphragm to near the navel. It had all closed up entirely and looked marvellously neat and tidy. Lipmann Kessel was pleased. He whipped out some of the stitches and dusted the place with penicillin powder. Then he looked at the splinter's point of entry in my left side and the other wound where the fragment had gone through my left thigh, both of which were healing well. He cleaned these and strapped everything up again. He then removed from just below my left eye a fragment of the mortar bomb that had killed Tiny Madden and sent me back to the little white room from which I had come. That, as far as I can remember, was on the ninth day after the operation.

Four days later I was told that I could sit up out of bed for ten minutes or so. This was a tremendous occasion. Up to then I had only been allowed, during the last few days, to hang my legs over the side of the bed and waggle them a little. I now sat in a chair facing the window. Outside I could see buildings and grass. There was blue sky with a few clouds. There were several trees whose leaves were troubled by a gusty little wind and sometimes fluttered to the ground. It was impossible to look at all this evidence of the existence of a world outside without emotion.

I was back in my bed again, dozing contentedly in that quiet time there is in hospitals after the midday meal, when I suddenly became aware that Piet was standing in front of me.

'How are you?' said Piet.

'Pretty good,' said I.

'Can you walk a little?'

'I expect so. I haven't tried yet.'

'If you can walk out of the hospital within a quarter of an hour,' said Piet, 'I can take you away. If not, I may not be able to get you out at all.'

I was wide awake now. This had to be quick.

'Get hold of Kessel,' I said.

In no more than a minute or two Lipmann Kessel was there. McGowan was with him.

I put it to Kessel.

'Can I go?' I asked.

'You're the only judge,' said he. 'Your stomach's all right. Do you think you can do it?'

'I don't see why not,' said I, and thought for a brief moment. 'Yes,' I said. 'I'll go. Let me have my stuff.'

All I had in the way of clothing was what I had landed in, with odds and ends found in the hospital – but no trousers.

'You will want civilian clothes,' said Piet.

Blue Johnny appeared. Piet spoke quickly to him and he ran off. Piet went too.

Left alone to wait as patiently as I could I thought a little more. I was going to have to walk. I had not yet walked further than from my bed to the chair and back again. Walking might not be easy. I would need a good stick. There, standing behind Robson's old bed in the corner, was something I had not previously noticed.

It came back to me all at once how Roy Urquhart had paid a visit to my brigade headquarters, a month or so before, at Knossington in Rutland. When he had gone I missed my walking stick, a good ash plant I had bought in Oakham a little while before and was much attached to. All I could find instead was a springy, sad-looking thing with a shiny handle. Perhaps Roy had picked up mine by mistake. At a conference a week later, when he was giving final orders for the Arnhem battle, he had with him a stick that looked like mine. It now had a 'U' carved on it. I asked him if it was mine and offered the other one in exchange.

'Nonsense,' he said, 'I wouldn't own a stick like that!'

I thought he took my offer a little amiss and, thinking back, I could scarcely blame him. The other stick was a horrible one. I gave my own up for lost and bought another, this time at Bland's in Notting Hill Gate. It was in my hand when we jumped and when I was hit but then I had lost it.

Now here in the corner was exactly the same sort of stick. It had a 'U' carved on it. Perhaps Roy had given it to Robson, who had then been parted from it when they took him off to Apeldoorn. It was coming with me now and one day I would give it back to the General.

There was no time for further reflection. McGowan had returned and was bustling about, packing my small-kit into the haversack he had found for me and the battle dress jacket and airborne smock and all the rest of my possessions into the large pack.

Blue Johnny came back holding a little suitcase. Proudly he handed over from it a pair of drab trousers and a black coat and waistcoat. I donned these over the hospital smock and while I was putting on my own boots, with a pair of army socks, heard how he had got them.

From the hospital he had gone to the nearby home of a young Dutch friend of his. The house had been evacuated, like most of the rest of the town, and men of the S.S. were picking over its contents.

'What are you doing in my house?' said Johnny. 'Go away!'

They laughed.

At least, he said to them, they might let him have a few of his own clothes. They saw no objection to that. He quickly took from the Dutch boy's wardrobe some clothes of about my size, stuffed them into a suitcase thrown aside by the S.S. men and ran back with it to the hospital. He had been gone less than ten minutes.

Piet and Kessel came in with a mass of blood-soaked gauze and bandage and tied it round my head. Everything was now happening very quickly. Sister van der Sluis put her head round the door. Her eyes opened wide in surprise and excitement. She said nothing and vanished.

Piet told me to leave the pack and haversack. Johnny would get these to me later. I was to travel in a car. It was already outside, with two Dutch passengers in it who would know nothing. I had to act like a very sick man and not speak.

I said a hasty goodbye to Kessel and McGowan and came to Kenneth Smyth. He was dozing.

'Goodbye,' I said gently. 'I'm off.'

There was no reply.

'Good luck!' I said.

He gave no sign.

I left the little white room and followed Piet into the strange world of passages and doors outside it, all wrapped in the thick quietness of a hospital in the early afternoon. In one or two of the rooms there were British soldiers lying sleepily on beds but for the most part the hospital seemed empty.

I found walking easy enough, to begin with at any rate. Anything would have been easy just then. We went down a long passage and were suddenly in the open air. It was cloudy, fresh and cool. There was a hint of rain. It was beautiful.

A narrow path ran before us with a plane tree beside it. On

the ground a few leaves lay. A young man was gravely sweeping them up. He was always there, as I knew, always sweeping. He was one of Piet's.

We were passing a red brick building.

'The mortuary,' said Piet. I knew that this was where his people had their arms hidden.

We were near the gate.

'You are sick now,' said Piet and gave me his arm. I lolled heavily upon it.

Peering under the bandages on my forehead I saw a car. A man and a woman were sitting in the back with a big bundle. We were in a tree-lined urban street, the ground under the trees scarred with slit trenches and strewn with branches. Piet helped me into the front seat and I let my head drop to one side without a word, eyes closed. The two people behind had been whispering together. They were silent now. There were aircraft overhead and somewhere bombs were dropping. German guns were firing loudly near at hand. I heard Piet muttering outside the car and then a rustling as though he were trying to clear a path through fallen branches. He was a long time about it. A frozen gloom settled on me. Then came sounds of splintering wood and a rasping noise. He seemed to be shifting some sort of wreckage. After an age he got into the car again with a grunt of satisfaction and set about starting it. No disaster would have surprised me. None happened. The engine started up. We were moving. Where we were going I did not know nor did I much care. I was out and away.

The car bumped on over rough paving stones while I sprawled on the front seat, relaxed, eyes closed, head sagging as though I were gravely hurt.

We slowed down and I felt tension in the air. We stopped. A German voice spoke. I lay very sick.

'Air raid casualty,' said Piet in urgent German. 'Very bad. Must get him to hospital.' I pictured the jerk of his head at my bloodstained bandages.

There was a gruff noise from outside and the car moved on, away from the hospital instead of towards it but that seemed not to matter.

Soon we were on a smooth road, travelling fast. After a while I opened my eyes. The surroundings looked vaguely familiar. A little further on and recognition burst upon me. We were crossing the Ginkelsche Heide, the stretch of heath on which the 4th Parachute Brigade had dropped three weeks before.

I remembered with the force of a blow the hard feeling that

came over me on that cool and cloudy mid-September afternoon as the green light went on over the door of the aircraft, where I was standing ready to jump. It was a feeling of being caught and held in some tremendous hand, powerless to act of my own volition and only able to do what clearly had to be done. But I knew that I had to see for myself what had to be done, whatever it might be. If someone else tried to tell me they might get it wrong. I did not jump at once, for instance, when the red light went out and the green light went on as the pilot's signal to jump I could see, still more than a mile away on the ground, the blue smoke put down by Boy Wilson's pathfinders on the spot I had chosen for my first command post. I would get there and be in charge of what had to be done that much more quickly if I waited a few seconds more before jumping. I counted five slowly and lumbered clumsily out into the slipstream, into the brief moment of peace after the canopy had opened, with nothing more to do than pay out the rope with the heavy weapons-bag on the end of it, making ready to land and trying to guess what might be waiting for me to do down there. The smoke and crash of mortar bursts and the crackle of small-arms fire showed that there was already fighting on the Dropping Zone itself. An inert mass was swinging down in a parachute harness beside me, a man from whose body the entrails hung, swaying in a reciprocal rhythm. As the body moved one way the entrails swung the other.

I dropped my stick during the descent and had to look around for it in the heather as soon as I was out of the harness. The air above was full of parachutes, like goose feathers blown in the wind or a legion of angels. It was beautiful and terrifying. Six frightened German soldiers tried to surrender to me as soon as I was on my feet but I had to tell them to wait. I must find my stick first. That happened very soon: they did not have to wait long.

I now looked around me under the bandages in Piet's car. The heath lay still and quiet, empty of people but littered still with debris. All that had happened there before seemed to me now to have been in some other time, some other place, in a different world separated from the here and now by a huge gap. I passed the very place, close to the main road, where the first brigade command post had been set up from which we soon moved on. There was the area to the north of it where 10th Battalion had reorganized after the drop and the spot where Kenneth Smyth had put his own headquarters. Here were the farm buildings where 133 Field Ambulance had started work at once with the early casualties; over there, towards the outskirts of the town I knew to be Ede, 156 Battalion had rallied, under that gallant Grenadier Dick des Voeux. I knew that I should remember this place forever. Just now it was remote. What had happened here, then and afterwards, was almost irrelevant. I was now thinking only of the present and how good it was to be free and I was at last beginning to wonder where we might be going.

It seemed to be towards Ede itself, well known to me already from the map. I now recognized the barracks on its outskirts, whose attack from the air just before the brigade came in I had so strenuously urged, to give 156 a better chance to organize after their drop. Soon the car stopped among some houses. Piet's two other passengers got out with words of thanks, taking their bundle with them. The car moved on.

'Where are we going?' I asked.

'To where Brigadier Lathbury is,' was the reply. 'When I tell you, take those bandages off and sit up.'

We turned a corner or two.

'Now!' said Piet suddenly, precisely at another corner. I tore off the mass of bloodsoaked bandage and strained to sit up straight. We were in a street of well-kept, prosperous little dwellings. Every one had a garden with a flagpole in it and that individuality in similarity which I had already noticed in Dutch houses.

He turned through a gate into a yard, with a barn or garage to one side of it. The car stopped and Piet helped me out. Then he led me into a bright modern kitchen where two women were at work. They gave me a friendly smile and Piet asked a question. The elder of the two answered.

'Lathbury's here,' he told me. 'Let's go in.'

I tried to brace myself up and look a little less decrepit. Standing up straight was not easy. Piet opened the door into a sitting-room with large windows through which I could see a couple of unarmed German soldiers walking down the street outside. This was a new experience to me. My attention was arrested and I watched fascinated as one of them turned round to look at a pretty girl. Then I saw Gerald Lathbury sitting in an armchair dressed in a sober suit of dark grey. He looked to me, as I told him later, like a somewhat seedy don about to give a tutorial.

It was not at all a bad entry. Gerald slowly levered his great length out of the armchair.

'Shan!' he said, with evident pleasure. 'The last time I saw you the doctors were giving you only a fifty-fifty chance of living, if that! And here you are!'

We were happy to see each other.

'Most unreliable people in the world, doctors,' said I, cheerfully enough but uneasily aware that I was being both untruthful and disloyal. 'You shouldn't believe a word they say.'

I now wanted a lavatory and for some reason felt rather proud of this. It seemed to represent another big stride forward. Gerald told me there was a real one in the house, with a chain to pull. I could scarcely remember when I had last been in such a splendid place as that lavatory. It was a great occasion. There was almost unbelievable satisfaction in finding that my internal machinery was working so well.

Piet was given a meal. He had much to do and could not wait till the rest of the household came for their supper. While he ate Gerald and I sat with him and talked to each other. Gerald told me what had been happening to him since he had been wounded by the splinter in his back and how Piet had got him out of the hospital. He was now living in this house. They could not, it seemed, look after me here as well. Piet, with this family's help, was going to try to find some other refuge in the neighbourhood.

When he had gone the family came in. There was a bright-looking young man with fair hair and a smiling face whom Gerald addressed as 'Tony'. My impression was that, in spite of his youth, he was someone of importance in the Resistance. There were two younger brothers, a quiet, good-looking sister and the mother of them all, silent and preoccupied. These were the two women who had greeted me in the kitchen. There were also two evacuees, a man and his wife.

It was now about six o'clock in the evening and we all sat down to supper, before which the evacuee husband said a long grace in Dutch. I realized now that I was very tired. I was also rather concerned that something seemed to be leaking inside the bandages around my middle. This has been going on for some hours now. I hoped nothing serious was wrong but I was pretty damp and did not like it. I had some food, bread and butter with a very thin slice of bacon and another of cheese and a dab of jam, with weak sharp-tasting tea. Gerald told me that he had now grown accustomed to do as everyone else in such households seemed to do, to eat bread and butter and things like that not in his fingers, as he would at home, but with a knife and fork. It was going to be some months before I would eat bread and butter in my fingers again, except away from the table or alone.

I understood that the name of this family in the house in Brouwerstraat was 'de Noy' and soon learned that it was spelt 'de Nooij'. Almost all of them spoke English, Tony rather well. Partly from shyness, I suppose, and partly I am sure from the tact which in the Dutch families I got to know never seemed to fail, they left me more or less to myself in a corner, with my leg propped up on a chair and a cushion behind my back. I was grateful, for I could not know what lay ahead nor guess what further calls might have to be made upon my dwindling strength. I sat still and withdrawn, husbanding what remained.

After a while Piet came back. It was nearly seven o'clock and getting dark now; for this was already the tenth or eleventh day of October. Piet said that everything was arranged. I was to lodge nearby with another household of the same family. I wanted to thank him properly for what he had done for me that day but before I could say anything he had gone.

When it was quite dark two solid, cheerful-looking, middle-aged men arrived. Tony said they were uncles of his. They would now carry me to the house where some of his aunts lived, a few hundred yards away. The two uncles put a very large hat on my head, largely to hide my face, and made a chair with their hands. I got up on this and put my arm round the neck of one of them. Then with a wave of the general's stick and something like a cheer from the company I was carried ceremoniously out of the house.

The way was short but for the two men who were carrying me over cobblestones, in the dark, it was clearly hard work. There were few people about. I had been told that there would be curfew at nine, quite soon now. After a few more minutes we turned a left-handed corner into an open place which, as far as I could see, was not quite a square and not quite a street. At the end of it there was a white garden gate, now open, and a pace or two beyond that a light was shining through an open door. Someone was looking out.

I was carried in through the front door of a house and put down in a narrow hall with a staircase straight ahead and two doors opening out on the right. In the light of a hanging oil-lamp stood a tall, fair young man with a long face. A pair of intelligent eyes looked down at me through gold-rimmed spectacles. Behind him, a head shorter and about my own height, a girl stood, a pretty girl with an honest, cheerful face, aglow with interest and excitement. They were both smiling. My hand was shaken with evident pleasure as though we were all old friends.

43

'I'm John,' said the tall fair young man in English, 'and this is my sister Mary. We are going to look after you.'

Mary was bubbling over with pleasure.

'We are very, very glad,' she said 'to have an Englishman here!'

There was also a quiet older woman with a round face and a sweet and serious expression. The younger two addressed her respectfully as 'Aunt Ann'. She too greeted me and told me I was very welcome. Her English sounded astonishingly good.

They said that I should now go upstairs. The uncles had left and they wanted to carry me themselves. I asked to be allowed to walk and did so, though climbing stairs, which was another thing I had not yet done on that eventful day, was far from easy. At the top there was a large landing, dimly seen, with three doors opening out of it. Around were cupboards, clothes-lines, tubs, a mangle. Through a door straight before us I was shown into a tiny bedroom, all white and friendly, shining kindly in the light of an oil-lamp. Everywhere about me was a feeling of goodwill and kindness. It was a feeling always present in that house, as I was to find out later. I came to know it well and love it.

They told me that a doctor was coming and I sat down on the bed to wait for him. He came soon, a young man of about thirty, good-looking with light brown slightly curling hair. This was Dr. Kraayenbrink. He told me later, when I had got to know him well, that I received him on this his first visit with reserve and that was probably true. A Dutch doctor treating a wounded British officer would be in a dangerous position. He was not, as I knew, a member of this family and so had not their involvement. The family had not even known him very long for he had only lately come to Ede.

Before we parted Lipmann Kessel had given me the field card from my bed detailing the nature and extent of my injuries. The doctor looked at it in silence. Then he took the strapping and bandages off my stomach and had a long and careful look. He was clearly deeply impressed with what he saw.

'This was brilliant surgery,' he said.

From the scar, however, there was now a fairly free discharge. Kessel's beautiful hair-line scar seemed to my untutored eye to be in something of a mess. The doctor said it was probably not very much, perhaps nothing more than decomposing sutures. He dressed it and the leg wounds with what he had brought and left. It was clear that there was not much that he, or anyone else for that matter, was going to be able to do about my injuries.

'You will either die,' he said, 'or get better.'

I knew that already.

Mary helped me to undress. I said my prayers, with a very great deal to be thankful for, and turned to the trim white bed under the crochet counterpane. Above it a sampler hung on the wall, an embroidered picture of the Sleeping Beauty in the fairy story. Underneath were the words, in Dutch, 'And she slept a deep sleep a hundred years long'.

This was the end of the very first day upon which I had been out of bed and fully dressed since the operation which had saved my life some fourteen days before. It had been a long day and a full one. Dead tired, in peace and complete content, I climbed gratefully into the little white bed.

4

WHEN I awoke next morning and looked around the small but friendly room in which I lay I thought this could not be anything but a nursing home. I could see a white painted commode and an enamel bedpan and bottle. There was a rubber draw-sheet on the bed and a rubber hot water bottle lay on the floor where I must have cast it out. On the bedside table in a glass jar stood a clinical thermometer and here and there were other things found in sick rooms.

A girl's face appeared cautiously around the door, the round pretty face under light brown hair, with healthy cheeks and cheerful smile, of Mary, the girl who had welcomed me the night before. When she was sure that I was awake she came in, now looking businesslike in a white apron and carrying a cup of tea on a tray.

'Good morning, Mr. Hackett,' she said in English, rather formally I thought, 'I hope you slept well.'

'Thank you,' said, 'indeed I did.'

Where was I? What was all this?

There was no real need for an answer. There seemed no need even to ask. The little world around me was a sensible and normal world in which I would be shown quite clearly what I had to do.

She put down the tray and bustled about the room.

'I shall bring your breakfast,' said Mary. 'Then you will be washed and made comfortable.'

My first day in the house in Torenstraat, or Tower Street, had begun.

As she moved around the room Mary told me about the nursing equipment. Earlier that year the father of the family, her own grandfather, had died in this house at the age of ninety. These things had been used in looking after him during his last years. Mary herself had trained as an emergency nurse. She was inexperienced, she said, and ignorant but I was to find her, in fact, most capable.

Presently she brought breakfast — porridge, bread and butter, milk and, rather to my surprise for I knew such things were rare, a boiled egg. Then she came back, washed me as efficiently

46

as any hospital nurse but leaving the dressings on my stomach and leg untouched, made the bed, finished doing the room and left me alone to doze.

I had noticed that this robust-looking young woman – aged about twenty, as I supposed – moved with something of a limp. Later I was to learn from her Aunt Ann that as a child she had been in a street accident with a tramcar and had lost one leg below the knee. She now wore an artificial limb which meant that she could not do everything done by other girls of her age. Indeed, she could not walk more than a little way or at any but a slow pace without weariness and pain. She never complained. In the months that I lived in that house I never heard from this sunny, serious, friendly young woman a word that was not good tempered and kind. Even when she spoke of Germans – or 'Moffs' as I now learned to call them – she did so without malice.

Of the rest of the household it was Miss Ann I met first, the youngest of the three unmarried sisters whose home was in the house where their father had died. It was Miss Ann who had greeted me the night before and shown me up here. She came and sat for a while by my bedside and I began to learn a little more of where I was.

The house, in the middle of Ede, near the High Street and under the shadow of the great church tower from which Torenstraat took its name, was simple and not large. It was old-fashioned – there was no bathroom, I learned later, and it had an earth closet – but it was solid and comfortable. The de Nooij family owned a paint factory, together with a paper-hanging and house-decorating business which in peacetime had flourished. The factory had closed down now and no one wanted house decoration, even if there had been anyone to do the work. The family also owned a drugstore. This was still in business, after a fashion, at the sign of the 'White Cross'.

Miss Ann, quiet in manner, with grave grey eyes behind her round steel-framed spectacles, had wanted to teach English and had been to England to study it. She had not, however, reached the standard she had hoped for and had gone into the family business instead, to become the book-keeper in the paint factory. She was one of the sweetest-natured and most charitable people I have ever known but at the same time a woman of great determination. Like nearly all others in that family she was a devout Christian. It was Miss Ann who had accepted the chief responsibility for my care, though Mary I was told, would do the nursing.

They knew, of course, the risk they ran in harbouring a

British escaper. This was the first time they had done it. They had once been asked, I believe, to help with escaping airmen but in their father's lifetime that had been out of the question and since his death they had not felt particularly inclined to do this sort of work. The airborne invasion had changed everything. Miss Ann told me that Mary had said the night before, when the ladies of Torenstraat had been asked to take in a wounded British fugitive and had agreed, 'Thank God I now have something worthwhile to do!'

John and Mary were the son and daughter of a fourth sister. This was a widow who had been carrying on her late husband's drapery business in the township of Renkum, about eight kilometres away on the bank of the Rhine, up to the time of the airborne landings and the battle. The shop and their house, together with another house they owned, had been destroyed, I heard, in the fighting. When Renkum had been forcibly evacuated on the first of October, about ten days before my own arrival in Torenstraat, the three of them had moved in with the other sisters. There was also a younger brother in the Snoek family, William, or 'Wim', who had been an active Resistance worker in South Holland and had been arrested and taken away by the Germans. When I learned more about him later and read the notes of his trial I was surprised that he was still alive. He was thought now to be in a labour camp in Germany. I was to find myself, in time, deeply indebted to brother Wim.

John came up to see me. He had a little dictionary in his hand, his finger marking a page.

'Good day, Mr. Hackett,' he said gravely. 'How is your corpse?'

I thanked him equally gravely and said that it was well. He discovered later from Miss Ann, to his dismay, that the little dictionary had not told him everything and he wondered whether he had been wholly tactful.

He had brought a chess board and we played. He was a much better player than I was. I had only learned how to play chess, as a matter of fact, three years before, when I was convalescing in Jerusalem from wounds in the Syrian campaign against the Vichy French. My wife-to-be was being allowed to take me out and we used to walk to a cemetery, where we sat on flat gravestones in the sunlight of a Palestinian spring and she gave me lessons on a portable board. Playing with John, on my first day in Torenstraat, I was lucky enough by sheer accident to win and he would never believe afterwards that I was as bad a player as I knew myself to be.

Lunch was brought up by Mary at midday — soup, meat and vegetables and a piece of cake, much more than I could eat. Then I dozed until Miss Ann came towards four with a cup of tea and biscuits and sat with me for a little. She left with me, to my great satisfaction, a Bible in the English Authorized Version and promised me some other books in English.

One urgent matter demanded my attention. Mary brought me paper and a pencil and I finished the last of my recommendations for awards. I put them together with the account I had written in the hospital of the action of the 4th Parachute Brigade and the letters to my wife and to General Urquhart. I did not know how, or even if, these communications would ever arrive but at least they had been written.

I was sitting up out of bed to write, still feeling fairly strong. This, however, was to be pretty well the last flicker of the splendid physical condition in which I, like all the rest of us, had left England for the airborne invasion of Holland a few weeks before. To me, commanding the brigade, it had been particularly important to be as physically fit as any other man in it. During the weeks of staff work and planning, not only for this operation but for the half dozen or so others that had not come off, with all the normal burden of work for a brigade commander in a time of intensive operational training, it had not been easy to achieve this. Finding time was the problem. Early in the day or late, whenever I could fit it in, I had been on solitary route marches round the fields and lanes of Leicestershire, going at a good pace in full marching order. The pack on my back had bricks in it to make up rather more than the weight usually carried by the parachuting infantryman. I had gone into the battle as fit as a prize fighter and certainly owed to this reserve of physical strength much of the resistance I had been able to offer to the stresses of the last few weeks. There was not much now left to drawn on. I was soon to fall so low that it would take much time and care to creep back up again.

It was several days before I had met all the members of the household in Torenstraat. They did not want to upset their patient, I was told, with too much excitement and so they were only brought up by Miss Ann to see me one by one, well spaced out.

Miss Ann, Mary and John had between them already told me much about the de Nooij family. The old father had had eleven children. As an ageing widower he had lived in the house at 5 Torenstraat with the three unmarried daughters, Wilhelmine, who was known as Mien, Cornelia whom they called Cor and Anna, until he had died there in early 1944. The fourth daughter Marie, known to her sisters as Rie, widow of the draper in Renkum, was Mevrouw Snoek, the mother of Johannes and Marie (she too was called Rie) who were my John and Mary, and also of the absent Wim.

Three of the old man's sons, Pieter, Zwerus and Ko had set up in Ede the Macostan paint factory. Pieter, now dead, was Menno's father and Menno had taken his place in the business. This had prospered and other enterprises had been added to it, like the drug store. The de Nooijs were a closely-knit family of a kind to be found everywhere in Holland, unassuming, prosperous and provident. Zwerus de Nooij, the old man's eldest surviving son, was now its acknowledged head.

It was on the second day after my arrival that Miss Mien, the eldest of the sisters, first came to see me. She was slight and silver haired with a gentle sweet face of delicate bone structure, a face in which there was also strength and shrewdness. She sat quietly by my bedside, smiling and saying little. She spoke no English but when I had learned enough Dutch to be able to converse with her I was to find the greatest pleasure in her company. Her comments were witty and wise, often pointed but never unkind, and she had an infectious laugh like a silver bell which I loved to hear.

Miss Cor visited me next, a taller rather more imposing person. She was respected, I learned, as the cleverest one of the family and was rather more highly strung than her sisters. It was she who ran the drug store. Her own health was not particularly good. From time to time she was confined to bed with migraine and had always to be careful over her diet. I came greatly to admire the fortitude with which she bore these additional troubles when life was already grim enough without them. Miss Cor suffered more, I think, from the strain of that sixth year of the war than the other members of her family. I had the feeling later on that she was also probably more affected than they were by the additional burden of my own presence in the house, though she gave no sign of this and always showed me the greatest kindness. She was well informed and very interested in what went on in the rest of the world, as well as being most instructive to someone as ignorant as I was about affairs in Holland.

The fourth of the sisters, Mevrouw Snoek, the mother of John and Mary, was the last to visit me. This was another gentle person, with a quiet sense of humour which I greatly enjoyed. She was always ready to laugh. She and I used to think the same sort of things funny and I would often look over to her, when I found something was particularly comical, and see from the twinkle behind her spectacles, under the greying hair drawn straight back over the head, that she found it so too.

A mother of sons had a good deal to worry about in those times. The boldness of Mevrouw Snoek's younger boy must have caused her much concern. Wim had been, John told me, rather restless at first. There was not much going on in the way of resistance in the very early stages of the war and the penalties imposed by the Germans were so slight as to make active opposition to them, in brother Wim's view, scarcely worth while. Then the penalties grew more severe and Wim, said John, cheered up. When early in 1941 it was reported that the Germans had threatened the death penalty for hoarding wool he was delighted.

'He was not at all happy to begin with,' said John. 'But of course it got better later.'

Everyone working in resistance of any sort had a secret name for operational use. Wim's had been 'Martien', John's was 'Duys' and Menno's, of course, was 'Toni'.

John too, had been active in resistance work. He was a cooler hand than his brother but no less determined and courageous. He showed me the scar of a bullet wound in the leg which was the result of a successful effort to save the life of a Jewish girl on the run.

John, out of consideration for his mother, had been obliged to moderate his own activities at first, though very sensibly not everything that happened was made known to her. What she did know was worrying enough. There was one occasion when the Germans had ordered all church bells to be requisitioned for the metal in them. John and Mary had determined to save from their own church in Renkum at least one of the smaller bells. They got it out all right, though it was far heavier than they had expected, and carried it home laboriously in the dusk. Whenever a German soldier or a known collaborator appeared they put the bell down on the ground between them and embraced like two lovers over the top of it. They spent quite a long time that evening in each others arms but they got the bell home in the end. Its presence in the house, however, was a continuing source of anxiety to their mother and they had to get rid of it. That was a long time ago now. As German pressure hardened so did the response all round and John now spoke proudly of the courage of his mother.

I knew that food resources were slender in Holland and

rationing was strict. How, I asked, was it possible for the family to feed me? This led them to explain to me something of the organization of resistance in the country. First of all, I had to understand that there were many men in hiding, mostly because they refused to work for the enemy. These were called 'Onderduikers' or Underdivers. There were 'light' underdivers and 'heavy' underdivers. My hosts were too tactful to emphasize it, but I was myself clearly a very heavy underdiver indeed! For the underdivers a rationing system had been set up parallel to the official one. In order to minimize distortions in food distribution ration cards were stolen where possible, but when enough could not be stolen they were secretly printed. Control of underground rationing was pretty well as strict as if the system were run with all the weight and sanction of government. For most of the Dutch, indeed, the complex system of Resistance Movements (if it could at that time yet be called a system) with the guidance of the more solid citizens and the support of the clergy, was all the government they recognized, though the orders of the German-controlled administration were obeyed when there was no alternative.

It had not always been like this. Early in the war there had been widespread indifference to German occupation and even a good deal of collaboration. This could still be found here and there, in some degree. There seemed no doubt at all, however, from the evidence that before long began to come my way, that by now, in the second half of 1944, the general temper of the population of Holland was very different and the Resistance organizations, of which there were several, enjoyed wide and growing support.

Of these organizations the Landelijke Organisatie, or L.O. was the most important. Its main task was the administration and maintenance of those working in any way against the enemy, or avoiding working for him, or finding themselves in difficulties as a result of doing either. Though there were local differences and no central structure of control, the L.O. operated everywhere on largely similar lines, feeding underdivers and providing them with fuel, clothes and papers, disseminating news, keeping a sharp eye on collaborators and doing whatever would help to stiffen morale. In Ede the young man I had met as 'Tony', but soon got to know far better as Menno when I began to be absorbed into his family, acted as its local head. It was he who produced ration cards for the essentials for me. He often brought in eggs, butter, bacon and other additions as well and in the time that lay ahead was to render me many other services.

Though the L.O. was not above doing a quiet bit of sabotage on the side this was largely left to the Landelijke Knok Ploeg, or L.K.P., which was a militant and aggressive body operating in small groups for that specific purpose. Its objectives were necessarily local, limited and dictated by opportunity. This offered more scope for the free play of personality: local divergences in policy and organization were more marked in the L.K.P. than in the L.O.

A third organization was chiefly to be found in the towns, the Raad Van Verzet, or R.V.V., with functions in part like those of both the other two. A fourth, the Orde Dienst, or O.D., was also in existence nearly everywhere, with the task of preparing a civil administration to take over when the Germans left. A high proportion of its members, who were often men of some substance, were ex-officers or former civil administrators. The O.D. was by no means free from criticism among the other organizations. The members of these sometimes thought it unfair that when the more dangerous work was done they were to be supplanted by people who had done less of it, some of whom had scarcely distinguished themselves in the brief campaign of the Dutch army and had shown no very high degree of resistance to the Germans since.

There were Germans, I heard, everywhere. The good communications in the neighbourhood of Ede, the railway, the great road on which it stood — a main east-west artery started by the Dutch and hastily brought half-finished into use, I was told, by the Germans for the invasion of England — together with all the facilities of this considerable township located only eight kilometres back from the Rhine bank, made of Ede a centre of some military importance. In peace time there had been a considerable Dutch garrison there, mostly quartered in those barracks on its north-eastern outskirts upon whose bombing I had so strongly insisted before our arrival. The surrounding countryside, with the heaths and coniferous woodlands on sandy soil which gave it such a strong likeness to the country round Aldershot, must have been a good military training area. There were now always considerable numbers of German administrative troops stationed in the neighbourhood and fighting units moved in and out. Many houses and other buildings had inevitably been requisitioned as billets.

Bit by bit, from what Miss Ann and John and Mary told me, I was beginning to get more in touch with my surroundings, even before I had been allowed to meet all the other inmates of the house. Some I never did meet. The room next door to mine,

I heard, was occupied when I arrived by a man, woman and child displaced by the evacuation of some other township. Within a few days they had moved on.

One piece of information which might perhaps have been thought of particular interest was conveyed to me quite casually — by John, I think — as something of no very great significance. The little garden of the house in Torenstraat, only a few square metres in size, adjoined another equally small, separated from it by a low fence. This was the back garden of a house whose front was on the High Street, no more than thirty or forty yards distant from where I was lying. That house was the billet of a detachment of Feldgendarmerie, the German Military Police.

5

WE were now in the third week of October and already, after four or five days in the house in Torenstraat, my life was beginning to settle into a pattern.

Mary would come in at about seven o'clock in the morning with a cup of tea, of a sort strange to me at first but now grown more familiar. It was made from a blend of dried woodland leaves, herbs and the bark of certain trees, thinner and more astringent than the stronger product of India or Ceylon, less fragrant than China tea, which were now all unobtainable. Very good it was, too, when you had become accustomed to it. The members of the household never put more than a drop or two of milk in their tea, even when milk was plentiful. I liked rather more and was often teased in the family, later on, for drinking what they described as 'kinderthee'. Pretty well from the beginning I was always given tea, or any other hot drink, out of the same china mug. It had a picture and the name of a cocoa firm on it and was recognized as 'my' mug, 'Mr. Hackett's mug', and reserved for my use alone.

A little later, towards eight o'clock, Mary would bring in breakfast on a tray — porridge with milk and sugar, bread and butter, a cup of milk and quite often, at least early on in my stay, an egg. Then she would come back, looking very efficient and crackling slightly in a starched white nurse's apron, to wash me like a child and make my bed and do the room. After that I would read a little, at first only in my Authorized Version and not very much of that, or lie there trying to sort things out in my mind, or doze. It was like being in limbo. I did not think a great deal about what had gone before. That was over and just for now did not matter any more. I did not think about the future or even reflect much on the hazards of the present. I lay in a sort of cocoon of security and kindness, thinking a good deal of my family and wondering what had happened to friends.

Towards midday I would be brought, my Mary or Miss Ann, a glass of white wine provided, they told me, by the senior uncle, Zwerus de Nooij, whom I had yet to meet. Then Mary would bring lunch, so plentiful that I could rarely eat more than half of it, and after that I would doze again or even sleep a little.

At half past three or four Miss Ann would come in with tea, in my own mug, and possibly a biscuit, and sit with me while Mary was relieved of her duties for a spell.

Miss Ann's presence brought to my bedside quietness and peace. She talked in her gentle voice, in slow, correct and charming English, of her time in England. She told me about the de Nooij family and how things were in Ede. After half an hour she would go.

Everything outside that little room seemed very far away. I cannot remember, for example, that in those early days it ever came much into my mind that there were German soldiers living in a house less than fifty yards away. If it did it would scarcely have seemed important. That was all a part of what was happening somewhere else, outside the limits of the little world I lived in.

I now began to learn more Dutch—though I did so, I am bound to confess, at first with a trace of reluctance. This was the consequence of an earlier experience. I had once spoken reasonably good Spanish, the rudiments learned by myself as a schoolboy in Australia out of Hugo's Spanish Simplified and later improved upon in Spain, in vacation time from Oxford. A few years after that, as a young cavalry officer, I had learned Italian for the Army Interpretership and done an attachment, largely for the riding, to the Italian cavalry. Very soon, to my regret, as my knowledge of Italian improved, almost all I knew of Spanish had disappeared. What frightened me a little now was that what I knew of German, at which I had been working quite hard over the years but had not yet mastered, would vanish in the same way if I concentrated on another language not very different from it. That was why, I think, I was slow in starting seriously to study Dutch. It was something I clearly had to get on with, however, and very soon I was having a daily lesson from one of the three with whom I had most to do—Miss Ann, John and Mary.

These three seemed to be, as it were, the executive committee in this enterprise. Between them there must have been many discussions, of which I knew nothing, about what it was best to do. I can picture now their putting major matters of policy to a sort of grand council, with the other three ladies present and Menno brought in when he was needed as a special adviser, all sitting under the chairmanship of Miss Mien. If further advice or assistance were required a wider family group could be convened, including some of the uncles. Of this, I assumed, Zwerus de Nooij would take the chair.

It was the executive trio, I think, that first came to the con-
clusion that I too, like so many others, would be the better for
another name, in addition to my own. It would be needed if
official documentation ever became necessary and would provide
a useful way, meanwhile, of referring to me amongst themselves
outside the house. With the family, of course, I would always
remain 'Mr. Hackett'.

Miss Ann, John and Mary had decided that my new name
must sound typically Dutch. It would also not be inappropriate,
they thought, if it embodied some allusion to the manner of my
arrival in Holland.

'We have been thinking this over very carefully,' said John,
'and we have decided to call you Mijnheer van Dalen.'

The name suggested, he explained, someone coming down
out of misty uplands.

'You came to us out of the clouds, you see,' said Mary,
with the happy smile I loved to see, 'so that ought to do very
well!'

I became, therefore, Mijnheer van Dalen.

Sometimes in the late afternoon John would come and play
chess with me, though I do not remember ever winning a game
after that first one. Later on Miss Ann would bring me the
news, an English translation written out in her beautiful rather
severe handwriting of the news broadcast in Dutch by the B.B.C.
in England over the channel known as 'Radio Oranje'. This
used to be taken down by resistance workers and copies circulated, from one of which Miss Ann would make her translation.

Once or twice in the first few days I had a visitor. Gerald
Lathbury came, to my very great pleasure, and Digby Tatham
Warter, an officer of the 3rd Parachute Battalion who was
also on the run in Ede. Digby was a brave and engaging person,
with a rather special mixture of eccentricity and panache: I had
got to know him quite well during our time of preparation in
England, though he was not, to my regret, in my own brigade.
His first visit to 5 Torenstraat put the household into something
of a flutter. He turned up at the front door one day, unknown
and unannounced, and asked for 'Brigadier Hackett' by name.
He had heard from Gerald where I was and it cheered me up
enormously to see him but Miss Ann took a rather grave view
of the way he had arrived.

'We have to be very prudent,' she said, in the nearest thing
to reproof I ever heard from her.

'It is best that people only come when a member of the

family brings them and we must not have too many. It would not do for the neighbours to see this house becoming an object of interest, with many strangers going in and out.'

Miss Ann would have been perfectly right, even without the presence of German soldiery living so close to us. I had to ask my visitors to be more circumspect.

Later, as night fell, supper would be brought to me — bread and butter, jam, cheese and milk. Sometimes there would be a cup of soup, even another egg. How they could continue to find such rare and precious things was baffling. Menno had a good deal to do with it, as I knew, but even that bold and resourceful young man must have had his work cut out to find the food they gave me.

It was growing dark sooner in the day now, as we moved through October, and in that little room under the roof, facing north, the light failed early.

'We must be very careful with candles and oil,' said Miss Ann, but early darkness did not worry me.

Electric current could only be used in Ede with German permission and its unauthorized use was a punishable offence. Any building not being occupied by Germans, or in use in their interests, had in fact been disconnected from the supply. Nonetheless, in the mysterious and almost casual way in which so many truly remarkable things seemed to happen in occupied Holland, soon after my arrival the house in Torenstraat was reconnected and the electric light came on again. One of his friends, John told me, worked for the municipality as an electrical engineer and he had quite simply, without asking any questions, done what John requested of him. He had connected us up. Behind the carefully arranged blackout curtains I could now read again at night, if I wanted to. I was still, however, not much inclined to read. Every day I read a little in my English Bible and prepared a small piece of Dutch for my daily lesson. That, for the time being, was all.

A search of the house was always possible and we needed a cover plan to explain my presence. It was decided (on a proposal from Miss Cor, I think) that I should become a patient from the hospital for consumptives which had recently been evacuated near Renkum. The family told me that I had a 'tubercular throat', whatever that might be, and John brought me a paper purporting to have been issued by the local authority, showing that Mijnheer J. van Dalen had lost his identity documents and was excused work on grounds of ill-health. We had a scarf ready to tie around his neck and a bottle of strong-smelling disinfectant to soak it in, relying on a well-established fear of tuberculosis among German soldiers and the probability that those actually carrying out a search would not be very well informed — or even very intelligent. My role (I was glad that I never had to play it in earnest) was just to look ill and not speak. In addition, everything I possessed which might arouse the least suspicion — army clothing and equipment, my own genuine papers, the silver pencil and cigarette case with their inscriptions in English, even my marching boots which did not, they told me, look Dutch enough — were put carefully away in the hiding place under the floor of the landing outside my room. My boots! They had been made to measure for me in Jerusalem, when the brigade was training in Palestine. We were jumping into Cyprus then, in preparation for the airborne invasion of Sicily from Tunisia. How long ago and far away all that was, I thought, as I watched the boots being packed up to stow away until I should need them again.

I was already getting into the habit of having nothing upon or near me which could excite the suspicion of Germans or even their curiosity. Even living quite close to them was something now quite normal. This had already begun to induce a frame of mind, a feeling of confidence and diminished vulnerability, which was to be of great value to me later on.

At first Dr. Kraayenbrink came nearly every evening, between supper and curfew, but Mary could do the dressings, for which the doctor left medicaments, and Miss Cor was still able to provide gauze and bandages (though not, alas, any new elastoplast) from her stocks in the chemist's shop. When Dr. Kraayenbrink was satisfied that the discharge was only caused by decomposing linen sutures and that all else was well (however much I might mourn the loss of Kessel's elegant hairline scar) he came less often, for he had very much to do. Like every other doctor who saw the evidence of Kessel's surgery, and heard something of the details, he remained full of admiration for what I have often heard described as a surgical miracle. He did not fail to let me know, more than once, that by rights I should be dead.

Now and then, as the frontal wound healed, the end of a thread would show and the doctor would pull it out. I used to dread this: it was an exquisitely painful affair which put me in mind of evisceration by medieval torturers. One night in mid-October, when I was still far from comfortable and had a trace of fever, he brought an abdominal specialist round, a young surgeon of some standing called Knook, who said all the same things over again, wondered at my good fortune in meeting such brilliant surgery in such an unpromising situation and confirmed that everything was in order.

A visitor I was always particularly glad to see was Dominee Blauw, the pastor of the Reformed Church to whose congregation my friends belonged. He was a young man whom I liked at once and came to admire deeply. There was a combination of simplicity and enthusiasm in him which compelled respect. He had a difficult task, to give comfort and encouragement amid so much hardship and calamity. In appearance he was rather frail and on his face there were signs of the strain under which he worked. I got to know him well and was always glad when I had word that he was coming. We had much to talk about. I never failed to be the better for his visits and for the prayer he would say with me before he went away. On about his second or third visit he brought me St. Matthew's Gospel in Greek and I now added a piece of this to my daily reading.

As Mary or Miss Ann moved about my room I was fascinated, as always in a Dutch house, by the overriding passion of Dutch women for cleanliness. The only sign of anything approaching animosity these gentle people ever showed was when they descended upon some offending particle of dirt like avenging angels and swept it away. There was a look in Mary's eye of the satisfaction of a huntress viewing her prey when she saw something that ought not to be there. The smaller it was the better she seemed pleased.

As my clothes were being stowed away Mary pounced on the shirt and woollen vest in which I had been wounded, with the holes in them and the bloodstains.

'I shall wash these at once,' she said. It was clear from her voice that this should have happened long ago.

I begged her to do no such thing. She was incredulous.

'Why not?' she asked.

I tried to explain to her, not without difficulty, for I scarcely understood it myself, that here in a strange country I was being nursed in a family not my own by women caring for me as my wife would have wished to do. I wanted these things left as they were. They would be taken home like this as a sort of token and washed when I got there as something of a share in what was now being done.

'But they will smell!' said Mary.

'Not very much,' said I, and Mary looked at me a little sharply.

But she did as I asked and put them away as they were and in the end I took them out on my journey home and handed them over like that, as I had intended.

So these early days passed. For long hours I used to lie still, my mind running on many things. I thought a great deal about my friends and the Parachute Brigade which I had raised and which had for two years been at the heart and centre of my life and which had now within one week been virtually extinguished. I thought much of what I now realized mattered to me even more — my home and family. They would not know where I was or what had happened to me. They would only know that I had been gravely hurt and left behind.

6

Miss Ann came.

'We are moving you to another room,' she said, 'a larger one on the other side of the house.'

This, I learned, was the room she had been sharing with Miss Cor. She herself would now move into the little room I was in and her sister would go downstairs and share another with Miss Mien.

My new room was splendid. It was large, bright and airy, with pictures on the walls. One was of the bridge at Cologne, another a photograph of a family group, a third a bridal photograph of Mary's mother. There was also a colourful picture of what could have been the coast of Palestine north of Gaza, complete with blue sea, white sand, Bedouin arab mounted on camel and white-sailed dhow.

Large windows looked out from this upstairs room on to the street into which we had turned that night when the two uncles had carried me here from Menno's house. This was Torenstraat, almost a tiny square. Our house was one of two on the north side, facing south. There was a large painted sign announcing an 'Electric Shoemakers' on a house to the right, facing ours. Beyond that, Brouwerstraat, where Menno lived and Gerald Lathbury had lodged, made a right-handed turn out of the square and beyond Brouwerstraat, still on the right-hand side of the square, a few houses curved over to the left to where a narrow lane ran out below the great church tower. On the immediate left of our own house was a garden or two, one of them belonging to the house where the German soldiers lived. Another narrow street opened off the square to the left, almost below my window, near the foot of the tower. The odd shaped little enclosure in front of our house, hemmed in like this, was all there was of Torenstraat.

Life was more spacious for me now. There was a sofa in the room. I used to get dressed in the black coat and drab trousers Blue Johnny had brought me in the hospital, wearing also a pair of someone's carpet slippers, and lie on the sofa while my bed was being made and the room done. I greatly enjoyed, as Mary moved about the room, listening to her honest and enthusiastic conversation and learning more from her about Holland.

I now also began to want to read and Miss Ann brought me

her English books. I also had more visitors. Piet came and told me what he could of the local situation. Gerald called to say goodbye. He would very soon be off, he said, and would take whatever I had to send out with him. I made up a bundle of the record I had put together of my brigade's action, the recommendations for awards for gallantry and the letters to my wife and General Urquhart. Gerald took them over. It was improbable he said that he would be able to come again before he left, so he would take these with him and promised to deliver them. I said goodbye to him, not without a pang of envy, and wished him well on his journey.

A man known as Bill, head of the local L.K.P. (the Landelijke Knok Ploeg) paid me a visit, brought by Menno, and talked a while in slow grave Dutch, with Menno translating. I was impressed by Bill, of whom I had heard something from Menno already. He seemed a solid, quiet, reliable man. He had been a sergeant-major in the Dutch army on the outbreak of war and when the brief fighting was over joined whatever was going in the way of opposition. He was now doing what he could to hamper the enemy in any way that offered. When it was all over he hoped, he said, to become a horse dealer. It would be very difficult, I thought, to sell him a dud. He was now busy organizing the escape across the Rhine of Gerald and his party.

The eighty or so men who were to make it up were scattered around the neighbourhood, lying up singly or in small groups with farmers or in houses in the villages. They would have to be concentrated and conducted to the bank of the Rhine where, if all went well, boats would have dodged enemy patrols and slipped across from the other bank (which was just there under Allied control) to pick them up. At this time there was still, strange as it now sounds, telephonic communication across the Rhine with that part of Holland which was occupied by British troops. This was through the line laid along with the electric power cables to the power house on the south side of the river. The power no longer flowed but the telephone circuit remained and at certain times it was possible for someone on the German-occupied side of the river to go to the instrument and speak to the staff officer making the arrangements at the British end. They told me this officer was one Hugh Fraser, the younger brother of an old friend of mine from Oxford days, Lord Lovat, who was himself a gallant Commando leader.

The day of the concentration was well chosen. On German orders the village of Bennekom between Ede and the Rhine was being finally evacuated on that very day and there was so much confused traffic on the main road that movement was almost impossible to control. The escapers arrived at a rendezvous, brought largely in Dutch lorries, lying under sacks on the floor, with a fair number dressed in civilian clothes joining them in well dispersed parties on foot. The plan was well conceived and almost everything worked. One of the battalion commanders from Gerald's First Parachute Brigade, David Dobie, had already crossed by another route, to assist in the planning on the British side with his knowledge of conditions on ours, and an admirable reconnaissance had been made of the northern approaches to the river by my own Tom Wainwright, an officer of 156 Battalion, and Sergeant-Major Grainger of the 1st Battalion in Gerald's brigade. The final move to the bank from the rendezvous in the woods was to be only two kilometres. The position of all German posts was known. Careful reconnaissance and silent, well controlled movement would prevent, it was hoped, interference from German patrols. The river bank was lightly occupied just here and defensive work had hardly yet begun. Conditions were therefore propitious. Moreover, this was the first time a mass escape had been tried in Holland and the Germans would not be expecting it. The escapers were almost entirely parachutists, or at least airborne troops, and since only a few weeks had passed since the battle they were still pretty fit. They were well trained and hardy besides being well disciplined, and they were operating under familiar command. The chances looked good. With reasonable luck, I thought, most if not all of them should get across.

On 21st October they concentrated and that night moved down to the river. One account I heard from the Dutch said that on the way from the rendezvous to the bank a German patrol discovered them, but was intimidated by the size of the party and interfered with only the last man or two. I was told that one man had been shot but I am still doubtful if this was so.

The main party, in any case, got across safely and a telephone message from Hugh Fraser reporting their arrival caused the Dutch on our side great joy. It was perhaps unfortunate that later on an account of the escape got into the English press. The Germans were more watchful after that.

The next attempt at a mass escape here in our part of Holland, on 18th November nearly a month later, was a bitter and costly failure and the publicity given in England to the first almost certainly contributed. One other unfortunate thing had happened recently. In talking about the airborne operations in Holland the B.B.C. had reported that information given by

64

Dutch civilians over the telephone had been most valuable. After that the Germans shut down the civil telephone service all over Holland at once, with a most serious effect on the work of the Underground.

Now that Gerald's party had left I felt rather more alone than before. I had for comfort the thought that my wife would soon have news of me.

From my window, while I was lying on the couch or moving slowly between bed and washstand, I could look down through the lace curtains into the street and watch the Germans. Usually there was an odd soldier strolling along, generally unarmed and almost always untidy. Often a platoon or some other detachment would march through, singing. I always disliked that singing. The accentuation sounded to me barbaric. In particular the emphatic shortening of the final note of any line, as though according to a drill, never ceased to annoy me.

I could often see motor transport of various kinds picking its way in and out of the narrow exits of the little square. There was also a good deal of horse transport and occasionally guns and tracked vehicles of various sorts moved through. All this was fascinating to watch. Like any other invalid I loved looking out of the window. There was much simple enjoyment in the contrast between the bustle of the outside world and the enforced calm of a sick room. There was also something else. These people in the street were my enemies, upon whose destruction I had been bent, as it seemed to me now, for a whole lifetime, just as they had been upon mine, and here they were passing to and fro most peacefully beneath my window within speaking distance. This lent added interest at first, but it soon became quite normal. No one can live on a high plane of excitement for long. After quite a short time you get adjusted to a new norm and are soon living what feels like your own life again, apparently without any difference between this way of life and whatever other you may have left.

The year was moving well on into the autumn now. The weather was often wet and windy. From my bed in the mornings I used to watch the topmost branch of a tree, appearing above the lace curtains in the window. Most of its leaves were gone and only a few still clung to the waving branches, daily growing fewer. Then one day every leaf but one had gone. Day after day I watched this leaf, feeling somehow a link between it and myself which I could not explain, until finally it too fell and the branch was bare. I turned at last wholly inwards to the life of the household which was now becoming my whole world.

Having met all the aunts in the household I began to meet the uncles of the family too. First came Uncle Ko, one of the two who had helped to carry me in on the first night, a youngish man, fresh and lively. He came to cut my hair and, with Mary translating, to give me all the more exciting local news.

Then came Uncle Zwerus, the head of the family, at last. I had been curious to make his acquaintance and was not at all surprised to meet an older man of considerable dignity with serious views. I knew myself to be already deeply in his debt. From the stores of the family business, he had been providing, either directly or by means of barter, many things for my comfort. Like the ladies of my own household he had early on in the war laid in considerable domestic stocks and used them providently. He was thus able to produce jam, which was now almost unknown in German-occupied Holland. He also sent me soap and cognac, razor blades and little cigars. The glass of wine which Mary carried in almost every morning on a tray, after the room was done and I was lying on my sofa, was the gift of Uncle Zwerus. He was not only a general provider in his family; I knew him to be a fountain of wisdom and good advice as well. His upbringing had included, he was to tell me, the getting by heart of the Book of Proverbs in his early teens.

I well remember his first visit. It suggested a meeting between two potentates of different nations in the eighteenth century. Zwerus de Nooij sat very upright on a hard chair, with his hands resting upon the stick between his legs, while I sat before him. Miss Ann interpreted. We talked soberly and a little ceremoniously about world affairs. We spoke about Holland in the seventeenth century and her relations with England under the Commonwealth; about the British Empire and South Africa. We spoke of the progress of the war and other things, with pauses on either side for Miss Ann's interpretation. After nearly an hour he rose to go, and notwithstanding his protests I struggled to my feet. We shook hands and said goodbye, and at the door he turned, very erect.

'God save the King,' said Uncle Zwerus.

He knew little English. Indeed beyond that sentence I heard only one other in English from him, which he remembered from school days and sometimes repeated to show that he had not forgotten:

'Under the feudal system,' it went, 'the state of the people of England was more,' as he called it, 'retzt than at any other time in her history.'

The wounds in my side and leg were now healing well. I had

66

settled into this family almost as if it were my own but physically I was still far from comfortable. It was very difficult to sleep. There were sedatives, but they were scarce and had to be carefully husbanded. I tried to sleep without them but with little success.

In particular the barking of dogs used to keep me awake. Night after night I lay and listened to their rowdy chorus, getting to know all the regular voices and to form in my imagination pictures of the dogs they came from. The two noisiest and most persistent were, as I imagined them, a yapping creature round the corner to the right, a small-sounding conceited sort of dog, and a rather rougher brute somewhere to the left, a dog with a coarse, elderly, irritable voice, apparently an animal of some size, but neither of good breeding nor good manners.

Miss Ann was worried that I slept so little and set out to remove the nuisance. She found that there was indeed a little dog, much as I had pictured him, living above a shop around the corner, belonging to the butcher. His owner protested that the poor little fellow was the best behaved and least noisy dog in the world and was never out after curfew anyway. He was told sternly, under threat of loss of the household's custom whenever he had meat to sell again, that no more must be heard from his little dog at night, and no more was.

The large dog presented a more difficult problem. He was traced to the German military police billet over the garden fence.

I cannot believe that Miss Ann was ever daunted by anything. Overcoming her repugnance to any sort of personal relationship with Germans, she presented herself late one afternoon at the front door of the house in the High Street. I could picture her kind round eyes flashing behind her spectacles as she asked for the person in charge. The officer came at once. In Ede Dutch women commonly shunned the German soldiery. They sometimes ostentatiously crossed the street to avoid having to share the same pavement. A visit to the house by a Dutch woman who was clearly of some standing was a notable event. The German officer greeted her very politely and invited her in.

'Do you have a dog?' she asked, ignoring the invitation.

'Yes,' replied the officer proudly. 'I do. He is a beautiful dog. There he is.' A big Alsatian stood behind him. He again invited his visitor in, to see the dog more closely.

'Look,' said Miss Ann, rather testily I think, and staying

where she was on the front doorstep. 'Someone in my house round the corner is very sick. This person cannot sleep because of that dog of yours and the awful noises it makes all night. Will you please have the goodness to see that at night it is kept locked up?'

The German meekly and readily agreed and Miss Ann withdrew. He was as good as his word. Thereafter there was more peace at night and I began to sleep better.

Listening as I lay in bed in the day-time I became familiar with other noises — more agreeable ones. There was a little girl who used to call every day in the street for a small boy to come out and play with her. 'Piet-je,' she used to call, 'Pie-e-e-et-je-e-e.' There was also sometimes a pleasant sound of a woman's voice singing next door. This I learned was Hennie, the wife of Henk, another nephew. They had been married during the war and things in their little house were not easy. But in that large and provident family everybody helped everybody else and Henk and Hennie got along. Hennie was Pietje's mother. I was to make Pietje's acquaintance later and found him a charming little fellow with bright fair hair and great blue eyes and a courage and self possession well beyond his four years.

I soon began to emerge from the gentle torpor into which I had sunk on my arrival in Torenstraat. I started to read. The books I had were all, with two notable exceptions, brought me by Miss Ann. They were not many but I could scarcely believe my good fortune when I found what they included.

There was first the big English Bible. It was in the Authorized Version, upon which so many in my own generation had been largely brought up. Then there were the complete works of Shakespeare in the one-volume Oxford edition and the Oxford editions of Wordsworth and of Scott's poetry. *Pickwick* was there and *Dombey* and the Christmas pieces. There were also (whether they were Miss Ann's I was not sure) *Love and Mr. Lewisham*, that charming tale; *The Street of the Fishing Cat*; *So Big* by Edna Ferber; a fine book called *The Christ of the Indian Road* and a long and rather dreary novel, *Susan Lenox*. Last, but by a long way not least, there was an anthology entitled *One Thousand and One Gems of English Poetry*, compiled towards the end of the last century by one Charles Mackay and published, as the reader learned from the Introduction, 'in a form and at a price which would recommend it to the taste of the rich without placing it beyond the means of the poor'. I acknowledge a deep and lasting debt to the 'Gems'.

Two very important additions to my books came from outside

the household, one early on and the other rather later, both brought at my request. The first was St. Matthew's Gospel in Greek, lent me by Dominee Blauw. The second was brought by Piet. It was *Vanity Fair*.

The Authorized Version was all I had in the very beginning and was all I needed for the very little reading I was at first inclined to do. It remained, even when I had all the rest, what I almost always opened first on any day.

Something like a set routine soon developed. I would first read a piece out of the Old Testament histories, usually in sequence with what I had read the day before, then a chapter of Proverbs and a passage from a Prophet. A chapter or two from a Gospel would follow and something from the Acts, or from St. Paul. I had been through the whole of the Old Testament before my stay in Torenstraat was over and had read some of it (or heard it read—but I shall come to that) more than once, though I am bound to say that on a second reading I used to skip pieces here and there, like the passages about who begat whom. I had also read the whole of the New Testament, first of all straight through and then in chosen pieces. I read the Epistles with care, making notes on what I found important— important to me, that is. St. Paul, with his combination of high conviction, sinuous mind and robust commonsense has always seemed to me a good companion in adversity.

In Dominee Blauw's St. Matthew I also read every day. I must have read the whole of St. Matthew in Greek at least twice before I left. I had also, I suppose, read Proverbs three or four times over, though I could never hope to know these as well as Uncle Zwerus did.

Begun as a rule in this way, my reading day went on with whatever, out of the limited but rich range before me, I happened to be reading at the time. To begin with I read all of Shakespeare, a tragedy in the morning and one or more of the comedies in the afternoon and then the historical plays, taken straight through like episodes in some tremendous pageant. Reading them like that, with a fresh memory of what had been said or done already, I noticed inconsistencies and contra- dictions which had escaped me before. I then went over the tragedies again, reading each at the pace at which I most enjoyed it. *Hamlet* I liked reading bit by bit, with pauses to chew it over. I lingered over *Lear* too. Ever since old Dr. Robin, my English master at Geelong in Australia, had given me A. C. Bradley's *Shakespearian Tragedy* to read and had led me deep into an awareness of the existence of a tragic world I had loved 'King Lear'. I had never seen it on the stage and did not wish to. I still have not. For some, and I suppose I am among them, it exists in the mind and is better left there. I found that, for me, *Othello* was best read at a single sitting, as it is bound into a powerful and baleful unity by the Moor's destructive passion, *Macbeth* had to be read non-stop too, and at a spanking pace, to get the best out of the swift and quickening surge of the action.

After the plays I read all Shakespeare's narrative verse, rather as something to be finished and put out of the way before I moved on into the sonnets. Here I spent much time gratefully and often came back to them.

Discovering Wordsworth was something of an unexpected adventure. I inevitably found my way almost at once to the 'Ode on Intimations of Immortality', well known since school-days but now seen in a brighter and wholly different light. I returned to be daunted yet again by the 'Ode to Duty' – 'Stern daughter of the voice of God' – though I could now accept its lesson more readily than before. Certain smaller pieces, already well known, enchanted me afresh, particularly some of the sonnets.

> *'Hermits are contented with their cells',*
> *And students with their pensive citadels'*

This was exactly right.

What I had never done before, however, was to read the rest of Wordsworth's poetry, 'The Excursion' in toto, for example and the sonnet sequences. Some of this was rather dull, as others have found, but the whole experience was highly rewarding.

In the Oxford edition of Scott's verse I also read every line. I romped through 'Marmion'. I read 'The Lady of the Lake', 'Rokeby' and 'The Last Minstrel' rather more sedately and after that turned to 'The Lord of The Isles'.

I was also reading every day in my monumental anthology, *A Thousand and One Gems of English Poetry*, with its five hundred closely-printed pages and nearly fifty thousand lines of verse. The 'Gems' gave me much enjoyment and much help. I did not look here for comment on situations resembling my own but very much of what I found and read again now appeared to me in a new and sharper light on account of it.

> *'I weep for Adonais – he is dead!*
> *Oh, weep for Adonais . . .'*

Shelley's beautiful lines on the death of Keats came close. Milton's lament for a beloved friend came closer still.

> *'For Lycidas is dead, dead ere his prime,*
> *Young Lycidas, and hath not left his peer.'*

How would it have been possible to read that and remain unmoved?

There was also my old friend *The Ancient Mariner*, first met in the nursery when my mother used to read it aloud to the five of us, four sisters and myself. I now read it with new eyes.

> *'Alone, alone, all, all alone,*
> *Alone on a wide wide sea!*
> *And never a saint took pity on*
> *My soul in agony.*
>
> *The many men, so beautiful!*
> *And they all dead did lie:*
> *And a thousand thousand slimy things*
> *Lived on and so did I.*
>
> *I looked upon the rotting sea*
> *And drew my eyes away;*
> *I looked upon the rotting deck,*
> *And there the dead men lay.'*

Then, as I read further, the water snakes came, 'blue, glossy green and velvet black' swimming in golden fire, and the spring of love for living things and his unconscious blessing on them set the Ancient Mariner free: he found that he could pray.

> *'The Albatross fell off, and sank*
> *Like lead into the sea.'*

There was now deeper meaning for me in this.

Milton's sonnet on his blindness, 'When I consider how my light is spent . . .', admired since my youth, also came much closer now.

> *'They also serve who only stand and wait'.*

A few lines from *As You Like It* gave me especial pleasure. I found them first in the play itself, where the banished Duke is reflecting in the Forest of Arden upon the unexpected compensations of exile, and picked them up again in the 'Gems'.

> *'Sweet are the uses of adversity,*
> *Which like the toad, ugly and venomous,*
> *Wears yet a precious jewel in his head;'*

71

They could have been written expressly for my own case. In this adversity of mine the jewel lay before me, clearly seen and unmistakable.*

What the extracts in the 'Gems' did for me more than anything else, however, was to show me that if I could have added anything to what I had already it would have been *Paradise Lost*.

I had been thrown not long before into yet another thunderous demonstration of man's inhumanity to man, its impact all the greater for the speed with which the airborne operation had developed. I had seen dreadful destruction, great kindness, cruel pain, high fortitude — a catastrophic mixture of opposites all of man's own contriving, not forced upon him but his own work, in a universe surely intended for some better end. What had gone wrong?

Perhaps Milton had the answer. He was certainly setting out to ask the right sort of question.

> '*Of man's first disobedience, and the fruit*
> *Of that forbidden tree, whose mortal taste*
> *Brought death into the world, and all our woe,*
> *With loss of Eden, till one greater Man*
> *Restore us, and regain the blissful seat,*
> *Sing, Heavenly Muse . . .*'

He was also seeking the right sort of help.

> '*. . . what in me is dark*
> *Illumine, what is low raise and support;*
> *That to the height of this great argument*
> *I may assert eternal Providence,*
> *And justify the ways of God, to men.*'

My anthology had other splendid passages to follow these. It had the Fallen Angels in the Burning Lake — marvellous lines — and Satan Presiding in the Infernal Council. There was Satan's Soliloquy in Sight of Paradise, his Expedition to the Upper World, where he meets Sin and Death, and much else besides. They fitted perfectly into my present frame of mind and I read them again and again but they did not develop the whole argument. They always stopped when I wanted more. I promised

* I spoke of what I had read in Ede much more fully than I have done here in a Presidential Address to the English Association in July 1974 under the title *Sweet Uses of Adversity: An Experience* (Oxford University Press). I am grateful to the English Association for permission to use the first two paragraphs from it in the Prologue to this book.

myself that when I got back to England I should ask for *Paradise Lost* as a homecoming present from my wife and read it all.

My life in Torenstraat went on as though it might go on like this for ever. I could remember saying in the past that there was a great deal I wanted to do which, because so much was always happening to distract attention, would only be possible with a long convalescence or a stretch inside. I now seemed, with advantage, to be in a situation combining something of both.

7

I WAS making good progress. I could get in and out of bed without help and whereas Mary had hitherto washed me every day I was now able to do this for myself. I used to walk up and down the room for a few minutes at a time each day for exercise and was hoping bit by bit to straighten out the curve in my back. The holes in my thigh where the little shell splinter had gone straight through had closed up and so had the entry wound of the bigger abdominal splinter, but there was still a discharge from the not yet fully healed incision in front where this had been removed. I was still far from comfortable unless I sat or lay fairly still. Trying to straighten up my back was painful and I realized how very weak I had become.

But I had already been downstairs. Miss Ann insisted that I make one trip, in case of fire or danger from air raids, so that I should know where to find the cellar or the front door if there were no one about to help me. She was anxious too that I should get out of doors again as soon as possible, though I was far from ready for that. There was nothing now left of the high state of physical fitness with which I had started off from Leicestershire, six weeks ago, and building up my strength again looked like being a slow business.

Time in that household still seemed to me to be almost standing still. I had not yet begun to think in terms of days of the week or dates, as one day after another moved on in its gentle routine from the morning to the evening. I had the total confidence of a child, without even giving the matter thought, that tomorrow things would happen again as they had happened today.

It was the arrival of Bat that made me aware again of the passage of time and brought me back into the calendar.

One afternoon late in October, Miss Ann came to my bedside with a serious face to say that there was a strange young man at the door, a Dutchman, who said he was a Dutch officer. He had asked for me and with caution used my own name. He said that he would give his too, if necessary, but that he would rather be known only as Bat. He had come, he said, to make arrangements for my escape. This sounded genuine, Miss Ann thought, but she could take no chances. I gave her a question or two to ask the caller about certain people whom he would know if he were all right. After a few minutes Miss Ann brought me up his answers. They were the right ones and he was let in. I asked him some more questions — though I knew he would be happier if I did not ask for his real name — and was satisfied.

Bat had been dropped by parachute with his wireless operator, who went under the name of Ball, to organize the evacuation of evaders. He had fought in the Dutch army and made his way to England after the collapse of Holland in 1941 and for some time worked with the British. He had been with the Americans on the recent airborne operations but had left them when the situation stabilized and returned to England. He had now been dropped in again. He gave me news of some of the others still in hiding on our side of the Rhine, of Graeme Warrack and Lipmann Kessel, and of several more. He said that plans were afoot to get a good number of us out as soon as battle dress and weapons and essential equipment could be dropped. He saw no reason why I should not be taken along too, though it would mean some form of transportation. The whole operation should not, he thought, take many days to lay on. We were now in the last week of October. I asked whether he saw any chance of my being out by the Fifth of November. This was my birthday, Guy Fawkes Day. When I was a child we had always had fireworks and a bonfire. It was wonderful to think of being home in time to spend it with my wife, who would at least now know, from the letter taken out by Gerald Lathbury, that I was safe. Bat didn't see why not, and said that he would probably come out then too and return to Holland later. He was determined anyhow, he said, to eat his Christmas dinner in England, turkey and all.

Bat was a pleasant fellow, speaking almost perfect English, nice-looking, efficient, enthusiastic and, as I learnt later, very brave. He paid me one or two more visits as he moved about the German-ridden countryside, visiting our soldiers in hiding and organizing their care. He always posed as an agricultural inspector. He had all the right papers, though he knew little of agriculture.

Graeme Warrack was to tell me later on how he had first met Bat, while he himself was lying-up at a farm, shabby, dirty and depressed. Bat and Ball had come in to the farmhouse, having just dropped by parachute, neat and shining in smart uniform and British army equipment, with red berets, airborne smocks carrying parachute wings on the arm, bright boots, blancoed webbing and creased trousers. It made Graeme a little home-sick, he said, to see them but it must have done him a great deal of good. The two newcomers had then changed into other clothing, hidden their uniforms and become two ordinary Dutch civilians. They then went off upon their dangerous and secret business.

Bat's visit added to my own confident expectation that some-how, at some time, I should find my way out of occupied Holland, the encouraging assurance that something was now being done to bring this about. He had good wireless com-munications, useful contacts and, I gathered, much experience. To know that he was busy on my behalf added a new dimension to my life in Torenstraat.

This continued to be a gentle reflective sort of existence, recently much enlarged by the reading I was able to do and the ample opportunity I enjoyed, with no hurry, no deadlines to be met, to think about what I read. It occurred to me that I was getting here the benefit of that much-needed and almost unheard of facility, a slow-reading course.

Reflective though this life might be for me, however, and of necessity physically inactive, it was not without excitement.

Searches were frequent in the town and were always possible in Torenstraat. The probability that our house too would at some time be searched grew with the passage of time. We worked out and practised a drill for my concealment, in a hiding place between the floor of the landing outside my bedroom and the ceiling of the hall below, and for the rapid removal of all traces of a compromising presence in the house. If a search happened at night one of the aunts would occupy my bed and act as a very sick woman. Another would help me to the hole, put the lid on after I was safely in and straighten up the carpet. A third would hold the enemy in conversation through the front door until all was ready. Everything that could knock a few seconds off our time for the whole manoeuvre was studied and every night before Miss Ann tucked me up she put anything in the way of English books or writing into a closet, together with odd things like English cigarettes, if I had any (Bat had brought me some), tobacco, male clothing and anything else likely to arouse suspicion in the room of a sick woman. All was hidden and enough clothes were set out for me, exactly arranged on a chair so placed that I could find it in the dark, to provide against the possibility of a prolonged search and a long cold spell for me in the hiding place.

To lessen the danger to some members at least of the household John and Mary had insisted that they alone should be regarded as responsible for my introduction to it. Their story would be that they had brought me there as a sick friend, and no one else in the household had dreamed that I was really a wounded British officer. If the Germans found me and accepted their story, John and Mary would almost certainly be shot and the house probably blown up as well, but the aunts might at least get off with their lives.

Nevertheless, privately I had other plans, for it was quite intolerable that any one of them should suffer on my account. I was determined that if discovery should be imminent or if pressure in the town grew too severe I would try to slip out of the house and get far enough away from it before I was taken to prevent the incrimination of my hosts. If necessary I could give myself up. To this end I found out in confidence from Dr. Krayenbrink the location of the German headquarters in the town, and had from him certain simple directions on how to get there.

Meanwhile Bat was busy, as I knew, but as the end of October came and went I realized that my thirty-fourth birthday was unlikely to be celebrated with my family. It looked like being spent in Ede.

Birthdays in Holland are events of some moment. A little calendar of birthdays was a common and prominent object in the houses I visited, carrying the names of close members of the family and those of other people whom the family wished particularly to remember: 'Our Mary', 'Uncle Hank's Jan', 'Mijnheer So-and-So', 'Mevrouw Someone Else'. It was especially impressive to find the birthdays of members of the Royal Family, the Queen, Princess Juliana, Prince Bernhard, the little princesses, entered in exactly the same way. I often took part in small treats to celebrate these, with the passing round of some rare sweets or pieces of almost priceless chocolate, or the eating of biscuits or small cakes.

My friends in Torenstraat had found out the day on which my birthday fell from the hopes I had expressed of getting home in time to spend it with my family. As the date approached it was clear that something special was being planned to mark an occasion so important in the life of the family's guest.

'It would be a terrible thing,' said Mary, 'for anyone to spend his birthday among strange people, far from home, and nothing be done about it at all.'

First of all Miss Ann smartened up my clothing. She borrowed a pair of shoes from the bookseller round the corner

77

and a more handsome shirt and tie from John. She pressed the trousers of the suit of his I was now wearing, whose trouser legs she had already had to shorten by several inches.

It was pleasing to discover that there was also to be singing around the harmonium. John asked me a day or two before the event to say what were my favourite English songs. I knew that hymns or sacred songs were meant and said at once that I was particularly fond of 'Abide with Me'. It was always played by the band in my own regiment after the Regimental March and before the National Anthem, a practice imposed upon us, it seemed, for bad behaviour in a convent in the Peninsular War. I very much wanted to hear 'Abide with me' again, both for the sake of its associations and for itself.

The day at length arrived. I was roused by Mary earlier than usual, this time at about 6 a.m. She came in and ceremoniously wished me a very happy birthday, followed at once by her brother John holding in his hand a card. He too offered his congratulations and handed me the card.

'These are the songs we sing for your birthday,' he said, and looking at it I found typed out the words of 'Abide with me' and all the verses of 'God save the King'. It was pleasing to see that I was to hear the robust words of all those later verses of the National Anthem which are today so rarely sung.

Then they went below again, leaving open the doors of my bedroom and of the Huiskamer below where the harmonium stood, so that I could hear. John played and the whole assembled household sang.

My feelings as I listened would be hard to describe. Such loving kindness to a stranger in adversity, on whose behalf these people had already accepted so many dangers with such modesty and courage, was a thing beyond words then and never to be forgotten afterwards.

Miss Ann explained to me later on that day why the singing had to take place so early in the morning. It would naturally have been better, she said, to have it when I came downstairs in the evening in that comfortable hour I had come to know so well. But that was the time when the German soldiers were in their greatest numbers on the streets, and it would not have been wise, she said, to arouse their curiosity with the British National Anthem, sung in English. It was considered best, therefore, that the singing should take place before they were astir.

After breakfast on my thirty-fourth birthday, Guy Fawkes' Day, in the last year of World War II, I was dressed carefully and the room tidied even more scrupulously than usual. There was, they told me, to be a morning reception, when the household would all come to drink coffee with me.

They duly came at eleven o'clock, Aunt Ann, Aunt Cor, Aunt Marie Snoek, John, Mary and last of all the senior member, Aunt Mien, with a happy look on her sweet face and in her hand a small blue and white Delft plate, a present from them all. One by one in turn they made little speeches wishing me a quick recovery in health and an early return to my own home and family. Then Mary brought in coffee and a huge apple cake. There was a skewer stuck in the top of this and on it a beautifully painted Union Jack. Around the flag a white margin had been left and on this, in delicate gothic lettering, a legend: 'Right or wrong, my country'. The cake, which was made out of a stock of condemned pre-war flour, in earlier days considered only fit to be used for paper-hanging, had been baked by a daughter of Uncle Ko. The flag was the work of a retired Dutch regular officer, a Colonel Boeree, who was said to be something of an artist in these matters. He was a much admired man of whom I had often heard, though we had not met.

We sat around on upright chairs in the best bedroom, where their guest was lodged, and drank real coffee made from the contents of one of the little bags of coffee beans dropped here and there in occupied countries by the R.A.F., always prized in Holland for great occasions, and we talked. The air was full of kindness, goodwill and hope.

When they left me I wept unashamedly.

In the afternoon there were other callers. Uncle Ko came, with the daughter who had made the cake. I congratulated her most fervently upon it and was given a fine cigar by her cheerful father, tied up in orange paper with a ribbon of the Royal colours. Uncle Zwerus came too. He gravely wished me a speedy and successful return to my home and duty and shook me warmly by the hand. In the evening I once more went downstairs and spent an hour with what it was no longer possible to regard as any but my own family.

8

I was now coming downstairs every evening. Curfew was at eight o'clock. After that there would be no more visitors and it would be safe for me to join the family.

How well I remember the first time I stepped into the Voorkamer! It was the room immediately under the big front bedroom which was now mine, opening out of the front hall where I had first arrived. The whole family was there, sitting at a circular table under a light hanging in the centre. I looked around. The wall-paper was brown, with a small pattern of flowers. There was a stove, two easy chairs and several wooden ones, a built-in cupboard, a chest of drawers, a bureau and a seat below a window, across which double curtains, of heavy stuff and lace, were now drawn. I saw a portrait of Queen Wilhelmina and photographs of the parents of the four sisters and of the brother who had died, Menno's father. There were also one or two brass ornaments but little else. Small objects of value and anything not in frequent use which could be hidden had, as I knew, long been put in hiding, for the most part away from the house. The room had in it now only what was thought essential but it did not look austere. It was a proper setting for the scene I saw before me.

Mary on that evening was doing an English lesson, John reading a book. The aunts (they were 'Aunt' to me too now) were all occupied. Aunt Mien was sewing, Aunt Cor reading the Bible. Mary's mother was at work on the wool mat that was to be the first furnishing of their new house, when they got one. Aunt Ann was translating the news into English for me. The atmosphere was one of peace and industry and contentment. It descended gratefully on the stranger and enfolded him.

Very soon after, at the end of the second week in November, when I had been down of an evening several times, Aunt Ann said it was time I was taken out for a walk. I had, of course, to do as I was told: my boots were brought out of hiding. Upon the very night after the announcement of this decision, just before curfew, well wrapped up in a coat of John's and with a hat of his on my head, with him in support on the one side and

Aunt Ann on the other and with the general's stick in addition, I was led out.

It was pitch dark and windy. Rain threatened. Like a blind man I was guided along, not speaking for fear of being overheard. We walked slowly across the little square and turned right into Brouwestraat, where Menno's house stood. When we came level with it, a hundred yards up, we turned back. That was enough, said Aunt Ann, for my first outing. We were now walking back along the same route over which the uncles had carried me on my first night in Ede. People passed in the darkness, some of them sounding like German soldiers.

A motor-cycle with dimmed lights had been following us at a snail's pace. This must be a German; there were almost no other motor-cycles on the roads. When we had reached our turning point and were retracing our steps the motor-cyclist slowly turned and followed. We drew away. He came after. A voice told us in German to stop. We were cornered. Aunt Ann asked him what he wanted. Could we tell him, he asked in makeshift Dutch, the way to the centre of the town? Aunt Ann told him (correctly, I wondered? I knew that on principle German soldiers asking the way were always misdirected) and in great relief and a sudden burst of high spirits we came home.

That was on 15th November. It was a very short walk but it came at the beginning of a new chapter. In a day or two, though Mary or Aunt Ann continued to bring me a cup of tea first thing in the morning and then gave me breakfast in bed, after which Mary would return to do anything necessary to the dressings on my injuries, I was being allowed down to join the family at their midday meal as well.

I would be sitting in the front room at noon as they began to gather, Aunt Cor from the drug store, Aunt Ann from the paint factory, where she always had something to do, Mary from her marketing, John from any of his many activities and his mother from a household duty or some errand. When we were assembled Aunt Mien would bring in from the kitchen what she had prepared for us. We all said grace, standing and in silence, and then sat down to Aunt Mien's dish. This was always a plentiful meal of vegetables in which there was sometimes also even a little meat. Aunt Mien was wonderfully clever at cooking up some combination of potatoes, turnips, beetroot, cabbage or whatever other vegetables there were, with gravy of some sort or pear- or apple-sauce. What she brought in was always good and satisfying and never dull.

When I first began to be allowed down to the midday meal I

was astonished at what seemed to me the enormous quantities of this food that John and Mary could take in. It was mostly bulk, however, and soon, as I grew stronger, I was eating almost as much as they were.

The de Nooij family in Torenstraat did better, I think, than most. They had laid in a store of food in the early days, when it was clear that there would be shortages. Some of this still remained. There were many relations and connections who would gladly come to the help of the aunts if help were wanted. John worked hard in scouring the farms for potatoes and other vegetables and there was occasional help from the Underground on account of the extra burden the household had to bear in looking after me. Above all there was the skill in household management of Aunt Mien, which was of the very highest order. All in all, though life was difficult and getting more so, this family was not too badly off.

Nonetheless, words could not express the gratitude I felt for the way they housed, fed and looked after me. A fighting soldier in war-time takes the dangers and tensions that bear upon himself for granted. It is quite a different thing to contemplate the actions of other people, to observe their bravery, contrivance and self-sacrifice, in protecting and looking after someone thrown by hazard into their care. There is nothing to be taken for granted here.

I had often tried to refuse the extra things the family provided for me, the additional milk, for example, and the occasional egg. There was also the jam and the daily glass of wine, among other things that came from Uncle Zwerus. I begged them not to give me any more than they had for themselves. It was a waste of time. When the ladies of Torenstraat had once made up their minds about something there was little more to be said.

The whole de Nooij family, and not only the household in Torenstraat, owed much to the stores of the paint factory and perhaps something to the drug store as well. From the factory stores, for example, there was oil to be had, and spirit, useful in themselves and valuable commodities for barter. From the stock of condemned flour, out of which my birthday cake had been made, one white loaf was now baked weekly for each of the family's principal households.

After lunch in Torenstraat grace was said again and a short passage read from the Bible. Then I was packed off upstairs, at first with a hot-water bottle. Sometimes, when I began to come down at midday, I slept a little in the afternoon but this was soon to become mostly a time for reading, lying fully dressed on the sofa in my room. After the midday meal Mother Mary rested too, for she was not over strong, and so sometimes did Aunt Mien. Later in the afternoon I would come down again, to be given another cup of pale tea — always in 'my' mug — and sit, usually alone, in a corner of the Voorkamer by the window, behind the lace curtains. Here I could go on reading, warm, comfortable and wholly absorbed. Only very occasionally did I look up from my book to see what was going on in the street outside and watch the German soldiers as they moved about.

As the afternoon wore on, however, I would find myself beginning to look up now and then at the hands of the church clock, keeping an eye also on the light. As soon as this began to fail I would get ready to go walking and whenever any member of the family was available (it was quite out of the question for me to walk alone) we would go off together at our slow pace through the gathering gloom, round the lanes and roads which I was soon to know, in this light, so very well.

Curfew did not stay long at eight. The Germans had good reason to suppose that the interval between curfew and nightfall was useful to their enemies and before long advanced the time to six. It was beginning to get dark, just then, about five and on the clear evenings rather later, so we had not a great deal of time in which to walk. This did not matter much for I could only take a little of this exercise at first. Every day we walked a little further, though still only very slowly. I used to come back tired, but in a glow, to supper.

Supper was a bread meal. There was a great dish of bread of varying shades of brown, from the light sort provided especially for Aunt Cor, down to almost black rye-bread, looking rather like slices of plum pudding without plums, very close to German pumpernickel. To put on our bread there was usually a little butter — a thin scrape for each slice or, when it was scarcer than usual, for every second slice: Aunt Mien would let us know which. Sometimes there were paper-thin slices of cheese or smoked meat. Earlier on there had been a sort of syrup (which gave out, I remember, quite soon) or what they called 'artificial honey', and there was still sometimes a sprinkling of castor sugar. The bread was always eaten, of course, with a knife and fork. In front of my place there was a pot of jam. This was always studiously ignored by all the others and only resorted to by myself to the minimum demanded by good manners. There was also very often a cup of milk for everyone and sometimes Mother Mary and I would each be given, as a very special treat, a boiled egg.

After supper grace was said again and we would settle down for the evening.

Aunt Cor would usually read and often retired early when her head was troublesome. Aunt Ann would mend and darn and sometimes read too. Mary would usually be working at her English, or would go over her English lesson with me, or correct my own exercises in Dutch. Her mother would be working away at the wool mat. Aunt Mien was usually sewing. John and I often played chess.

As the family's day approached its end a passage would be read from the Bible.

I can still hear Aunt Mien saying in that gentle voice, as she lifted her silver head from her needlework, 'Shall we read now?'

This was the signal for one of us to get up and bring out the Bibles from the cupboard in the corner, one for each. The big English Authorized Version, now living once more downstairs, would be handed to me where I sat, usually in the same place at the far end of the table from the door, or in an arm-chair just behind it. A different member of the family would read a passage every night, each in turn, while I followed what was read in the English version.

Then, for as long as they lasted, there would be an apple for each one of us. Aunt Mien, without being asked, would peel one each for John and me if we sat engrossed in a game of chess. The apples were running low now.

During the evening sessions in the family John and I began to teach the ladies chess. They all played, each in her own characteristic way. Aunt Cor learnt quickly and played logically, though sometimes a little impatiently. Aunt Ann played quietly, carefully and slowly but made terrible mistakes of which she was ashamed. Mary played keenly and gently, with much sympathy for her opponent's predicament, but could be disconcertingly tough—not so much in exploiting the other person's blunders as in helping him to make them. Aunt Mien played merrily and liked to see the pieces fall. Mother Mary hardly tried at all. She soon laughed and gave it up. There was trouble enough, she said, with one chess player in the family. John had been known to be a little difficult over his meals when chess was much on his mind and where would they be if she caught the same complaint and forgot to cook?

So she went on working on the wool mat for the new house they would move into some day.

There was only one set of chessmen and play was limited. As we sat, the seven of us, in the warm Voorkamer, after the oil lamps had been got ready for the time when the illicit electric current would be cut off about nine o'clock, with a kettle on the stove for the hot-water bottles, the day's work over and apple-time still some way off, we talked a great deal.

There were particularly interested in Palestine. I had spent several years serving under the British Mandatory Government in Palestine and Transjordan before and at the beginning of the war, first for a few months in my own regiment and then for four years in a cavalry squadron of the Transjordan Frontier Force. I used at one time to live with the squadron, which was composed mostly of Arabs and Transjordan Circassians, on the southern shore of Galilee. I knew Palestine, on the whole, pretty well. My Dutch friends never tired of asking questions about the Holy Land, the one place Aunt Mien wanted to see above all others.

None of them, in fact, had travelled much. Aunt Ann had spent a summer in England and showed me the travel folders she had brought back with her. They were full of things I had never seen and promised myself to see when I got home again. Aunt Cor had made a journey up the Rhine and another, I think, to Switzerland, and was often appealed to as an authority on foreign countries.

About Palestine they asked me, was it not a truly wonderful thing to be in the country which had seen Christ? Aunt Mien said she found it very strange to be talking to someone who had lived there.

Even for a committed Christian, however, it was just not possible to go on living indefinitely in a state of wonder at being where Christ had been. Nazareth, with all its associations, had been most recently for me the place where the headquarters of my parachute brigade had been located, in a monastery, during the months we had spent training in Palestine the year before. My answers to the questions put to me in the family, and my explanations, had therefore to be given with care to avoid causing even the slightest offence to susceptibilities I could readily understand.

What I could not easily explain was something I was only beginning to understand a little better myself. However unusual the environment in which you find yourself—however extraordinary the circumstances—if these persist you adapt to them surprisingly soon. You have to get on with the business of living and this is immensely difficult unless you can come to accept the way in which you happen to be living as normal. As I sat of an evening with the rest of the family in the Voorkamer, warm and secure, surrounded by kindness, reading in my one-volume Shakespeare or the 'Gems', or any of my other books, playing chess with John, doing my own lessons in Dutch or giving English lessons, or talking about Palestine to a group listening with rapt attention, it never occurred to me to give much thought to the strange and dangerous circumstances in which it was all happening. This was now my life: it had become for me the norm.

9

PLANS were now well advanced for the next party of airborne evaders to make their escape. for which the date chosen was the night of 17th/18th November. It was already apparent that I would not be going with it. The German defensive works along the river bank and the depth of the forbidden zone made it impossible to concentrate the party close to the intended crossing point. There would therefore have to be a long approach march at night. This would be quite beyond my strength and a stretcher-party to carry me could hardly be considered. I therefore became an onlooker and had little opportunity of influencing certain aspects of the planning which made me feel uneasy. The success of the last big escape operation, in late October, had generated quite unjustified confidence in this new plan, which was necessarily different and very much harder to carry out.

To begin with the private telephone line had gone. It had been interrupted by shellfire within the forbidden zone, we were told, and the break could not be got at and repaired. Communications were therefore much more difficult. Secondly, the party did not have the preponderance of fit, well trained infantry that there had been in the first, in which the men were also mostly operating under officers well known to them. All of those in this group had been in hiding several weeks more and were that much less fit. Very many of them, moreover, were not infantry soldiers at all. A considerable number came from the R.A.F. Few, if any, of these had much idea of how to carry out a difficult infantry operation at night. Thirdly, to reach the chosen crossing place required movement through an area where German patrols were active, Dutch forced-labour was at work by day on defences under German supervision, and gun positions were manned all round the clock. Finally, this ill-organized body was to conduct its operation under leaders whom few of the men had ever seen before. Many did not even know their names.

The party was to number about one hundred and twenty, about the size of a strong company, and the march from the final rendezvous to the bank would be about twenty-three kilometres.

87

A good infantry company, well trained in night work, fit, fully equipped — the smoothly working machine of interlocking parts which all good infantry companies become — would have found it no easy task to move at night, in silence, through unfamiliar and almost completely unreconnoitred country in which hostile troops were preparing defensive positions. To have done anything so demanding would be a feather in the cap of the best company you could find. What chance had this random collection of men, however keen they might be?

I sent word for Bat to come to see me and, busy as he was, he came. It was really no business of mine, but I asked him what recent experience he, or anyone there, had of an infantry company operating at night. Very little, it seemed, if any, either on his own part or that of anyone else involved. I pointed out some of the weaknesses, and urged him above all to take particular care over the organization of minor commands. The equivalent of sections should at least know their section leaders. But even that, in the circumstances, could hardly be arranged since many of the men could only be brought together for the first time on the day of the final move, or at most a day or so before.

The difference between this plan and the last was what most distinguished good plans in war from bad ones. The other had a high probability of success if it did not run into really bad luck; this one would need very good luck indeed to have even a sporting chance.

The trouble was that, particularly among the Dutch side, there was so little experience of ordinary infantry work that they could not even see the problems.

'What happens,' I asked 'when they are discovered?'

'They are a large party,' was the confident answer, 'and armed. They can fight their way through.'

This answer, which could only come from total unawareness of the problems of command and control in an infantry action at night, filled me with foreboding. A tragic muddle seemed to me a virtual certainty.

No blame attaches here to anyone. The circumstances were too much for the promoters, that was all. I say now what I said to several people before it came off, to the Dutch during the period of heart-searching and recrimination that followed its failure, to those on the far end of it when I met them and to more than one sad officer since then who has tended to blame himself too much for the failure: it was not a good plan because it demanded too much good luck for success; it was probably the only plan possible under the circumstances; since the need to get these men away was pressing, both for their own sakes and to relieve the hard-pressed Dutch of their presence, it was possibly a justified risk.

As it turned out the operation ran into bad luck quite early on. The main party was discovered on the move. There was shooting. Confusion resulted and such little control as there had been, on follow-my-leader lines, now vanished. A few got through to the river and some were killed. Most were recaptured. My indomitable friend Graeme Warrack got himself as far as the bank, but at a place where there were no boats and so had to make his weary way back to hide somewhere else until he could try again. He later made a second attempt to break out which was an even more gruelling experience and again nearly succeeded and again just failed. Finally, he would come out with me, under the arrangements which John Snoek was to make in the fullness of time.

Before daylight on the morning fixed for the crossing, the 18th November, I heard distant shooting from my bed. I knew only too well what this must mean. Then the news began to trickle in. First there was a rumour Aunt Cor brought, one of Uncle Ko's I think, that an American patrol had come across the river and penetrated as far as Wolfhezen, and that an officer had been captured. This, probably meant that one of the U.S. Air Force officers with the escaping party had been taken. The area and the time fitted in, and so did the absence of American troops on the south bank just there. Then more and more details filtered through while sporadic shooting in the distance suggested that the Germans were beating the woods. By early afternoon I could guess the extent of the failure. It seemed virtually complete.

During the next few days, though confined to the house in Torenstraat, I found much to do. There were Dutchmen closely involved in the enterprise who felt very badly about its outcome and blamed everyone in turn, themselves included, for its failure. Every sort of rumour circulated. Uncle Ko, who had no part in the undertaking, brought me some of these—that every man had run like a rabbit at the first shot, for instance, and that most of the men had been drunk anyway. I did my best to calm things down. No one should be blamed. For the very best of reasons they had tried to do too much.

It was agreed in the family that in a search of the house by day the best plan would be for me to be found in bed, and for them to say that I had been injured in an air raid. I was no longer to be 'tubercular'. There was good evidence of violent injury on my person and the family felt that they could tell a convincing enough story. Anyway, the intelligence service of the Dutch Underground was swift and good and we expected to get some warning of a daytime search.

That in fact was how it happened.

One morning Miss Ann came in and put down my breakfast tray.

'There is no cause for alarm,' she said, 'but we are told that German soldiers are searching the houses and that they are coming this way. They are taking blankets and clothing, so we are putting away everything that we can.'

I could already hear a considerable bustle outside my door. Anything woollen that was not being worn, or was not in use in some other way, was being stowed away in the hiding places. We did not know what the Germans might be looking for but whatever it might be they always took any woollen things they found.

We had had these alarms before and the arrangements were in good working order. This time, the hiding places were full of textiles, so there was no room in any of them for me. I was dressing slowly when I heard someone climbing the stairs. Mary came in hurriedly, breathing hard.

'German soldiers are moving up the street and look like coming in here,' she said. 'Go back to bed.'

I flung my clothes off but before crawling into bed again caught a quick glimpse through the window of three German soldiers of the Luftwaffe, all armed, advancing across the little square towards the house.

Mary stood at the window and waited. I lay in my bed looking up at the ceiling; a long time passed. The air seemed to be heavily charged.

Mary was looking down through the window.

'They are coming to the door,' she said.

I heard a heavy knocking followed by loud male voices. Female voices answered, several at once. There seemed to be an argument. The noise rose swiftly in pitch and volume. Then bedlam seemed to break out. Aunt Cor was having an attack of hysterics delivered, it was clear, with truly exquisite timing. The enemy were already wavering under the verbal barrage. Aunt Cor's hysterics, as the aunts told me later, broke them.

'They are going away,' said Mary.

I lumbered out of bed and over to the window.

Well armed though they were, the Germans seemed to be

almost slinking away from the door. A cloud of defeat brooded over their heads.

Presently Aunt Cor came in with a little dish in her hand, once more her usual placid self.

'You must have a piece of our pre-war chocolate,' she said, 'to celebrate. It is almost the last we have and we were keeping it for some great event. We shall eat it now.'

I had always known, I suppose, that no very young man, however well armed or whatever other advantages there might be on his side, was any match for an angry elderly woman, let alone for three or four all talking at him at once in a strange tongue. Here was proof. I felt almost sorry for the Germans.

I heard later that they had gone straight in to Hennie next door, rather truculent, and taken several of her blankets. Hennie protested vigorously.

'You need not talk like that,' said the Luftwaffe corporal in charge, 'you're all right. What about the poor old ladies next door? They've got nothing!'

Hennie, who lived largely on the generosity of her aunts, particularly where things like blankets were concerned, was struck almost dumb.

'Well!' she said.

10

GERMAN pressure was now increasing steadily both in Ede and in the surrounding countryside. The Todt Organization, with its cruel-looking old men in their yellowish uniforms, at once hateful and pathetic, was here in some strength, conscripting what labour there still was for work upon defences. More bicycles were being taken, whenever they could be found, and houses were often searched for them. Seizure of food and textiles was common and personal papers were more rigidly inspected. There was talk of raids to flush out and imprison men in hiding; this was already happening in the cities. It was reported that 800 Grüne Polizee (the armed support of the Dutch Nazi organization, the N.S.B.) had moved into the village of Barneveld up the road. The system of permits (to possess a bicycle, for example, or to travel) was being reviewed constantly and sometimes the papers in use were cancelled suddenly and new ones issued for which fresh application had to be made. Menno and his friends were kept hard at work procuring the new issues and putting the right signatures on them.

These were often masterpieces. I spent a long time comparing the signature of Herr Groll, head of the local N.S.D.A.P., on the handsome Ausweis which Menno had furnished to exempt Mijnheer van Dalen from digging for the Germans, with that on the similar document held by Dr. Kraayenbrink which Herr Groll had in fact signed himself. I could detect no difference. The curls and pressures looked exactly right and a red pencil of identical shade and texture had been used in both.

Once all Ausweise for any purpose were withdrawn suddenly and an entirely new sort issued, with an underprint of small 'N.S.D.A.P.'s all over it. This too, with the intention of providing a new control on unauthorized exemptions, had to be applied for afresh. The printer was a man trusted (and also highly paid) by the Germans but he found it possible to run off a few hundred of the new sort for Menno at the same time, which were then signed up and held ready for instant issue. Menno's people already held similar stocks of passes for the 'Emergency Zone of Ede' (if ever there should be one: this had not happened yet) and for other contingencies. They had to be careful, of course, not to issue such things too soon — before, that is to say, the Germans had sprung their own surprise, cancelled the old sort and brought the new ones into use. The whole business made a great deal of unnecessary work, Menno told me, and wasted far too much of his people's time.

One day Menno, on his way to see Bat in his hiding place in the country, had a narrow escape. A Todt man halted him and told him to come along with him and bring his bicycle with him. Menno tried to slip off but a shot over his head from the Todt man's revolver suggested it was wise to do what he was told. At the N.S.D.A.P. headquarters in the Amsterdamscher Weg he was told to leave his machine outside and come in. He did not like this at all because he had with him at the time several beautiful facsimiles of Herr Groll's signatures, on blank permit forms, to take to Bat. If these were found it would be a serious matter. Other people were being questioned inside. Menno seized a moment when no one was looking, walked boldly out of the entrance, told the guard that he was to send in any others waiting and strolled off towards Torenstraat. He came in and told us what had happened and Mary went back and wheeled away his bicycle. We all laughed over Menno's time with the N.S.D.A.P., probably in relief more than anything. We also teased Mary for her lack of scruple in taking German property. The bicycle had been requisitioned by the Germans, after all, and so was legally theirs. Mary, we told her, had been stealing!

Then we learnt how narrow Menno's escape had really been, and were appalled. He had been going out to meet Bat in his hiding place about the middle of the afternoon. The Todt incident had made him too late to go that day. At ten past four a lorry-load of troops drove up to Bat's house and a second came up from the other side. The troops dismounted and closed in. There was shooting. Bat ran for it but was hit in the leg. He was now in the hands of the Security Service of the S.S., the Sicherheitsdienst.* Menno's temporary detention by the Todt organization, therefore, had fortuitously kept him out of really bad trouble. He was always lucky. But Bat's capture was truly disastrous, for Bat knew everything.

How much he might give away under examination, stout hearted though he was, could not be guessed and apprehension was general. Next day it was reported that searches and arrests had begun and a descent upon Torenstraat was possible at any time. It would be best for everyone if I were away from it.

* The SD operated more or less openly, whereas the Gestapo, as its name implied (the Geheimestaatspolizei) worked in secret.

Fairly early that morning Mary and I left the house and went down the lane to the left, to a house in the corner of the High Street. It was that of the bookseller from whom Aunt Ann had borrowed the shoes for my birthday. Though the journey was one of only a very few minutes I was careful then, as always, to show neither unfamiliarity with my surroundings nor curiosity about what was going on around me. To look about is dangerous. In consequence I saw little enough on the way. It was exciting in the highest degree, all the same, to be out in the street in broad daylight for the first time. We took books and Mary her sewing and when we reached the house I had my Dutch lesson from her and she her English lesson from me. Aunt Ann brought us food at midday, into the upstairs bedroom where we spent our day, and after we had eaten Mary read aloud the 91st Psalm from the English Bible. Later I passed some time at the window, looking down through the curtains at what was going on in the High Street, where there was much more movement and more troops could be seen than from our own house. It was certainly interesting. I noticed that the companies of marching (and singing) German infantry were all made up from different units and some were parachutists. None of the several companies I saw was all from one unit.

In the evening the danger was judged to be over, at least for the time being, and I was allowed to come home. Aunt Ann excused me from my walk in the dark that night. She said I had had enough exercise already.

Then we heard that among other arrests there had been one even more serious than Bat's. The Commander of the L.O. in the Veluwe area had been caught by the Germans at work in his headquarters, with his papers spread before him. Not only had the Germans got from his lists information which would put many people into grave danger, but it was feared that the man had given way under interrogation and told them still more. This seemed unlikely, because he was said to have behaved very stoutly when examined on two former occasions, but a rumour to that effect was widespread.

Almost immediately afterwards a raid had been made on the local resistance centre at Otterloo, a village a few miles from Ede, where Piet was now based. Sixteen people had been arrested and were now being held in a bank building in Velp, just east of Arnhem. They were not there long, for a raid was made by Dutchmen from the local L.K.P., with the connivance of the Dutch police guarding them, and the whole lot removed to safety, Dutch guards and all. But one result of this was that the Germans now posted Luftwaffe guards on that building instead, and when Bat was held there later, with both legs in plaster as we heard (though only one was injured) and a German guard beside his bed with orders to shoot him if there were an alarm, he could not be got away.

Piet now took over command in the Veluwe and found himself obliged to change the whole cover scheme for the organization. He himself became a food control inspector and set out by changes of local headquarters, designations, courier systems, addresses and personnel to cover up all traces of the old system.

Piet had many narrow escapes himself. He was arrested and interrogated more than once and even he did not always know how he got away. Once about this time he came to see me in Ede on a motor-bicycle and told me that a few days before he had been stopped while he was driving his car. He knew that in the car were papers which would be his death warrant if they were found. He then had to stand by while six Germans searched it, singly and one after the other. They found nothing. But they confiscated the car and drove it away, papers and all. The papers were under a piece of matting fastened down to the floor. There was no evidence that they were ever found.

Before very long Bill's headquarters near Ede were raided. The warning given by the outposts was adequate and weapons, compromising papers and other dangerous things were hidden in time. But while the Germans were still there a girl courier arrived on her bicycle. She was a Jewess. When she saw what was happening she turned round and started riding away as hard as she could. After only a few yards one of her tyres punctured and slowed her down. She was caught, searched and beaten savagely, and then taken away. The house itself and that next door, owned by the same family of farmers, was blown up.

Bill was fortunately away at the time, but like many others had to go into hiding. He was chiefly worried, as so many of them were, about his wife and child. Menno was hiding too. Inquiries by Gestapo men seemed to have been directed plainly at him, and I felt that if I could get out of this country soon it might be wise to take Menno with me.

In all these circumstances the family in Torenstraat thought it best that I should move away for a while. A kind offer had come from Colonel and Mrs Boeree to take me in: it was accepted gratefully.

I had now got in touch, through Menno, with another agent whom we can call Sam. This young man had been operating not far from Ede for some months now. He belonged to a famous and often brilliantly successful raiding and sabotage organization but, as business had become a little slack for them when the fluid conditions in which they operated best had given place to a more stable situation, he had been dropped by parachute in occupied Holland to do a mainly Intelligence job. His stuff, I believe, was quite first-rate and I always admired the soundness of his security arrangements. Not even the underground knew much of his whereabouts. No one ever went directly to his place but only to a rendezvous, to be met by his own courier who then took the business over to hand on to him. We had corresponded freely, though always with the delays inevitable in his system, before I met him. This happened, only by accident, almost two months later.

Sam had two plans to get me out.

One was that I should be picked up by a light aircraft. This had been suggested to the other side by Bat, I think, over his own link, and turned down at the time as not practicable until the ground, then soaked by autumn rain, should harden. There were also many other difficulties, of which I was later to learn in England, but I must confess that as the frost came and the ground rang iron-hard underfoot I wondered if this plan had been forgotten. It was probably impossible for someone planning it as an operation on the far side to see with our eyes how easily it could be done on this. I knew many pilots who would have come with pleasure. If only I could get hold of that brave and brilliant airman and best of friends Joe Crouch, Commander and trainer of the U.S. Troop Carrier Command Pathfinders, who had dropped me so often and jumped with us too, I should be home in almost no time! But though the idea of evacuation by air was raised on our side more than once for re-examination at the far end, nothing was ever to come of it.

Dutch friends in Ede were inclined to suggest sometimes that my own people at home were not trying hard enough, that they were ungrateful. I tried to help them keep a sense of proportion. The people on the other side would get me out if and when they could, but only if the risk was considered worth the possible return. My value could not, in my present state, be all that high.

The other possible plan was to get me down to the Rhine bank somehow, to be picked up there by a patrol from the other side of the river. The Germans had flooded much of the country in the Betuwe, on the south side of the Rhine, and our troops had had to withdraw here and there, while small German posts had been pushed across to the southern bank. It would need careful planning and timing on the far side to bring a patrol up through no-man's land and get a boat across between the German posts. Weather, moon, German movements, height of the winter river, ice, direction of wind, other plans and many other things would have to be considered. Moreover, on our bank the Germans were digging hard. There were infantry posts and detachments of the Todt organization and a belt of country from which even the farmers had been evacuated, through which we would have to penetrate, and I was still very weak and could walk no more than a slow mile without exhaustion.

We had an absorbing time planning all the same. Menno was coming too, and when a signal arrived through Sam that the other side had agreed to a plan along these lines and would confirm a day for the attempt round about Christmas Day, we two settled down to making the detailed arrangements. We were full of hope.

In the meantime I had been taken down to the house of Colonel and Mevrouw Boeree. Mary, Aunt Ann, John and I walked one cold dark night through the town, in and out of groups of German soldiers off duty and past the Ortskommandant's headquarters (which, after Dr. Kraayenbrink's directions, I had been curious to see) and at length I came to the house in Stationsweg where a warm welcome awaited me from Mevrouw Boeree.

It had taken twenty minutes to walk the distance and I was tired out. Luggage, clothes, books, dressings and things like soap and a little butter were taken along by the family, and of course I had with me General Urquhart's stick. There was also a bottle of cognac from Uncle Zwerus for which I was very grateful. A stomach upset was quite common in Ede just then and I too had fallen a victim to it. It was quite painful but brandy calmed it down. It never even occurred to me that this abdominal pain might come from other causes. My confidence in what Lipmann Kessel's surgery had done for me was complete.

11

THE Boeree household, to which I came at the beginning of the third week in November, in my fifth week in Ede, was that of an elderly retired regular officer of Artillery in the Dutch army. Our two backgrounds were not greatly dissimilar and I was at once at home. There was a girl staying with them, the daughter of a Scottish officer killed in the First World War, who had been brought up in Holland and had never been in England. All three spoke English, Mevrouw Boeree knew it very well indeed. She had translated books from English into Dutch. Her husband was of a precise and scholarly turn of mind and had written what I was told was an excellent book on the history of an ancient family near Bergen op Zoom.

I was now able to thank him for the flag on my birthday cake. I told him that I had kept it and would in due time take it home with me.

We had much to talk about—the war, our two armies, books, horses. The conversation of my hostess also gave me much pleasure and I greatly enjoyed our little walks in the dusk through the wooded and unfrequented outskirts of the town. The whole household, including the elderly maid-servant, who used to sit with us in the drawing-room in the evenings to make the best of what little fuel there was for the stove, could not have been kinder or more charming.

The Boerees had bought this pleasant little house for their retirement. It was not very far from the barracks and had been one of the buildings to suffer in the allied air attack just before our landing in September. One side of the house had been partly blown in and there had been a good deal of other damage, including some to the spare bedroom in which I now slept. They had not yet been able to do much in the way of repair. I was now being sheltered in a house quite unnecessarily damaged as a result of my very own action. I kept that to myself.

This family could hardly have differed more in habits, outlook and background from the one I had just left. They found it very much harder to manage, for one thing, without the resources available to the de Nooijs. Later when I had left and came back one evening by a cautious and circuitous route to dine with them, Mevrouw Boeree had been to a farmer and exchanged some linen for the butter she wanted on her table.

Menno used to come to see me and give me what messages there were from Sam. John used to come too.

'That boy,' said my hostess of John, 'looks simple. But I do not think he is.'

There was a newly made hiding place upstairs, a part of the bathroom partitioned off and painted by the de Nooij firm to look like the rest. I spent one cold and dismal morning in it, crouching in the dark and sickened with the smell of new paint while German soldiers searched the houses of the neighbourhood for bicycles.

The Boerees' house stood on the road leading out to Bennekom and Renkum and there was constant passage to and fro of German troops, as many going down as came back. I saw nothing to support the view, held by some, that the Germans were moving out. It was fascinating to stand at the broad windows of my hostesses' drawing-room on the ground floor, a few yards back from the street, and watch the Germans across the piece of front garden. By far the greatest number wore the blue uniform of the Luftwaffe, though they were being employed as infantry. I used to watch them marching, well dispersed under the threat from the air, almost crippled under the heavy load of kit they carried; or riding in groups on bicycles that had clearly been requisitioned, machines of all shapes and sizes, men's and women's. Some had tyres, others had none and rattled along on their rims. Down this end of the town, close to the railway and the German positions, allied air activity was nearer and much noisier. My hostess's little dog was terrified by it and used to cower under the chintz-covered sofa at the first faint drone he heard. The Germans were almost as much affected as the dog. They often got themselves into difficulties on their bicycles by looking up when aircraft were about. I remember watching one who was pedalling slowly and noisily along on a bicycle without tyres, wobbling more and more as he kept on screwing his head straight up to see what was happening overhead, until the inevitable happened and he took a crashing and spectacular fall only a few feet from me. I enjoyed that.

But my stay in the house in Stationsweg was soon to be cut short. The Colonel's work was in the evacuee organization and he spent all his day at it. One evening he was late for supper and as time went on apprehension grew. Finally he came. He had, perhaps unwisely, gone that day to ask for straw at the very same farm where Bat had been arrested. It was still under

German guard and he had been detained. They had taken him to Lunteren and subjected him to a close and, it seemed, offensive examination. He was able to answer all their questions about the papers in his pockets and his movements. Later on he was allowed to return to his home, but he was convinced that he was still under suspicion.

Quite apart from my own presence in his house, there were other things connected with my host in which the Germans would have been interested. He had formerly been local head of the O.D. Although this was now, in Ede, being merged into other bodies, he was still liable to stern punishment at the hands of the Germans if his former connection with it were to be discovered.

It was therefore time for me to move on again. The Colonel had been rather shaken by his unpleasant afternoon, and the shadow he was now under, but he did not think there would be any follow-up that night. The next day, however, it would be wise for me to go elsewhere.

Word was sent that night to the de Nooijs. On the evening of the next day (it was 25th November) Aunt Ann and Mary came round to collect me and take me back to Torenstraat.

My return to the little house I had so lately left was the occasion for a great reunion. It was like the homecoming of a member of a family after a prolonged stay with friends at a great distance. Their pleasure at seeing me back seemed to be almost as great as my own at being there again.

Aunt Ann told me that when they heard that I could no longer stay in Stationsweg there had been earnest discussion in the family about what it would be best to do. Should I return to their house or go somewhere else? For me now to go elsewhere had seemed at first the obvious course but the more they looked at it, she said, the less they liked it.

'We considered one or two other places,' said Aunt Ann, 'but we did not think you would be well enough looked after in them. We feel anyway, as you know, that we are responsible for you; we would really be happiest if you stayed with us until you leave for good.'

There was nothing I could say.

'It seems to us a sort of task,' she went on, 'in which all of us in the household are expected to play a part. You have your own part to play in it too. It is best, really, that you have come back to us and this is where you must stay.'

How happy I was to sit with them all around the table by the stove again, with the curtains drawn and their kind faces smiling at me! Everything was as it had been before. I suffered a crushing defeat at John's hands over the chess board that very night. There was the evening apple for everyone, the portion of the Bible to be read, the B.B.C. war news to be discussed, the preparations for an alarm to be gone through before we went off to bed. The whole atmosphere of friendliness, kindness and quiet security enveloped me once more as it had in the past. I was truly at home again. It signified little that I was also back in the centre of the village, in a more dangerous place than the one I had just left. Even to be back within fifty yards or so of the dog-loving German military police gave something of the comfortable feeling induced by the return to familiar things.

I was now no longer to live in the large front room but went back instead to the little one I had first come to, on the other side of the upstairs landing, facing north. Aunt Cor had often been unwell with her migraine and it was clearly best that she should have the more comfortable room. It was, I must confess, very cold where I slept now. Often — indeed on most mornings — I had to break the ice in the pitcher before I could wash. At Aunt Mien's request the windows were kept closed at night. Apart from the danger of cracked bedroom china and glass, there was very little fuel to heat the house now and we had to use it as effectively as we could. The temperature in my little room when I woke up was sometimes minus ten or twelve degrees centigrade, even with the windows closed.

We were approaching Christmas. In our household it was its Christian significance that mattered. As in the rest of Holland, if presents were given it was upon St. Nicholas's Day, 5th December that this happened. I now learnt about Black Piet. He goes along with the Saint carrying a bag with gifts in it for the good children and a stick for the bad. In Holland he is a very famous person. In the scrapbook the Snoek family had kept of what they called 'Nazi Nonsense' since the invasion of Holland I noticed a Dutch Nazi paper's account of an English atrocity — the bombing of Ravenna. The tomb of St. Nicholas was there. On the cutting brother William had written: 'As long as Black Piet's all right, what's the fuss about?' Most villages have a visit from the Saint and Black Piet of their very own. The eagerly awaited pair would mostly arrive in their splendid clothes in a cart, or on a sleigh, but to the villages along the Rhine bank they usually came by water.

The girl with the Scots name staying with the Boerees sent me on St. Nicholas's Day a gay little packet, addressed to Mr. Van Dalen, containing a pretty little painted matchbox holder.

It was touching to see the lengths to which people went, and their ingenuity, in finding presents to give each other from amongst their meagre possessions. There was nothing to buy in the shops and as the sixth year of German occupation approach the Dutch people did not find themselves at all rich in earthly goods. But somehow they found gifts for relatives and friends and for strangers in their midst.

Back in Torenstraat planning for my escape with Menno was going ahead. With his advice, having weighed up comparative ease of approach, depth and degree of German occupation and other factors, I had chosen, upon maps borrowed from Colonel Boeree, places on the Rhine bank from which we could possibly be picked up. A message drafted by me had been got by Menno to Sam, making suggestions for a signal to be sent by him to the other side, and at length the reply reached me in the same roundabout way. The troops nearest to the chosen spot on the south bank would be prepared to send a patrol up through the German outpost lines with a boat or boats, and bring back two of us, myself and anyone else I chose. It was my intention to take Menno. Then followed an interchange of messages in which the exact rendezvous was checked. My map, one of those borrowed from Colonel Boeree, did not have an English grid. I had to send off to Bill and he brought back his own map, and then at last I had the spot fixed. It was a Steen Fabriek, or brick factory, on the south or river side of the great Rhine Dyke which contained the winter flood water. Though the factory stood out in the river it was not entirely flooded even in midwinter, with a little raised path running out to it from the dyke itself. Our journey was going to be bitterly cold. The countryside had been lying white under heavy snow for several days now. This would also make concealment harder.

We now arranged with our own people on the other side a bracket of dates: some time between 20th and 24th December was their stipulation, times and exact date to be agreed later. I also arranged the exact point in the factory where we should meet the patrol, having a horrible vision of both sides doing their job so efficiently and quietly in the darkness that we should be sitting silently a few yards apart and never meet, and then as silently separate. I also arranged, as I hoped, means of identification, a time margin on either side of the meeting time, a single repetition of the patrol if we failed to meet (when Menno and I would lie up very close to the bank but would not be able to do this for more than 24 hours) and the time by which I must hear in Torenstraat on any one day if the attempt were to be made that night. I was not going to start off at all unless I had last-minute confirmation. Whether the messages arranging all these details ever got through I cannot be sure, but Sam was clearly doing his best.

In Torenstraat Menno and I went into every detail of our own approach to the river. He made a reconnaissance by bicycle down to the edge of the forbidden zone, not four kilometres from the Rhine Dyke, and marked down a farm on our side which would be our first intermediate objective. Here we would leave our cycles. He also marked down an evacuated farm over the boundary of the forbidden zone where we could lie up during the early night and eat and rest. Here I would change into uniform. Menno had the whereabouts of the German posts, the Todt detachments, the paths, irrigation cuts, drains and bridges fixed most accurately as far as the second farm, and we discussed in great detail a scheme for crossing the last bridge under the very noses of the Todt men. There must, I insisted, be no misunderstanding about who was in command at any particular time. Menno would be in complete control up to the second farm, where he knew the ground. I should be in command from there to the bank, where neither of us did. Then I set about a minute examination of possible routes down to the bank, getting a fairly recent 1:5,000 local government map through a friend of John's, and measuring and learning not only all distances between any marks on our actual path which would be noticeable in complete black darkness (dykes, cuts, banks and so on) but also those over a fair area on either side. My aim was to guarantee dead reckoning navigation from the second farm to our rendezvous in the brick factory in any conditions (it would certainly be pitch dark for one thing) even if an alarm made us change course several times on the way. I had time enough to rehearse endless problems, going back to the figures whenever I found myself lost and learning every distance not only in metres but in the time it would take, walking cautiously in the dark, as well. I tried to imagine what each bank, ditch, fence or path might look like as we approached it, and was irritated when confusion in my own mind or a lacuna on the map left me uncertain. I had never prepared an operation more carefully.

As Christmas drew near I thought of poor Bat, now lying miserably, as we were told, in Velp. There was a rumour that he had been drugged to make him talk, and another that he had been in a delirium for weeks and given everything away, but nothing was known. He was at least still alive. The Germans were usually very deliberate in their examination of suspects and in the preparation for their trial. But there would be no Christmas turkey for Bat in England. I remembered how lightly we had dismissed, in October, any possibility that we should not both be home in time for that.

The German military police in the neighbouring house also clearly had Christmas in mind. They were fattening up a fine goose and the night air was often hideous with its clamour. In our household we were a little jealous that anyone else should have a Christmas goose, besides being greatly vexed that probably the only people in Ede who did were Germans. It seemed to me, after careful study, not impossible that if I waited for the right moment I could nip over the fence and lift that goose. I mentioned this one evening in the family gathering. Mary's mother looked up from the wool mat. It had made such progress since I saw it first that it could now hardly be recognized as the same one. She smiled in her usual warm and friendly way.

'We have a proverb in Dutch,' she said to me, 'which you probably ought to know. It says "Do not go out into the sun with butter on your head".'

I laughed. She was right of course and the plan was dropped. A few days later the goose must have begun the final stage of its journey to the Christmas table of the German military police, for its voice was heard no more.

For our own Christmas dinner we had been given a rabbit, the 'Underground Rabbit', but as it did not seem likely that I should still be there on Christmas Day we planned to eat it on Christmas Eve instead.

Menno and I hoped that we should be crossing on Christmas night, since on that day work on defences stopped at 3 p.m. and from then on it was probable that German watchfulness would be less. We joked about how these honest fellows would be sitting in their shelters, weeping alcoholic tears over little fir trees and talking of their homes, while we slipped by. Notions like this appealed to Menno and to me too.

Many people came to wish me God-speed. The uncles came, and Menno's mother, Bill came, and Piet. The last named talked to me for a long time on underground politics and the present steps being taken for the unification of all the varying forms of resistance work under one central organization, the N.B.S. The smoothness of the process of reorganization in the different area depended entirely on local personalities. Here in

Gelderland it was going pretty well but elsewhere there were difficulties.

Piet also gave me a list of tasks he wanted done outside, if possible, to ease the co-operation of his organization with liberating troops, and gave me a letter to the army command responsible.

I spent some time, in return, trying to set out the point of view of the commanders of liberating troops and in explaining, as far as I could, how things would work when British troops moved in. I was particularly anxious to spare them the disappointment which would inevitably follow if expectations were pitched too high. I reiterated warnings, already given more than once, on the troubled aftermath of liberation. There would certainly be people even prepared to say that things had really been better all round under the Germans.

I now carefully assembled my kit. Mary made me a little black silk cover for my luminous wrist watch. John lent me a flannel shirt and some useful odds and ends. The 'Escape Kit' was broken up and the parts distributed over my person. The flat transparent plastic box it had been packed in was given to Aunt Cor for her sewing materials.

It was now Christmas Eve. We had been warned by the other side that the attempt must be made before the 26th on account of the moon, though I had asked that it might be as late as possible, both because my strength increased a little every day and because more time would assist Menno's plans for the approach move. We should probably try on Christmas Day.

I did not like the weather. It was freezing hard. The nights were bright and clear, and already the moon was getting uncomfortably big and late. On those two days the sun shone brilliantly. I sat wrapped in a rug in the little summer house of the tiny garden each morning, basking in the winter sunshine and watching our Spitfires very high in the clear sparkling air.

We were waiting for a message. None came.

The planning of this operation had been an interesting intellectual exercise, not without rigour, but there was more to it than that. I was in the not unusual position for a military commander of having to make an important and irrevocable decision before a critical point in time without being in possession of essential information.

Were we to go or not?

At midday on Christmas Day I gave my judgement, with reluctance but in the certainty that it was the right one. The operation was off and we would stay where we were.

Two days later a note from Sam told me that on the other side they had thought that the moon was already too big, in conjunction with the white frost and the brilliant weather. They too had decided the operation should be called off. A fortnight must pass before we could try again. Sam was also investigating another possibility.

I have to say that, in spite of all the careful planning and preparation we had done and our high and fervent hopes and expectations, I do not remember being either disappointed or surprised that so much concentrated effort had come to nothing. Again we had done all we could. In the end everything would work out as it was meant to.

12

DAY by day I was taking a little more exercise, extending my halting walk in the dark upon John's arm, or Aunt Ann's, by a few minutes each time and coming home after every outing uplifted, exhausted and content.

After supper one evening I was taken into the Huiskamer and shown a hiding place in which there was a wireless set. It was a small broadcast receiver which could bring in the B.B.C. from London, they said, though no one could tell me exactly where to find it. I was allowed to try.

I had made many attempts to pick up London on the little wireless set, all unsuccessful. Then one night after communication in what could have been Hungarian, another in Spanish, some music, German propaganda from Radio Arnhem, some news in French, more music and more German, I heard as I twisted the knob a cultivated voice saying '. . . On the nawrrtherrn bawrrrderrrs the Rus-sians underrr Marrrshal . . .' and I almost shouted with joy. It was the voice of a B.B.C. announcer to whom I had in the past taken a possibly quite unreasonable dislike. The precision and care with which he pronounced his consonants, particularly the r's, sounded to me not only un-English but rather precious as well. That voice, however unwelcome I had found it once, was music now.

I listened to the English news nightly from then on. The Germans used to cut off the electric current in the town supply at nine o'clock, or just after, and our reception was sometimes interrupted. They were not always punctual. I was usually able to hear the broadcast right through, sometimes with the commentaries that followed it as well.

The volume of sound from the loudspeaker had always to be kept low because of the proximity of Germans. Operating a strange set under these conditions had its hazards. More than once, before I got used to it, I turned a knob the wrong way or too far. I had let loose one gigantic clang from Big Ben upon the startled air, or a single bellowed syllable from some stentorian announcer before I could turn it back. Every time this happened I could hear my heart beat in the ensuing silence. What Germans might have heard that? What could they have thought of it?

107

The rest of the household listened to Radio Orange, the B.B.C. broadcasts from England in Dutch. That is, John and Mary listened as a rule. They later retailed the main points of what they had heard to the rest of the family at our evening sessions round the table in the Voorkamer, where we sat in the family circle, comfortable and warm by the stove, with the Germans — and wild weather too, as often as not — outside.

One evening Mary dashed in from the Huiskamer with her eyes shining.

'The Queen,' she said. We rose hurriedly and trooped into the other room.

I understood only about one word in three, but the dignity and power of the voice impressed me greatly. Its effect upon the others was remarkable. An orchestra played the Dutch National Anthem afterwards and we all stood in silence.

In these days John was much concerned about the lack of informed comment on the news. It was essential, he maintained, to keep public opinion rigidly opposed to the Germans but there was too little guidance. He said that we must start a newspaper. That was the birth of the journal which we called, with no great originality, *Pro Patria*.

Our paper came out as a single sheet published weekly, mimeographed upon both sides of the paper from a typewritten wax. The circulation target was two hundred copies. I was asked to contribute and after a little hesitation agreed to write a weekly commentary under the heading 'Notes on the War in the West'. I wrote my piece in English and Miss Ann, with suggestions from John and Mary, translated it painstakingly into Dutch. It was, of course, a highly distinguished and very enjoyable position to hold — that of 'Our Military Correspondent' to a Dutch Underground newspaper — though I could do little more than explain some of the implications of the wireless news and hope to forestall and lessen disappointment by discouraging false hopes. Knowing well enough how long big operations took to mount I thought I could serve a useful purpose here. But I made a mistake in our very first issue. I pointed out that the timing of the next big allied offensive must depend upon the clearance of the Scheldt (where the Canadians were still fighting for Zeeland) and the establishment of a base in the Low Countries. I knew nothing at all of the plans of 21 Army Group. It seemed sensible to suggest, however, that rather than cross the lower Rhine from south to north in Gelderland (as these people hoped and expected) and then to fight eastwards across the River IJssel, Montgomery might well prefer to establish a crossing over the Rhine from west to east further to the south and then, having moved north, cross the IJssel from east to west. I had no way of knowing how long the clearance of the Scheldt would take, nor indeed anything else much except what could be gleaned from the brief B.B.C. broadcasts. Nonetheless I was rash enough to say in print that if everything went well there seemed no reason why Gelderland should not be free by Christmas.

The day after the publication of our first number Mary came back from her daily weary wait in the bread queue and said that the woman behind her had asked whether it was true what she had heard, that Mr. Churchill had promised to liberate Gelderland by Christmas? The source of the suggestion, it seemed was our *Pro Patria*.

The rest of the paper, apart from my own column, was good — pointed and uncompromising comment, admonition, exhortation, reproof. There was also occasional verse of pretty high quality, as far as I could then judge and can now remember. John had no difficulty in distributing the whole of the weekly output, which was mostly carried round by Mary on her bicycle.

There were air-raids fairly often now, as Allied fighter-bombers kept up their pressure on German communications. The low-flying attacks on the railway and on road traffic along the great main road or on administrative transport or troops quartered nearby were both frequent and frightening. At night I used sometimes to hear the Lancaster bombers droning over, as they had done over my home in Oakham during the summer, while we in the 1st Airborne Division had waited to be off and into battle. The sound was doubly comforting now. At night, too, I used to hear the German horse-transport convoys, very long and slow, clip-clopping through the deserted streets and out on to the open roads whose use was denied to them in daylight by the R.A.F.

Sometimes bombs and cannon-shell from our own aircraft did more damage to the Dutch than to the Germans: there was one painful case of a bomb dropping on a funeral with results both shocking and grotesque. But in general the R.A.F. was praised for its accuracy. Even when its bombs went astray the R.A.F. used to be given the benefit of the doubt: they had tried hard, it was said, and made unavoidable mistakes; or they had been defeated by the conditions. It would be difficult to imagine more loyal friends and Allies than the British had in Holland in that last winter of the war. But a good deal of feeling had been aroused, I learned, by the bombing attack just before the drop of my own brigade on 18th September. It had been carried out, my Dutch friends said, in a wild and irresponsible manner and had resulted in widespread damage and many casualties in the town. The barracks on the outskirts, which were supposed to be its target, had suffered no damage at all.

I was the person who had made the plan for this bombing mission and had fought hard to have it accepted and carried out. My own feelings about its outcome can be imagined. There was little consolation in the fact that the damage had not been done by British airmen but by a hastily assembled collection of assorted allies.

I had another visit from Piet. He could not stay long. He gave me some of the local news and asked me if I wanted anything. Miss Ann's books gave me plenty to read but there was something I realized I should greatly like to add to them. I asked Piet to find me some Thackeray. I felt a great longing for a glimpse of that cool, orderly world and the taste of elegant and lucid English prose. It was *Esmond* that I wanted most, I think, for I knew it best. I had found it for myself at school when I was fifteen and fell at once and for ever under its spell. It was *Vanity Fair* I asked Piet to get for me, if he could, all the same. I had an instinctive conviction that this would be the better medicine for the condition in which I found myself, rather more restless now and uncertain, facing a future of which little could be predicted with confidence except that it was unlikely to be an easy one. I felt rather as a fish might, panting on a river bank. Piet found me a copy of *Vanity Fair*, in a looted house, and left it for me in Torenstraat. I plunged at once into its cool and limpid depths in deep and heartfelt gratitude, read it straight through and put it by refreshed.

The end of the year was not far off now and the weather was very cold. The snow lay thick on the ground and looked as if it would be there for ever. In the mornings Mary was still bringing up breakfast to my cold little room and lighting up a paraffin stove to take the bitter edge off the air before she did the dressings on my stomach. We were now very short of surgical plaster and even Aunt Cor, still working in the drug store, could not find any more. One set of strappings, of poor quality even to begin with, would be put on again and again for dressing after dressing, until it seemed, Mary said, that only drawing pins could keep them on much longer. But I loved that paraffin stove for which the stores in the paint factory furnished fuel. It had a red glass front which sent out a friendly glow and made me think of an open fire. My Dutch friends were puzzled at this fondness for a fireside and surprised to hear that the wood or coal stoves in general use in Holland were almost unknown in England. Aunt Cor pointed out that the stove was a far more efficient form of heating, with which I had to agree, but Aunt Ann who had been in England, though only in summer, said that there must be some advantage in an open fireplace because in England she had seen hardly anything else.

One morning as Mary was changing my dressings we heard a sound, like and yet somehow unlike, an approaching aircraft. It was very close.

'What a heavy noise!' said Mary.

It passed not far from the house, and when the thing itself had gone the noise it left behind was even louder than before. I had heard this in London. I knew that it was a V1.

From now on a steady stream of them passed over us, six to eight a day. They were launched, we heard, from near Apeldoorn. The map showed that Ede lay on a straight line from Apeldoorn to Antwerp. I supposed that the Germans were trying to interfere with the Allied build-up by attacking the port.

Not all the V1s were to pass over. In a day or so one of them came down and burst not very far from the Boereis' house. It was said to have killed seventeen people, though I was sure this was exaggerated. Every day one or more could be heard exploding somewhere. The worst day was when three landed right in Ede, or just outside it, with considerable loss of life.

During twilight walks in the snow with members of the family I used to watch the V1s on their vicious fiery way, very low above us, moving ahead of the ugly, shattering noise they trailed behind. More than once we saw them fall. The bitter cold weather, I supposed, was presenting problems of icing which were now being experienced operationally for the first time and had not yet brought under control. Quite a large number were falling soon after launching. I watched several wandering crazily about the sky until their fiery tails went out. Then, after a breathless pause, there would be the rending crash we had now come to know so well. Others seemed to motor straight into the ground still going full blast.

One evening Aunt Ann and I were walking in the beautiful dim hush and the pale after-light that follow the setting of the sun in a time of hard frost. Suddenly, in the north-east, there swam slowly up into the clear upper air a thin feathery trail of white vapour climbing in majestic white zig-zags to an

111

enormous height and then levelling out to travel straight on to the south-west, where it was lost in the gathering gloom. There were now V2s as well.

We continued on our walk, following and gradually gaining on a group of men walking ahead of us, workmen going home perhaps. As we got nearer in the dusk something about their hats troubled me: too many were of the same shape. Aunt Ann saw no cause for alarm and we had almost overtaken them before I realized what they were. It was a detachment of members of the Todt Organization, clearly moving with a purpose.

We had often before walked behind one or two of these men, quietly mocking their bent limbs and shuffling gait and making little jokes about the pathetic old dotards that so many seemed to be, for all their savagery and strutting. We used to call them 'apes'. But there was nothing to laugh at here, and we thought it best to turn back. Later we heard that this party had been on its way to cordon off and search the very quarter to which we were going.

Such manhunts were frequent now. The German grip was getting tighter. Compulsory billeting, food requisitioning, seizure of goods, all were happening more often now and more severely. Control of movement was getting still stricter. Mary was often stopped on her way to and from the shopping queues.

Once her papers were being examined by a soldier when one fell on the ground. A boy of about nine years old was passing.

The German soldier jerked his head at the child.

'Pick it up,' he said.

'No,' said the boy.

'What?' said the German in great surprise. 'Pick it up!'

'Can't bend down,' was the reply.

'Why not?'

'Rheumatism,' said the child and walked on.

John told me of another incident. An 'ape' ordered a workman to get off his bicycle and hand it over. The workman put on a burst of speed and disappeared round a corner. The 'ape' discharged his pistol ineffectively and then ran through a vacant lot cursing, to cut the workman off. At the other side he had to climb over some iron spikes. His clothing got caught on one of them. Just then the workman cycled by, in time to see the 'ape' suspended by his pants and struggling hard.

'You may burst before you get my bicycle,' said the workman in a tone as John described it, so calm as to be almost friendly, and rode on.

112

I heard from Menno about another man, a farmer, who was riding his bicycle down a country road when a very young German soldier stopped him and ordered him to hand it over. The farmer was a large quiet man.

'I will not,' said the farmer.

'Then I will shoot you,' said the soldier, unslinging his rifle.

The large man got off his bicycle.

'No,' he said. 'You will put that rifle down. And then we shall fight with our hands over whether you have my bicycle or not.'

After a little silence the soldier slung his rifle on his shoulder and walked away. The big man got on his bicycle again and rode on.

Aunt Cor used to bring home something of interest every day from the drug store. Her great gift for mimicry made her stories always well worth hearing. She described to me once the scene outside the shop while the Germans were 'organizing', of all things, perambulators. A German soldier stopped a mother wheeling her baby, took the baby out, handed it over to the mother and pushed the perambulator away, blankets, shawls and all.

'What on earth can they want with kinderwagens?' asked Aunt Ann.

'You have only to look at the soldiers they are now getting,' said Aunt Mien. 'It's for bringing troops up to the front.'

Aunt Cor gave us a spirited account one day of what she described as a gaunt, sad, stringy looking Moff who had come into the shop and pointed to his throat. He was so hoarse he could only whisper, which he did in execrable Dutch. We laughed at the way Aunt Cor stretched up her head and imitated him.

'Something for my neck,' he had croaked, 'something for my neck.' But Aunt Cor had had to say that there was nothing for him.

Mary raised her gentle face from her needlework and spoke almost tenderly.

'What about a rope?' she said.

13

As the pressures of the occupation increased, some of the special problems of our household inevitably grew more acute. Serious consideration, for example, had to be given to our little paper *Pro Patria*. Was it sensible, we asked ourselves, to run the risk that the S.D., or even the Gestapo, might trace a copy back to where it was produced and in their investigation of the house discover my presence in it? We thought not and, with regret, ceased publication. The change in the hour of curfew from eight o'clock to six gave us a further problem, as it did for many others who found it advisable to move about only in the dark. Since my walking exercise was getting a little longer every day it had been becoming increasingly difficult to fit our walks in, even before the time was changed.

My physical condition had greatly improved in the past week or two and I was now walking without help (except from the General's stick) for a fairly brisk half hour every day. I was able to take still more. We could not lengthen the time much without too great a risk of being seen in daylight. We therefore increased the pace. The family used to take it in turns, more or less, to accompany me, for it continued to be unwise for me to go out alone. There was, as it were, a 'duty' Aunt. The Aunts wore each others' hats and coats to present unfamiliar figures, but sometimes friends recognized one of them in the twilight as we walked, and greeted her. The greeting was rarely acknowledged.

'We are being very unfriendly,' said Aunt Ann, 'we do not visit other people now or invite them to visit us. But though I expect we have offended some old friends they will know later why it was, and they will understand.'

'What do people think,' I asked Mary, 'when they *do* recognize you and see you walking with a queer looking stranger?'

She looked at me seriously, and then said in her charming English, 'They will only think, I suppose, that we are taking a Jew for an airing. It is often done.'

Persecution of Jews by the Nazis, and by the N.S.B., which embodied the Dutch version of National Socialism, had been particularly severe in the cities, from which many had been deported to Germany for extermination and others had fled to the countryside. The hostility of the occupying regime had given the Jews an almost automatic claim to protection by the Resistance and in consequence many were being looked after in hiding.

I was by now a confirmed underdiver and knew something of underdiver habits. I claimed to be already suffering from what I called 'underdiver's neck', a state of strain in the neck muscles due to a continual effort not to look round. I was also getting able to recognize a colleague. Sometimes we would pass a solitary young Dutchman hurrying by in the half light along one of the less frequented streets, with no sign of returning from work about him, no tools, no basket, no bundle of firewood, his eyes fixed straight ahead. I would nudge Aunt Ann and whisper 'Collega' and she would laugh softly and agree.

I loved these evening walks. They were the great event of my day.

Ours was a busy household and the time just before curfew was a busy time in Ede everywhere, so that it was not always easy for any member of the family to get away at the right time. I used to sit around and wait, I was told, with a look in my eye just like a dog's. Sometimes I used unconsciously to heighten the similarity, taking my hat and coat, gloves and stick, and waiting rather conspicuously somewhere in the house, almost as though holding a leash in my mouth, until I was noticed and taken out.

Walking with Aunt Ann I was led around the main roads and the streets of the town's outskirts and I got to know them all well. It was often beautiful. Walking along the Amsterdamsche Weg past the Todt organization headquarters one brilliant star-lit evening, with the great trees reaching up into the sky along the street like pillars in the nave of a cathedral, I saw Sirius hanging between them at the end in frosty glory, like a chancel lamp. Sirius was an old, old friend. I remembered the iron-hard winter nights of the Transjordan uplands, as I rode up with my squadron out of the warmth of the Jordan Valley and Sirius blazed above. I had watched for his coming in many different lands, as the year approached its end, and was glad to see him now.

Aunt Cor chose different walks. She used to take me round the byways, the narrow lanes and alleys between the tidy gardens and the prim, dignified little houses of the older part of the town. With the snow on the ground, the gentle mist of winter twilight, the steep gables, men in their wooden shoes returning from work, the ample figures of the womenfolk waiting at lamplit doorways and the fresh faced children in their bright, gnomelike woollen caps sliding on the icy roads, it was a picture by Pieter Brueghel.

Things in their domestic aspect got harder now. The bread ration was cut. The meagre allowance of gas for cooking ceased entirely and there was no coal. Central kitchens were being organized in the town to make the best of the miserable rations and the scarce fuel, and one or other of our household stood every day in a queue with a pot, to receive the daily half litre per person of vegetable stew — potato and cabbage — which was the allowance. After a time that too stopped. There was insufficient food even to fill out the ration. This only amounted, according to Dr. Krayenbrink, to about six hundred calories a day anyway.

Fuel was a pressing problem. Around Ede there were considerable areas of young coniferous woodland from which the fuel ration was found. The coupon for the ration only entitled its holder to a young standing tree. This had then to be felled, hauled away and, green as it was, sawed and chopped up into billets small enough for a stove. It was not easy to get this done. The Germans had impressed into working for them every male in Gelderland up to forty-five years of age upon whom they could lay hands. Many were sent to Germany. Beyond the age of forty-five and up to sixty there was no liability to transportation but men in this age group had to work for the occupying forces locally. Nearly every day I saw sad files of dispirited Dutchmen shepherded by savage-looking old men of the Todt Organization, on their way to or from the defences. The plight of the really old in this hard winter, or of the families whose menfolk had been taken away, was very great.

Day after day droves of men and women pulled sledges or carts out to the allotted areas of woodland, felled their trees and dragged them back, to cut them up when and how they could. They helped each other as far as they were able. There was usually someone to help the wholly helpless. But where there was so little to go round, with few to work and everyone so weary, it was a grim struggle.

The scarcity of labour on the land had made it impossible to get all the crops in, a specially important matter where that staple food the potato was concerned. The Germans organized potato-lifting, taking some of what was got for themselves and leaving the remainder to the getters. Young and active people

116

like John, or Menno's younger brothers, brought in fair quantities of potatoes, and occasionally procured odd barrow-loads of beet, or a little grain from friendly farmers. Most of the farmers were doing all they could to help people less well off than they were, in the cities and townships, though some of them, it is true, were not.

The Germans cordoned off the potato pullers one day and took away all young males (of whom many, as they knew, must be underdivers driven by the necessity of their families out into the open) to labour camps. They were impressing young women for cookhouse work to save their own men. They cancelled the papers of all men working in that vital office, the food distribution, and ordered each man either to report to a German labour centre for work on defences, or to find a substitute to go in his place. Their proclamations grew more savage and their penalties more severe. For feeding an underdiver you would now have your furniture thrown into the street and burnt. For using the electric current without leave your house might be blown up. The penalties for harbouring Allied fugitives needed no restatement, for they were well enough known already. They could scarcely have been made more severe.

The members of my own family knew all this. They could not fail to. Carelessness or ill luck, a simple mishap, might at any time destroy them. This would be their reward for taking in a stranger. Yet they went about their daily lives calmly and cheerfully and never showed to me, the cause of the mortal danger in which they stood, anything but solicitude and kindness. There was no trace of fretfulness. If any of them longed for their guest to be gone, and the threat removed which was embodied in his presence, they gave no hint of it. There was no appearance of anxiety in that household, no sign of fear, no tension. The atmosphere was one of confidence and trust and sometimes there was even gentle mirth. My admiration for these people touched on awe. I wanted urgently to be away and would go as soon as I could. Till then I would go on living among them in gratitude and love.

Meanwhile the pillaging of all that could be useful to the Germans, either locally or in Germany, went steadily on. I saw numbers of cattle being driven away, and knew that the Germans hoped to leave no more milking cows than would suffice to keep the local butter factory going for their own benefit. From this factory hungry Dutch parents of hungry children used to see almost every day loads of priceless butter going off to their enemies. Machinery was being dismantled in factories and workshops for removal to Germany, looted textiles were being taken off in convoys. I heard of desperate struggles on every side to keep from German hands the last necessities of a decent life.

German troops still moved freely but there was little singing now. The Ardennes offensive had been halted: there seemed to be a widespread conviction among the enemy that only by a miracle could they avoid losing the war.

'Of course we are taking all your men,' Herr Groll was reported to have said, 'It is possible that we may have to leave this country before very long. Would it make sense to leave behind anyone who could work for the Allies?'

I used to stand at the window of the Voorkamer and watch an O.T. man, in the yellowish uniform and red brassard marked with a black swastika on a circular white patch, stopping each passer-by and demanding his Ausweis. The Todt men were often to be seen in Torenstraat, especially on Sundays, because two streams of churchgoers met there. There were no young men among them. Only the older men, the infirm and the women passed that way.

As each man was stopped a little drama was played out, always different, always the same. It was shaming to see the look on some of those faces, haunted by the fear that the document of exemption, procured somehow and now being scrutinized, should not prove good enough, and that a labour camp lay ahead with the home left in destitution. There was an obscenity about those bent and rheumy-eyed old men who were the examiners, propped up by self-importance, carefully adjusting their spectacles for a close scrutiny of the papers, clearly enjoying the fear they caused and prolonging it, while in an attitude of resignation but with terror in his eyes the man stood by and waited, and a woman clung to his arm in dumb misery.

One morning Aunt Ann came in early.

'My brother Ko has been arrested,' she said.

Agitated hours followed as report after report came in. This one had been taken, and that one. Then the climax – Uncle Zwerus had been taken too.

In restless calm the family waited. Further scraps of information were brought in. There had been a drive against any citizen suspected of anti-German sympathies. They were being detained by the Dutch S.S. in Lunteren. They were in a cellar, ill fed and badly treated. Their heads had been clipped like criminals. There had been savage interrogation and beatings.

In a day or two Uncle Zwerus was released and came home again, looking a little worn but with his dignity hardly impaired by the close clipping of his grey head. He had not been beaten, though others had. He had apparently held his own against the interrogators, who lolled insolently in easy chairs flanked by men with rubber truncheons. But Uncle Ko was sent to a labour camp nearby to dig.

Through the boldness and energy of Uncle Ko's two daughters contact was soon regained and little comforts were taken to him. Aunt Cor, who was very close to this brother, told me sensational stories of the hardships he was suffering. When I learnt the facts it seemed that he had probably been no worse off in reality than troops often are. I said this to Aunt Cor and she was fair-minded enough to agree that it probably was so but she had not, she said, known before how soldiers did live, and anyway, it was worse for a member of one's own family. Uncle Ko, it is true, was not a young man and the sort of life he had led had not prepared him for campaigning. He began to suffer from his stomach and was put on light work in the cookhouse. Later on Uncle Ko was to be sent home again as too weak and sick to be of use.

One very small practical effect of his absence upon my own life was soon apparent. I badly needed a haircut and Uncle Ko was no longer there to give me one. Aunt Ann knew of a barber who sometimes cut the hair of Jews and other underdivers in secret. He would be far too frightened, she said, to cut the hair of a British officer, and was hardly to be trusted with so dangerous a secret even if he were not, but we might perhaps deceive him.

In parts of Germany and Holland there was then in use a very sensible device. This was a little button which could be worn by the deaf to make their disability known. It was round and white, with a broad red band on it bearing the letters S.H. in black — Schlecht hörend in German, or Slecht horend in Dutch. A few days before this Aunt Ann had brought me one as a provision, typical of her, against the embarrassments which might arise if I were publicly addressed in Dutch by a stranger. I always wore it now when outside the house and there were many small jokes about it at home. I was now to wear it for my haircut and for this occasion was to be a deaf Jew.

Going out, even for a haircut, was something that had to be carefully planned. In the middle of the afternoon John left the house and a few seconds later, as we had arranged, I followed him. We moved independently of each other in case something

119

went wrong. It was cold and I was wearing a sad black gaberdine overcoat Menno had procured for me. We called it the Gestapo coat. I was thrilled to be out in broad daylight for a change, no longer just to watch through a window what life there was on the streets but to be a part of it. German soldiers passed me, singly and in pairs. We made way for each other in the most natural manner in the world. Once as a pair approached me, silent, relaxed, absorbed in their own thoughts, I scanned their unsuspecting faces from very close and thought how odd all this was. I pushed past others as they looked into shop windows (where there was little enough on display) and once, looking into a shop window myself, caught a glimpse in a mirror of a bent figure in a black waterproof, pale, drawn, muffled up to the chin, wearing a dark-coloured oversize hat pulled down to the ears. It was hard at first to recognize my own self, for this was also someone else, a person who only existed in a movie or a novel.

I was led into the family's paint factory, in whose largest bay another de Nooij family was now living, evacuated from Oosterbeek. During the minutes we had to wait Aunt Ann showed me around. I saw the little office where she used to work and the whereabouts of the underground containers in which most of their valuables lay. Then the barber arrived and in the factory office I sat down to have my hair cut. He was a small man with a knowing face and a rather contemptuous look on it. He talked to Miss Ann all the time, full of misleading little items of information most confidently given. I was sure from the way he looked at me that it was indeed as a deaf Dutch Jew that I was accepted. He did not seem to like me much but he did cut my hair. Aunt Ann paid him and I followed her home again. It had all been for me a great and exciting adventure.

I now met Pietje, the little boy from next door. He often used to come into our garden to play, his friendly little face bright from the cold with a red woollen cap pulled over his fair hair.

'That is Mijnheer Pietersen,' Aunt Mien said, indicating me, the first time he came.

She told me later with a smile that she had called me something other than 'van Dalen' out of habit: they were so used, she said, to not calling underdivers by their real names in public.

'Mijnheer Pietersen is sick,' she said to Pietje. 'He must not be worried. Now say good morning.'

Pietje gave me a little bow and said, solemnly, 'Goede Morge, M'Neer Peters' and ran off to play.

I met him often after that and always had the same solemn little greeting. He was a beautiful manly child and my day lightened whenever I saw him.

There was also Diena, the workwoman, who came in once or twice a week. While I was still confined to my bed the only security precaution necessary in her regard was that we should not talk too loudly in English while she was near my door. Now that I moved freely about the house, the security problem was greater. She was told I was from Friesland, where they spoke a dialect she could not understand which sounded I was told, quite like English. They said that I had come down to Ede on a visit and was now stuck here with no means of getting back. I was sick too. It was a common enough sort of story. I made guttural greeting noises when we met and she seemed to suspect nothing.

Meanwhile correspondence with Sam continued. It was now considered no longer possible for a crossing to be made where we had planned. On our bank the forbidden area had been greatly deepened and on the Allied side patrol activity was less. This may have been, we thought, a consequence of withdrawals of troops in connection with the Ardennes battle, or at least a general policy of holding one's hand elsewhere while the enemy's main effort was defeated in Luxemburg and southern Belgium.

I was now to meet an old friend again. Blue Johnny turned up one night. It was only now that I realized that Blue Johnny was yet another member of the de Nooij family—another Zwerus. He had a tale to tell. Soon after he had helped me in St. Elizabeth's Hospital, when the remaining patients had been taken off to Apeldoorn, he had been picked up on suspicion by the Sicherheitsdienst. They had searched him but found nothing, which was lucky for Johnny, for he was in fact carrying papers which would have got him into bad trouble if the Germans had found them on him. Among other things, for example, he had a letter from Lipmann Kessel saying that he was a dependable person who had helped at least twelve British officers and men out of the hospital. The S.D. men had missed this, and he still had it and showed it to me.

He was detained nonetheless and soon found himself in Amersfoort labour camp. Here, with many hundreds of other Dutchmen of all kinds, he was kept under guard and employed upon local work. The conditions were no better than would be expected and he got thin, pale and weak. When I saw him, with his shaven head and ragged clothes, he was like a scarecrow.

Before long the Germans had begun to move the Amersfoort workers into Germany and soon Johnny too was packed into a train, with about eight hundred others. He saw little attraction in the prospect before him and when the train slowed down near Apeldoorn he and one or two more jumped off. There was shooting but Johnny got away. He lost the others and started a long tramp down to Ede. Farmers gave him food (bread with butter on it, he said, and a bit of bacon from one of them) and the next day in the dusk he arrived, worn out, at his aunt's house in Torenstraat. They put him to bed in John's folding bedstead in the closet in the Huiskamer and he slept for about twenty hours.

I was delighted to see him—as Zwerus de Nooij now—and we talked cheerfully about our time in the hospital and people we both knew. His brothers came in from other parts of the town, and then his mother from the little house into which they had moved when Bennekom was evacuated, and there was great family rejoicing. In a day or so young Zwerus slipped off to his mother's house and went into hiding there. His arrival and brief stay in Torenstraat brought vividly back to me what I had almost forgotten—my time in St. Elizabeth's Hospital. His departure left me again in the present but thinking more and more about the future.

14

My own chief task as the year approached its end was very simple. It was to get stronger.

One day I went out to the barn just outside the kitchen door and found John, single-handed, sawing lately-felled firewood. There was a two-man saw there. I took a turn with him on it for a minute or so. This was tiring, but I found that it was within my strength and did not, surprisingly enough, disturb too much the bandages around my middle. I was thrilled. I now took up sawing seriously. Every day I worked in the barn by myself with the small saw, first for a few minutes and gradually for longer. John now and then joined me on the larger two-man saw. I rejoiced to have at last some physical work to do, especially something with so stimulating a rhythm. John was pleased too. He had plenty on his own hands in other ways and was grateful for any help he could get.

The ladies fitted me out for the work with a long grey cotton coat, in which I looked rather like an apprentice grocer. Soon I was spending part of every morning in the bitter cold of the barn, taking off gloves and muffler as the exercise set my blood moving.

After a while, carefully and experimentally, I started to use the axe too, first on kindling wood and then on the sections of young fir trunk I had already sawn. Before long I was swinging out merrily, though not without caution. There were still open places on my stomach. These did not really worry me, except sometimes a little when the dressings stuck, though with the more violent movement required by the use of the axe the dressings themselves used sometimes to come off. I would have given a very great deal for some good broad elastoplast.

The hours spent in that cold barn, though physically exacting, were enjoyable and stimulating. I was rarely disturbed. Diena used to come in now and then on her working days and say 'Good morning' as she started on her tasks. I was always afraid that she might try to engage me in conversation and find out that I was not a Dutchman after all, whether from Friesland or anywhere else. So I would reply gruffly to her greeting and saw away without even glancing up, trying at the same time to

123

look like an angry and disagreeable person who was better left alone. If she still stayed around I used to leave the barn and stalk as grimly as I could into the house, there to wait timidly until she had moved elsewhere.

It was very cold. In the Voorkamer, the front room on the ground floor, the stove was kept going. It was now, to my great satisfaction, burning the billets of wood I had myself chopped up. The main living-room just behind, the Huiskamer, from which doors to one of the bedrooms and the kitchen led and where the radio was housed in a wall cupboard behind a bookcase, could not be warmed as well. To listen to the radio news I had to sit in this unwarmed room. The aunts at first used to wrap me up against the cold in a coat of John's, with a muffler and gloves, and put me in a chair with a rug upon my knees. Later, as I grew stronger, I became more hardened to the cold.

It was into the Huiskamer that I was bundled whenever there were visitors to the house whom it would be wiser for me not to meet. The visitors would be received in the Voorkamer and I had many a cold wait in the other room while they stayed and chatted and the aunts longed for them to go. It was to the Huiskamer that I used to retire too, when Aunt Ann had with, joyful face brought me a fine Dutch cigar, wheedled out of some provident and unsuspecting friend. To smoke my treasure in the Voorkamer might upset Aunt Cor and I did not want to do that.

It was amazing how the family contrived to keep me out of the way in so small a house when callers appeared as often at the kitchen door as at the front. I would be sitting in the Voorkamer, in what was now my accustomed chair in the far corner on the right, looking through the lace curtains and a hole rubbed in the mist on the glass at the Germans passing in the street, when there would be a knock at the front door of the house in the passage outside. I would at once get up and go out, waiting in the passage, if no member of the family were with me at the time, until one of them came through from the back to answer the knock on the door.

'Is the Huiskamer free?' I would ask. If it were I would go and sit there until the visitors had gone. Aunt Ann would come out from time to time to see how I was getting on and if the visitors were given coffee she would bring me some.

'They have a great deal to tell,' she would say sometimes, coming to give me a progress report, 'but I believe they will go soon. You must keep well wrapped up.'

If there were also people in the Huiskamer when visitors

arrived, however, I would have to go straight upstairs instead and sit in my little bedroom. That was very cold indeed.

Even the private pattern of the family knock sent me to cover. A family visitor might have a stranger in tow: we could take no risks.

The aunts wisely kept the number of people whom I should actually meet to a minimum. All the time I lived in Ede I did not even meet Henk and Hennie from next door, the parents of my little friend Pietje. No doubt many members of the family, and others too, realized that there was something unusual afoot in the house in Torenstraat. I do not think, though, that there were many people who would care to press my hostesses for more information about their private affairs than they were prepared to offer.

One habit became deeply rooted in me. Long afterwards, even in my own home, it occasionally reasserted itself. I never entered any downstairs room in Torenstraat, unless I had been expressly told beforehand that only members of the household were present, without first giving the door the gentlest possible push with my foot — and then waiting. The movement of the door would be noticed by some member of the family, who would then quietly get up, if there were strangers present, and leave the room as though on some household matter. If she spoke to me on her way through the passage I would know that it was safe. If she passed me by without speaking I would know that it was not and would creep off somewhere else to wait until they told me I could come back.

The habit of touching the living-room door with my foot, and then pausing before entering, and others of similar origin — like that of constantly listening for significant sounds or changes in the sound background, or of never going to bed without first disposing everything according to a practised drill in case of a night alarm, or of never looking round in public and above all of never allowing myself to meet a stranger's eye — all these developed almost automatically. I did not realize how strong a hold they had taken until later. It was only when the tensions lessened and there was no longer any reason for them that I found how much I had been overdrawing on internal resources to adjust to the situation in which I had been living.

For protection against the intense cold my hostesses had furnished me with my own brown woollen gloves and muffler, to which I had now become much attached as always happens when possessions are few and valuable. What worried the aunts was that I had no warm underclothing. Mary's mother had written to business connections in Amsterdam and pressed them to find somewhere a woollen vest and pants, knowing better than any of us that such things were rare as pearls. She did not doubt that they would come eventually but this would certainly take time.

Meanwhile, Aunt Mien tackled the problem of woollen underwear in her own characteristic fashion. She set to and made some up.

Their old father, towards the end of his life, had been kept warm about the legs at night by long, thick, knitted sleeves. Aunt Mien found two of these, one white and one a pale blue. By unravelling something else she found wool enough to knit together what were, in effect, two readymade legs into a pair of long pants. So there I was, dressed a little like Harlequin underneath my trousers, but warm.

Later the woollen underwear ordered by Mary's mother arrived. Their advent, prosaic though anyone who can find no poetry in pants may think, gave pride and pleasure to the household. It was a pity that all were not able to enjoy them in a public display. Only John could see and admire these new treasures on the wearer. When I first put them on I felt as important as a battleship about to be launched and regretted the lack of ceremonial suitable to the occasion. The Harlequins we put away for the journey. The aunts had found another tremendous piece of clothing for me. This too was a woollen garment made for their father. It was something like a cricketer's sweater, knitted in heavy white cable-stitch, with a high yoke neck and a great, buttoned, double-breasted front which reached almost to my knees. That too now went into the war chest, with the Harlequins.

New Year's Eve came, and the seven of us had a little family celebration. All day long, upon the fiery kitchen stove, the pot-shaped thing known by its trade mark as the Little Devil, upon which, after the gas was cut off, all cooking was now done, Aunt Mien had been preparing a surprise. I was told it was something traditional and very good. And indeed it was. She had made little apple cakes fried in batter, which were brought in to the expectant family group with some ceremony. There were two for each of us, with a small glass of wine provided by Uncle Zwerus.

Aunt Mien said we should each wish, as we ate our little cakes, for what we wanted most in the New Year though we must not tell anyone what it was. I had secret doubts whether Aunt Ann would entirely approve of such frivolity but saw on her face an indulgent look as we all sat for a moment in silence, reflecting on what we would wish for, and she said nothing. I noticed that Aunt Mien was looking at me, her eye resting more on what I was wearing — and particularly my sad black jacket — than on anything else. She looked up and our eyes met. With the tiny flash of an almost guilty smile, as though she had been found out, she looked away.

I was still abed very early in those days. I had been asleep on New Year's Eve for several hours when I awoke out of a violent dream of battle to loud noises, whose ominous familiarity made it hard for a moment to think where I was. I knew the sound of many German weapons almost as well as I knew that of our own. You could not afford to be in doubt whether it was a Bren you heard, or a Spandau. I had also myself fired all those commonly used by the enemy. In the training of airborne troops we used to practise the use of the enemy's weapons to make up for a possible shortage in action of ammunition for our own. I had therefore made a close acquaintance with the M.G.34, the M.G.42, the Schmeisser and various other weapons. I carried a Lüger myself.

Now here they all were, firing away in a tremendous chorus of malignant sound, every instrument in the German small arms orchestra, in harmony, in unison, in fantastic fugue-like parts, in crashing chords, in vicious staccato solo.

I listened in the dark, unhappy and confused. The noise was very close. The nearest weapon sounded only a few yards away. But why? This was not the odd shot you heard nearly every night, loosed off by a patrol at curfew breakers, or by drunken soldiers at a gleam in a blacked-out window. Could it be an attack by the Allies? That was impossible. There were no British weapons to be heard there, and nothing heavier than automatic small arms anyway. What else could be happening?

I looked at the luminous face of my watch. It showed a few minutes after twelve. The noise was already dying away. The Germans had been welcoming the New Year.

15

I n the very first days of the new year, 1945, we began to make another plan for my escape. A note came from Sam to say that he saw a possibility of getting two or three of us across the Waal by Driel, if we could first be got down over the Lower Rhine somewhat to the west of Ede. At this time the possibility of my being picked up by an aircraft was still being considered on the other side, the chief difficulty being in the choice of a landing ground. Sam had reconnoitred and suggested several but on the far side they did not like any of them and no progress was being made. He thought this new plan looked quite promising and he was going ahead with it, though the journey might be a hard one for me. I would again be allowed to bring someone else. For the moment, however, I must wait while he explored further.

Piet came to see me again, travelling on his motor cycle as an official of the food control. He told me he had seen something of Graeme Warrack, now back in hiding again near Barneveld. When the unhappy mass attempt at escape on 18th November had broken up in confusion he had pushed on alone, like several others, but found no means of crossing the river. He had then made his courageous and solitary way back to the household which had hidden him before and been received and taken in again with pleasure, for they had all become fast friends.

As far as my own planning was concerned, Menno had now decided, after much thought, that he really ought to stay in Holland. His work was here and he must also look after the family for which he was largely responsible. I determined to take Graeme in his place and we began to plan accordingly.

Piet thought that this might be our last meeting before I left and he had much to say. First he talked for a long time about affairs in the Resistance Movement and efforts being made to establish a higher degree of central co-ordination and control over its parts. This was not easy in something which had sprung up spontaneously and grown piecemeal, with many differences of organization and practice under the influence of strong personalities and local circumstances. Problems of security and poor communications increased the difficulty.

Progress was being made in the setting up of the N.B.S., the Nederlandsche Binnenlandsche Strijdkrachten, which was intended to be the command structure of the Dutch forces of the interior. Meetings were now taking place to co-ordinate provincial resistance activities under two leaders in each province, one military and one civil, making use of such men and organizations as appeared locally most suitable, all under the general guidance of the N.B.S. Prince Bernhard was often mentioned as a mainspring of this movement and there was widespread praise for what he was doing.

Piet, who was now the Military Commander in this Province, also gave me a letter to the Commander of the British Second Army. It contained suggestions for joint arrangements and liaison, on the assumption that that would be the formation coming in. Piet also spoke of the difficulties arising from the lack of a wireless link between the Resistance, as such, and Allied troops opposite. There were already several links operating in Gelderland but each had a special function — intelligence, evasion and so on — and there was none whose main purpose was to provide communications between Allied commanders on that front and Resistance commanders operating in depth behind it. To have to rely on the occasional goodwill of agents was very frustrating, particularly since these knew only too well that their own effectiveness and the security of their links depended largely on their sticking closely to the tasks given them.

I suggested to Piet that it was unwise to assume that the main attack would come from south to north. It might go in further south, to cross the Rhine from west to east. What I wanted to do as far as I could was to ease the disappointment of these heartsick people if their hopes were further deferred, as they well could be.

I also warned Piet that it might not be easy to get him a liaison link of his own while they were waiting. The men who operated these were scarce and valuable. He suggested that such a link might be set up just before an offensive. I had to say that though this was a good idea there could be security objections.

I also tried to help Piet clarify his notions of what to expect when Allied troops finally came in, as I often did with others, only regretting that my own familiarity with the work of the Civil Affairs people on military staffs was now not great, since I had not seen them at work since the North African campaign nearly two years before. Again, I was trying to moderate expectations. Liberation when it came was bound to be a tremendous experience. What had been so painfully pent up

could all now come out. The excitement and jubilation, however, might be followed by something of a let-down. They might
expect too much, for example, from the behaviour of troops. I
knew the average British soldier as a very decent person but
towards the end of a hard campaign not all soldiers in any army
are saints.

There was also the question of reward, of no interest at all to
some — like those in my own family, for instance — but of high
concern to others. I was confident that reward and recognition
would be generous but delays could be expected and there might
even be injustices.

They would certainly be better off with the substitution of
British troops for German. Their fears, for example, that the
arrival of much larger forces would result in an even greater
scarcity of food were easily set at rest. The Allies would not look
for food in Holland as the Germans did. They would bring their
own and would have food to spare. There were many other
features of the German occupation in which I could promise
them a certain change for the better.

Sitting now, outside the cage of alien occupation and so far
from it all, I can only remember with diminishing clearness the
strength of my feelings about these things. Anyone who has
never seen it from the other side, never shared the hopes and
longings of people behind the bars, may find it difficult to
picture how much these hopes and longings could mean to
someone who was there, how passionately one longed for all
to go well with them, and how much one hoped they would
be spared disappointment and disillusion.

Piet handed over the letters he wanted carried and we talked
a little more. I wanted to thank him as he deserved for what I
owed him, for I was greatly in his debt. This was quite impossible but I also had the impression that nothing of the sort
was expected. Piet did not regard what he had done for me, I
think, as any more than another part of the task he had taken on.
What I could thank him for, and did most warmly, was *Vanity
Fair*.

I was now much less of a sick man, though my left leg was far
from strong and I was still, of course, heavily bandaged about
the middle. The abdominal incision-wound continued to discharge here and there and scraps of stitches would still occasionally appear and be pulled out. With the good care I was getting
in the family, however, and the daily exercise in the wood-shed
and on our walks I was getting stronger every day.

Almost the most remarkable of all the amenities provided for me in that remarkable household, was to be able, before my bandages were put on again each day, to lie for half an hour under an electric radiant-heat lamp. This was for the pains in my back which the doctors used to tell me were from fibrositis, whatever that is. They had often plagued me in the past and were now there again. It did not really surprise me, for some reason, that when I spoke of them to John he went off and found from somewhere this electric appliance and then arranged with his friends in the town to have the house supplied with electric current during part of every morning, as well as in the evening.

After breakfast and the sun lamp, when I had been re-bandaged by Mary (I do not think any other member of the family ever did this: she was the expert) I would go downstairs and sit, well wrapped up, in the unheated Huiskamer to start my reading. What I read at this time of day was almost always only Scripture. There was no time to read anything else in these morning sessions in the cold Huiskamer for I had other things to do. My other reading had to be left till later in the day, after the midday meal, or in the evening.

The morning reading done I would put on the grocer's coat and go out to the wood-shed (dodging Diena if it were a Thursday) to saw up the steadily increasing quantity of wood I was setting myself as a daily task. While I was at work Mary would usually appear with hot coffee in my own mug, made as always out of burnt barley but good and warming, and just before the midday meal I would come in to be given in the Huiskamer a glass of the white wine from Uncle Zwerus.

After the midday meal I would usually read for a while in the Voorkamer and then go out to the wood-shed to finish my task for the day. I was getting through a great deal of wood. By the end of the first fortnight in January I had already cut up all the logs in store in Torenstraat, to the immense satisfaction of John, for this had been a very time consuming task for him and he had many other things to do. He now brought me in a few logs to cut up for other households in the family. It pleased me very much to be able to do this. I spoke of putting up a business plate outside the wood-shed door.

When my afternoon task in the wood-shed was done I would come inside and drink some tea and then sit reading until it was time for me to be taken out and exercised.

I always greatly looked forward to the family gathering at the end of the day, the exchange of news, the friendly conversation, the company of such good people sitting quietly in perfect harmony, never idle. Quite often Aunt Cor or John would play hymns or sacred songs on the harmonium and sometimes the others sang. Every one of them could play, more or less well. I was learning too, trying to remember what I had been taught on the piano at school and had much enjoyed there but had soon allowed to lapse as an undergraduate — probably because I was not good enough and some of my friends did it better — and had determined, as I lay in hospital, to pick up again and learn thoroughly if I ever became a prisoner-of-war. There are difficulties, however, in the way of practising a musical instrument in a small household full of people to whom you do not wish to be unkind. The aunts were full of encouragement and praise for the progress I was making but I never got as far as solo performance in public at a family gathering.

One evening I saw Aunt Mien was sewing curtains.

'They are for the barn,' she said, in answer to my question. 'Where you cut up the wood. It is not usual to have curtains in a barn, I know, but the windows are so close to the street that I put them up when we first began to have underdivers.'

She went on sewing and sighed a little.

'That was a long time ago,' she said. 'The underdivers have lasted longer than the curtain.'

16

I⊤ was essential to my way of life in Torenstraat to behave as though it would go on like this indefinitely. Hopes and plans for my return home, absorbing and important though they were, could not be allowed to upset its even tenor. Twice already now I had sat upon the very edge of departure, with everything packed up, all preparations made and the farewell visits over and all of us in the family, myself included, looking upon my departure as a certainty. Both times I had found myself fully prepared for what would happen if, for some overriding reason, I could not go. Everything would be just as it was before. The elaborate impedimenta for my journey would be unpacked and what had to be hidden put away again in hiding. The familiar and satisfying thread of life in the family would easily be picked up again and I would sit down to read or play chess with John as though nothing else had ever been intended. That was what had happened both times. There were no post mortems, no discussion of what might have been. We had tried our best and it had not come off. We would try again and perhaps next time it would. There was no place for fretfulness over failure among people to whom the phrase 'Thy will be done' was something more than a form of words.

Nevertheless, I felt the need to remove myself from the household in Torenstraat growing more pressing every day. The family had now been burdened by my presence for more than three hard months. Food was more difficult to find than ever: the meagre bread ration had just been cut again. Things were getting harder all round. Bill came to tell me that it was urgent to see what could be done to get the scores of other fugitives, still in hiding round the countryside, away and out of the country. The farmers who looked after them did not want to give them up to the Germans, he said, but to keep them hidden and to feed them, even on the farms, was getting more and more difficult. Quite apart from the problem of maintenance the risk of detection inevitably grew greater with the passage of time.

I was only too well aware that in my own household, here in the very centre of things, it could only be a question of time before something went wrong, before some trifling accident brought discovery upon me and ruin on my friends. There had been more frequent visits to the house by Germans of late. Some came demanding the things that were being seized all round, food, woollen goods, more bicycles, even skates. Others came looking for billets. Ede was now being used as a rest centre for troops relieved from forward positions. There were weary looking men to be seen around the streets, never allowed, I was told, to rest for very long. Billets were much in demand and this, for us, was particularly dangerous. If any of the soldiery looking for a roof turned truculent we should be in an awkward position. We had a scheme, and on one occasion had to put it into operation, for spreading our beds to show that the house was already full of evacuees. This was good enough as a temporary expedient but could not stand investigation.

Work was being energetically pressed on in the preparation of defences to the south and the Todt Organization was very active. Every day processions of dejected-looking men and boys were to be seen marching out under the grey skies to dig, shepherded by the old men in their yellowish uniforms with the swastika armbands, pistols in holsters on their belts. Raids and searches for more men were frequent.

'It is such an anxiety,' said Aunt Mien, looking kindly at John and me, 'to have a man about the house.'

I think the nervous strain told on Aunt Cor most. She was far from well. One day news was brought to her in the drug store that in a family well known to her a mother had just been killed by a bomb and her baby's arm blown off. Aunt Cor collapsed and was brought home in pain, suffering from a crippling attack of what they called lumbago which lasted several days.

I often spoke to Aunt Ann, to whom among the older members of the family I was nearest both in age and outlook, about the possibility of my again moving elsewhere. She was unwilling to admit that there would be advantage to their household if I did move away into hiding somewhere else but was prepared to look around for another place. We tried several openings but found nothing that would work.

In the end she said: 'I do not think this is the right thing to do.'

'Why not?' I asked.

'First of all because nobody can look after you as well as we can. We are all settled here. We get a good deal of help and you are part of the family. It is not easy in the household but you know that as well as any other member of the family. You do all you can to help carry the burden. It is more difficult for some others here in this house than for me, and there have been times when I have wondered whether they could really go on. But they find they can. What we all want you to do is to stay in this house until you start on your journey home.'

She spoke with quiet dignity and great warmth of friendship.

'You are a Christian, too,' she said, 'and this makes it even more our duty to look after you. We regard this as a task, you see, and we want to finish it.'

There was nothing I could say.

Aunt Ann put her hand on my arm and looked at me with her kind and friendly smile.

'Beside,' she went on, 'we like having you. It is not often we can get to know someone who has been so much about the world. It has been of great benefit to John, you know, to have you here. So it is not only a duty to look after you. It is a pleasure.'

She got up to go.

'Make your plans,' she said, 'and in good time, if God wishes, you will go home. Till then this is your home.'

She left me, sitting in a corner of the Voorkamer, in silence.

As the January days went by John was getting more and more restless.

'I do not think your own people on the other side of the river are trying hard enough to help you,' he said.

I tried to persuade him there was no reason to think this. I knew enough of the planning of military operations at several different levels, both more orthodox and less, to sound, I hoped, convincing.

'Besides,' I said. 'Nobody owes me anything and I can't really believe, even now, that a big effort to get me out would pay much of a dividend.'

He then suggested, more than once, that the Dutch on our side should be trying harder.

Again I thought he was wrong. Resistance work in Gelderland was being done under great and increasing difficulties. Too much had been brought into the open at the time of the airborne landings and the Germans had come down on it. Since then there had been serious mishaps. The underground, already under strain, had been driven more and more on to the defensive and now had its work cut out to stay in business at all. I was fully aware that they found my own presence an embarrassment and I did not doubt they would welcome an opportunity to help so heavy an underdiver to move on.

John's position was a delicate one. This was not his area. His own village of Renkum had been evacuated only a week or so before I came to Ede and the work he did for the Resistance Movement was still primarily concerned with Renkumers evacuated like himself. However great his friendly interest in myself, he had no responsibility for me outside the household and he had to be careful about making suggestions or offering advice to those in whose area of responsibility I happened to be.

John had gone on trying all the same. A month before he had had the idea that if I could be got to the tubercular hospital at Renkum (now evacuated, and the place from which I was supposed to have come when my cover story was that of a tubercular patient) it would be easy to arrange for me to be met there by an Allied patrol from across the river, since at that time our patrols often came over and moved about around there. The proposal, when suggested tentatively, was not received by Resistance leaders with enthusiasm. They pointed out that a plan for evacuation by air was also then under consideration. This was thought to offer a better chance than John's and there would in any case be difficulty in getting me to Renkum. I could not walk so far and vehicles were forbidden in defended areas. So we dropped this idea for the time being, but when the air evacuation project was abandoned and other prospects looked unpromising we began to consider it again.

John found a farmer who had helped Lathbury's party, a man whom he described as 'One of those splendid people who are too stupid to be afraid'. This man had sometimes received a permit from the Germans to take a waggon down to the hospital with three or four men, to get in potatoes, or do other work in the hospital's vegetable garden. He was prepared to do this again, whenever he could get permission, and he would take me down in his waggon too. I let my beard grow against the time when I would have to appear as an agricultural labourer.

In time the farmer got his permission. We were just about to send a signal to the far side through Sam proposing a rendezvous when we heard, through him, that Allied troops had been withdrawn from the south bank and no more patrols would be coming across the river just there. We were too late, and John swallowed his disappointment with as good a grace as he could.

Then came Christmas, and further failures.

'What about South Holland?' asked John. 'Perhaps there is some way across the Waal down there in the south-west, now that the Lek looks so unpromising.'

Should we try to find out how things were by Gorkum, or whether it was possible to get into the Biesbosch, that huge labyrinth of swampy waterways on the south of the Waal, the lower edge of which was said to be in Allied hands? What about Sliedrecht? We asked Menno to find out more for us.

A few days later Menno came back to Torenstraat with the answer. It was no use even making further inquiries, he said. Two girls had just come all the way up from Sliedrecht, with a recommendation to him from the L.O. chief in that area. The girls badly wanted to get to their families on the south side of the River Waal in Brabant, but Menno's opposite number in South Holland had been unable to find any way across. They had heard down there, however, that it was possible to cross the Rhine in Gelderland, up in our part of Holland, and so get down into the Betuwe as a useful first step. 'Could Menno help?' they asked. It made us smile a little to think of anyone coming up to Ede to be helped across, in what was said to be the most sternly repressed rural area in Holland. It was clear that Menno and his friends had a big reputation. But that seemed to finish Sliedrecht as a possibility for me.

Meanwhile we were waiting for more news from Sam. He sent me a note to say that planning for another attempt was going well. Warrack would be in the party. Dates were not firm, but the other side had accepted a proposition in principle. Was I fit enough for what might be a strenuous journey? I replied by Menno's courier service that I was. I told them of the two hours' work in the wood-shed I had now been doing daily for a week or two, and the fast walking, up to an hour every day, often in foul weather and always in snow. I was now, in fact, a very different person from what I had been a month or two ago.

That was on 11th January. I began to prepare once more for departure.

A couple of days later I heard a disquieting report from Menno. Sam had gone. I thought it possible that he had merely changed his location, but Menno said the impression was that he had left the country. Then I had a note from Sam. It said that plans had changed. His headquarters in England had ordered him to come out now, without waiting for the relief originally intended. The journey he was about to make looked like being a rough one, Sam wrote, down to the Lek some way to the west of Renkum, beyond where the German line curved southwards, across the river at night — loose ice and German vigilance permitting — and then down by foot or bicycle to the Waal bank near Tiel, where a patrol from the Allied line across the Waal would pick him up. Sam doubted if I could endure such a journey and made his opinion clear that if I came I might hold his party up.

To this I wrote back that I was the only possible judge of my own fitness and that I was coming anyhow. All I wanted from him was a rendezvous. But he never received my note. He had already left.

The same day I had a note from someone known as Vandyck. I had often heard of this operator from Bill and Menno, though I am not sure if Menno had actually met him. His whole task was to provide for the maintenance and movement of Allied escapers and he had arrived in Holland by parachute over a year ago to do it. He spoke perfect Dutch, I was told, and was accepted as a Dutchman but whether he was Dutch or English I did not know.

Vandyck was known to have been doing a fine job, though deprived by unkind strokes of fate of much of the success he deserved. So far he and I had not been in direct contact, for I had been a client of poor Bat, and then of Sam, and Vandyck had sensibly left me alone. But he had sent at my request a list of all the Allied fugitives in hiding in the Veluwe, and I had rejoiced to find in this the names of several friends I had thought dead, like Sammy Carr for instance, of 10th Battalion, about whom I had heard a grim story during the battle. I had searched the list in vain for the names of others about whom I badly wanted news, like Dick des Voeux and Teddy Ritson, the Commanding Officer and Second-in-Command of 156th Battalion, Lionel Queripel and John Howard of the 10th, and George Lea commanding the 11th.

It was only much, much later that I was to learn that Dick des Voeux, my old friend, that gallant Grenadier, was dead, and so was Lionel Queripel, with a posthumous Victoria Cross, and John Howard was dead too, and so was Teddy Ritson, and of all these only George Lea, a large, cheerful, imperturbable man who had been my Brigade Major and remained a greatly valued friend, had, thank God, been taken alive.

Vandyck now proposed in his letter to look after me. I wrote back to him, by the courier, to say that I was rather in the doldrums, asking him to find out whether anything was happening about the aeroplane, since for the moment nothing else seemed to be developing, and suggesting that we should meet.

By now my friend John could contain himself no longer.

'None of these people,' he said, 'Dutch or English, has done you any good. I am quite certain that if anybody had really put his mind to it you could have been home months ago. You say they have too many more important things to do. Well, I have not so now I am going to try for myself.'

His proposal was simple. There must surely be some way out through South Holland. He would go down and find out.

Though the journey did not look an easy one, he readily secured his mother's agreement to it. They had lived in Gorkum and she had friends and relatives there which made the prospect rather less daunting. She would be glad to have news of them and they would be pleased to hear from her. John had one special advantage. He was Wim's brother. The memory of the bold and distinguished Resistance worker in South Holland known as 'Martien', whom the Germans had caught and carried away, was still green. John believed that a very old friend of his own was also mixed up with the Underground business somewhere in those parts and this was an added advantage.

He had good papers. His Ausweis exempting him from work for the Germans and another allowing him to keep his bicycle were exemplary and he had got himself an authority from the neighbouring village of Veenendaal to travel south to inquire into the circumstances of other Renkumers evacuated down there. In Veenendaal there was an official who had hitherto been a tool of the Germans but did not particularly like the way the war was going. He was now inclined to render small services to people who had not collaborated, as a form of insurance. John told me that the official kept a copy for himself, against the future, of any document that he issued of this kind. I was later to find myself indebted to the official in Veenendaal.

John provided himself, out of the family's stores, with provisions for several days. He took bread, cheese and a small piece of bacon, and packed these and a few other odds and ends into a suitcase which he strapped on to the back of his bicycle. From a friendly tobacconist he procured a pound or so of loose tobacco. Into his pocket he put a photograph of a family group which showed his mother, his brother Wim, his sister Rie and himself, and off he went into the bitter weather, a tall, lanky, fair-headed youth, with a large mouth easily chapped when the wind was chill, gold-rimmed spectacles, keen grey eyes, and a sharp straight nose which in the cold used to turn rather red.

My walks in the evening, as the days lengthened, got even shorter.

Aunt Ann delivered a stern judgement.

'I am sorry to say, Mr. Hackett,' she said, 'you will have to get up early and walk before it is light.'

In hard mid-winter weather this was not a very attractive prospect. For a day or so longer we put it off and continued walking as best we could in the evening dusk. These little twilight walks were interesting and sometimes even exciting. One of them was possibly more exciting than prudent. There had been a suspicion, probably without much foundation, that some of the doctors were beginning to collaborate with the enemy. If they were, and the tendency spread, the danger to all resistance work would be very great. A batch of circulars was prepared and addressed to several score citizens pointing out the danger to everyone if this fortress of non-collaboration should be breached, and asking for their moral support in buttressing it. To Aunt Ann fell the task of posting the letters. On one evening walk, therefore, instead of avoiding the centre of the town as usual, we went straight through it to the Post Office.

In front of the Post Office building (I can see it clearly still) there was a group of German soldiers, perhaps about a dozen, lounging about and gossiping, with nowhere in particular to go and nothing much to do. We pushed our way in through the group, between the untidy grey-green figures, and begging the pardon of those leaning against the letter box itself pulled out bundles of envelopes from the pockets of our coats and thrust them in. Having committed a good deal of highly inflammatory anti-German propaganda to the post we apologized again to the soldiery for disturbing them and elbowed a way out to continue on our walk.

Here, as I write this story, I have to pause in something approaching incredulity at what I have just put down. Can this possibly be true? How could this mild and unassuming woman find the courage to behave like this, the boldness to move straight into the very eye of danger with someone at her side whose simple presence was her death warrant if he were discovered — even using him to help carry letters almost as lethal to her if she were found out? And yet, incredible though it sounds, I know it happened for I was there, and as we walked away Ann de Nooij's demeanour was as untroubled as if she had done no more than a little household shopping.

On one other walk, taken rather earlier than usual in good light, we were approaching the door of the German military police billet just round the corner on the High Street, upon whose back garden our own adjoined, when we met a group of Feldgendarmie just going in. I badly wanted both to touch one of these and speak to him—to say anything at all, just to address him. I walked abstractedly into the middle of the group, cannoned into a couple, and apologized.

'Very sorry,' I said in German. 'Terribly cold, isn't it?'

'Terribly,' said one. The others grunted.

That was all: I only wanted that. It was like being a little boy at the zoo.

I was walking with Aunt Cor and Mary's mother on another snowy evening when we were stopped by a German soldier on the outskirts of the town. He asked us in German the way to some place or other. Whether it was well known to my friends or not made little difference to them: it was much better on principle not to tell him.

'I don't know,' said Mary's mother. 'I'm an evacuee.'

The soldier grunted impolitely and turned to me.

'I don't now either,' said I. 'I'm an evacuee too.'

This I found good fun but that evening on our walk there was what looked like being a real disaster. Mary's mother lost, without knowing it at the time, one rubber overshoe in the snow. The total impossibility of replacing it and the extreme scarcity of shoes and shoe leather made this a serious loss. When we got home and she discovered it I went straight back, out of the house alone for the very first time, searching along our path until caught some way from home by six o'clock and curfew, still unsuccessful. I hurried home late, without the overshoe, wondering if I might not provoke a worse catastrophe still by getting arrested as a curfew breaker and having my identity discovered, with all the danger to anyone who had helped me that might follow. But I got back safely and next day, to our great relief, the overshoe was found.

It was typical of the ladies of Torenstraat that Aunt Ann had long since got from somewhere a good pair of rubber overshoes for me, and that now Uncle Zwerus had contrived to have my marching boots re-soled too, though both rubber and leather were said to be almost beyond price.

My most pressing fear in Ede was always that I might be picked up by the Germans for some trivial reason, and that it would then be realized (as it would have been almost at once) that I was not Dutch but British. The outburst that would have followed the discovery of a British officer living there in their midst, with the searches, the reprisals, the taking of hostages and the summary punishments was dreadful to think of, even if direct implication of my own friends could by any chance be avoided.

For this reason the Todt men, whose business it was to bring in any male who looked young enough to work, were always my chief enemies. I remember sitting one morning, in the clear frosty sunlight about the turn of the year, in the little summer house of the de Nooij's tiny garden and looking up for a moment to meet a baleful eye over the hedge. A seedy, savage-looking old Todt man stood there, wearing the hateful ochreous clothes with the swastika arm band, looking at me with a speculative eye. My heart almost stood still. After a minute I went inside and warned the family, and then crept upstairs to watch him out of the window, with the hiding place hatch open. I was in great fear. Supposing he came to inquire who that male in the garden was, as he almost certainly would if he had been as interested as he seemed? But as I watched it appeared that he was there only to intercept pedestrians in the little square and inspect papers. I looked on for a while at the usual dismal little comedy until he went away.

It was precisely with this sort of danger in mind that John had begun to talk about getting better papers for me before I set out on a journey. The procurement of personal documents had long ceased to be as easy as when Gerald Lathbury and some of his party had been so readily furnished with official identity cards, photograph and all. We now looked back on those days as a Golden Age. John decided, nonetheless, that I must have a real identity card. The procuring of a photograph presented the first big problem.

There was only one professional photographer left in the town and he had no electric current for his lights. Even the cable to his house had been removed. John went to see him and spoke of an interest he had in a deaf Dutch Jew. The photographer was not unwilling to help, but could do nothing without current. John went to the friend who was the municipal electrical engineer and told the man the same story about the Jew. He trusted the electrical engineer but still had to be prudent. Certainly, said his friend, who never asked John any questions, how would it be if he ran a temporary cable across to the studio for twenty-four hours? And of course, said John, it would mean turning on the current for a while during the day-time, and that meant turning it on for the whole town. That too could be arranged, said his friend. He would tell the Germans he had to test the circuit.

Next day the same little procession set out from Torenstraat as for the haircut, with John fifty yards ahead and me following, thrilled again to be walking up the High Street in daylight.

This time I followed him across it and along the far side. Nearly opposite the paint factory he turned up an alley to the left, under a new-looking black power cable sagging overhead. I soon found myself in a little photographic studio silently shaking hands with the photographer. John reminded him that I was deaf. He motioned me to the throne and then demonstrated in dumb show what I had to do. The photograph was soon taken and we went back to Torenstraat and tea, the photographer promising to have his picture ready in a day or two. I wondered what people had made of it, Dutch and German alike, when the electric light suddenly went on everywhere that winter afternoon, and after a short time as suddenly went out again.

Then John went off on his journey to South Holland. Before he was back Vandyck had been to see me.

17

AUNT Ann came in and said 'There's a young Dutchman asking for you at the door. He says you have been expecting him and his name is Jan.'

Well, that was as good a name as any and quite as authentic as Vandyck, and Aunt Ann let him in. He was a strongly-made young man, not over tall, with a slightly turned-up nose and thoughtful eyes under dark brown hair which curled a little. He wore rough tweed trousers thrust into high loose black boots, a thick white sweater of natural wool with the grease in it, and a tweed jacket. They were borrowed clothes, he said. The Sicherheitsdienst had moved in on his last location and he had had to move out quickly, leaving all his own things behind.

He said it had not been easy for him to get through the nearby township of Lunteren since the Dutch S.S. were now operating a control post there. He took a careful look around the lace curtain out of the window of the Voorkamer and then sat down away from it.

We were pleased to see each other at this first meeting: there was much to talk about. Towards the end of his visit we got around to my own situation. Sam had gone, as I had heard, and three other officers of his own organization with him. They had not, it appeared, yet got across the Waal and were said to be trying at another place. Vandyck said he saw little prospect of my getting over down there and even less of crossing the Lek up here. He was now exploring a route which would take me round behind Arnhem to the north and then down south and across the Rhine, further upstream, from east to west.

I told him about John's idea. He did not like it. I hardly thought he would. He told me I was a client about whom he had been told to be especially careful. His distrust of the amateur operator in a business in which he was a professional was natural and caused me no surprise. I said I would send John up to see him as soon as he got back. Menno would arrange a rendezvous through someone called Mark, with whom both he and Menno were in contact. It was clear that I should have to be careful not to make things difficult for Vandyck. He had enough difficulties as it was.

Aunt Ann gave us tea and my visitor after another peep around the lace curtain, went out of the front door, got on his bicycle and rode away.

Life went on in our household much as usual. I was reading a great deal. Sawing and chopping up wood was helping me to get slowly stronger. The principal change was what I had seen coming and rather dreaded. Aunt Ann's stern decision had been implemented. I was now, and had been for a week past, taking my walking exercise on those grim winter mornings before daylight.

Aunt Ann was right, as always. It was the only thing to do. At half past six she would call me and light a candle, a sad little yellow flame flickering in air like black ice. The thermometer on my bedroom wall never showed, as I put my clothes on, a higher temperature than eight degree centigrade below freezing point and sometimes went as low as minus fourteen. Downstairs we each had a cup of tea from a thermos, with a piece of bread, and then set out in the dark. Often it was snowing hard. The snow always lay thick on the ground, except where there were irregular and malignant patches of ice upon which we slid and stumbled in the darkness. Gradually the light grew. Soon it was possible actually to see the broad snow flakes as they fell, instead of only feeling their ghostly fingers on your face. We walked fast. The blood stirred as exhilaration grew, and hunger mounted. Soon dim figures of men could be seen in the growing light plodding to their work, huddled-up shapes like birds in the cold. Others on bicycles were struggling through the snow. A cart would pass with the horse pulling strongly, the wheels squeaking against packed snow, or crunching and clattering on the ice. There would be a glow in the dark where a man stood still for a moment and the sharp surprising tang of tobacco smoke would drift over on the morning air. Perhaps the first V1 of the day would pass overhead, streaming fire and leaving a shuddering in the air all around long after it had gone. Then as the light sprang up from all sides it was time to hurry home, with face tingling and limbs aglow, and something of a feeling of superiority over anyone who had not been out walking too. There would then be hot tea and porridge for breakfast.

One afternoon John came back. It was clear at once that he had been successful and brought important news, for his mobile face was full of pleasure. My urgent questions met a quiet reproach from Aunt Mien. There is a proper way to do these things. After supper, with the whole household gathered round him in the Voorkamer, John told his tale. It was in

145

Dutch, and some of it I could not follow, but it was clearly a concise and complete recital of his adventures from departure to return, with many allusions to friends and relatives and what was happening to them. It was listened to with close attention. There followed keen questions and gratifying exclamations of interest and approval.

Then John and I withdrew to the Huiskamer and held our own conference. First of all he told me the outline of his story again in English. He had had his first set-back when trying to cross the Lower Rhine into South Holland over the German-controlled ferry. The Germans in charge had refused to take him and confiscated the paper he carried authorizing him to inquire in South Holland about evacuees from Renkum. They were even rather annoyed and more than a little suspicious that he should present such a thing. They might well have detained him.

'But I look such a silly fellow,' said John. 'It is always easier for me. They let me go.'

He went a little further downstream and bribed a boatman, with some of the tobacco he had brought from the friendly tobacconist, to take him across together with his bicycle. Floating ice had piled up, loose and dangerous, for some way out from each bank. The crossing was by no means easy, but the boatman had managed it. Then he had found his friend. This young man, whose name was Kars, had been a university student of mathematics before the war. John described him as a burly and argumentative person with a booming voice. He was very fond of him.

'A beautiful man,' said John.

Kars had told him of someone to whom he should go in Sliedrecht. John cycled down there, found the man, said who had sent him, and got out his family photograph.

'Do you remember Martien?' he said to the man.

The man looked at him thoughtfully. 'Yes,' he said at last. 'I do.'

'I'm his brother,' said John. He produced the photograph. 'Here we are together. Look—mother, sister and us two sons.'

The man looked at the photograph for a long time, and then for a long time again at John.

'Yes,' he said at last. 'That's you all right, and that's Martien. He was a good boy and a great loss to us. What can I do for you?'

'I've got a British officer,' said John. 'Can you get him across into Brabant, to the Allied lines?'

'I believe that can be done,' said the man. 'I can't do it myself, but I think I know who can. Come with me.'

After that John was in the groove. What had looked impossible before now seemed very simple. He found that there was little to be arranged. I could be taken across into British hands by a courier service which operated in two-man canoes and had now been working for a month or more. Wind and weather permitting, they ran down the Waal on a couple of days each week. Getting escapers out was not their real job. They were carrying correspondence and intelligence material for the Dutch Government in Britain and for a department of the British Government linked with it. They had been keeping out of what was called the 'tourist traffic' because the two functions were different and could not be combined without loss of efficiency and security. They would certainly want to oblige a friend of John's standing, however, and would take out anyone he suggested. How about 5th February, conditions permitting? The journey down the river would take about three hours, all told.

John clinched the deal and undertook to get his client down to Sliedrecht in time to cross on 5th February. Then he worked his way back along the route by which he had come, to arrange our journey from Ede to Sliedrecht. Kars would accommodate us on the last stage, just south of the Lek. When he was told that the officer coming down was higher in rank than any he had yet seen, Kars asked if he might put on a guard of honour from the local L.K.P. They might not be smart, said Kars, but they would all have Sten guns. John said that he thought a guard of honour was hardly necessary, but it would be splendid if Kars could provide a chess set. He then arranged that we would cross the Lek on 1st or 3rd February. We might fail the first time and have to withdraw from the river bank a little before trying again. John then came back over the Lek where he had crossed before, again with the help of the friendly tobacconist, and cycled on to Ede. On his way he booked us in provisionally for night stops at a safe place he knew along the road.

This all sounded good to me, but would Vandyck like it? I had to think carefully of that. John arranged a meeting through Menno and Mark and went up to see Vandyck.

Vandyck cycled over to visit me next day. He was worried. He was, I knew, quite an old hand at this game. He had told me that earlier on he had worked on one route along which shot-down Allied aircrew were being moved. After some time it was discovered that these men were being fed straight into German hands through a stoolpigeon in Belgium. He knew nothing of the route we now spoke of and, since he had no instructions about it from his control on the other side, he was unwilling to trust it. He had, he told me again, been instructed to consider me as a more than usually valuable subject and he wanted to take no risks. His own plan, which was to open a route further east and feed all those he was looking after through that, was far from complete, but it was making progress.

This was all very awkward. Vandyck did not know John and I did. I would have complete confidence in any plan of his. Vandyck thought it all sounded too good to be true and not unnaturally treated plan and promoter alike with reserve. The last thing I wanted to do was to make things difficult for Vandyck. He was under orders and had a job to do. That, as a matter of fact, was all that prevented me from embracing John's proposal at once. Vandyck said that his instructions were perfectly clear and he was responsible to his superiors for carrying them out. If I went off on this enterprise against his advice he would have to have from me a certificate of clearance for his chiefs. I listened with the utmost sympathy. Nevertheless, I was anxious to be off. Everything proposed so far had come to nothing and I was tired of waiting for more plans to mature. Above all, I wanted to spare my friends in Torenstraat any further danger. I had been there too long already.

In the end we compromised. I would set out with John and be lodged securely somewhere on the way. John would then go on alone and find out whatever Vandyck wanted to know to convince him that what was proposed made sense. Vandyck himself would go off to find out how promising his own route looked. He was hourly expecting news about it to arrive back in his own location: if he moved about a bit he could find out much more. We could all meet in a few days at wherever I had been left and compare results. I reserved to myself the right to decide at that time which way I would go, but I hoped to be able to do this without embarrassment to Vandyck.

John agreed at once, though a good deal was being asked of him. I was very sorry for Vandyck: he was a good man doing a most difficult job. He said he did not even much like my moving west from Ede, when I should probably have to move a good way to the east, even from there, where I now was, in the long run. He would only agree to my setting out on certain conditions. What John had to find out for him was first of all whether there was a wireless link working in connection with the canoe route. He must then discover what the operator's operational name was, what Allied troops, designated by rank, name and number, had recently passed that way and whether confirming signals had been received of their arrival on the far side. He must also be told about any failures there had been.

This was going to be hard for John. He had no idea at all whether or not there was a wirelss link working for that route. So far as he knew there was not. He was well aware, too, that any passengers, they might have taken would almost certainly have been Dutch and not English, and even if the boatmen had taken Englishmen, what would they know of names, ranks and numbers? John agreed all the same.

But Vandyck went further. Even if it looked fairly promising, he said, he might still have to insist on their sending a couple of others through first before he would agree to their taking me.

John bridled at this. He pointed out that these people were not working for Vandyck and were unlikely to accept his instructions about who was to go. The offer to take me had been made, John said, as a concession among friends. It was only as a concession, moreover, that he could hope to get the information required of him.

Vandyk, conciliatory as well as firm, said that he could at least find us a good staging post near Doorn. He had sent several people there, and even now they were looking after a party of British officers on the run.

This, I learnt, was none other than the party that had started off with Sam. They had failed completely and been forced to come right back, almost to their starting point. In the group, I heard to my great joy, were Graeme Warrack, Lipmann Kessel, Theo Redman out of my own field ambulance and Derek Ridler, who had been Kessel's anaesthetist. Sad though I was at their failure, I could scarcely have been more pleased at the prospect of seeing all of these again. I had not met a soul from the Division since Gerald Lathbury went off three months before. These were all friends of mine, to one of whom I was more than usually indebted, and I could hardly have chosen people it would be more pleasant to meet. I accepted Vandyck's offer at once.

We differed on one final point, however. Vandyck was used to moving his clients round furtively, usually by night, often in bunches, rarely with Dutch papers, and almost always with odd bits of incriminating evidence on them. Moreover, whenever they could get them, they carried weapons. This did not suit me at all. I was by now used to living as a member of a Dutch family and had long since grown accustomed to carrying nothing, even a cigarette tin, which could be traced to an English source. I had come to rely on the false papers provided for me and was by now so used to the proximity of Germans that I did not mind moving freely among them. Weapons for me would be liabilities. Having complete confidence in John's guidance I was sure that, once we were away from Ede, by far the safest plan would be for me to cycle together with John freely and openly, by daylight, along the main roads. I would be Mijnheer van Dalen wearing the deaf button, as usual, as a sort of Tarnhelm. We should travel 'clean' as I chose to call it, with nothing about us to cause anxiety. The added confidence this would furnish made it all the more likely that we should get through.

Vandyck hesitated. It was unusual but he could see that it all made good sense. He agreed.

We then arranged our rendezvous near Doorn. John received further detailed instructions and Vandyck left.

John and I, in good spirits, set about planning our cycling tour like two schoolboys going on a holiday.

18

I T was good to see before me at last a real chance of getting away from the household in Torenstraat. The depth of my gratitude to its members was the measure of my pressing anxiety to be off and relieve them of so dangerous a presence. It did not surprise me in the least to learn, much later on, from John Snoek himself, that a rumour had already, at this time, reached German ears that there was a parachute brigadier of the British army somewhere on the run in Gelderland. It was high time to be gone. This was one more reason for following John's plan rather than Vandyck's. I could get away sooner.

There was added satisfaction too in the thought that the person who would eventually contrive to get me out might be a member of the family. The prospect that John, the amateur, might end up by wiping the eyes of all the professionals was not unpleasing.

The photographs for my new identity papers had not yet come. Several messages had been sent to the photographer, but he always replied that he now had no electric current and could not print them. He was looking around for the loan of that rare object, an accumulator.

John was a little annoyed. He went round to see him.

The man worked now and then for the Germans didn't he, and was well in with some of them?

Yes, of course he was.

'Well,' said John, 'borrow a battery from the Germans. What could be easier?'

The man did so that very day, printed off my photographs at once, and sent them round the next.

John bicycled off with the pictures to Veenendaal to see his uneasy friend there, the municipal official, and brought back the same evening an identity card, complete with photograph, for Mijnheer Johan van Dalen, an employee in a farmer's bank, born in Renkum but evacuated from there to Veenendaal and now living in the province of Utrecht. Everything was in order: the card had been stamped, numbered and signed by the issuing authority. All that was now needed was Mijnheer van Dalen's fingerprint on it and his signature. Those were added that very night.

I was now a citizen of the province of Utrecht, and thus felt a happy community with Beachcomber's Dr. Strabismus, whom I had long revered and of whom I had often spoken to John. Dr. Strabismus, 'whom God preserve, of Utrecht' was something of a cult figure in my own generation of undergraduates. Fantasy apart, citizenship of the Province of Utrecht had advantages. In Gelderland, where I was actually living, every male was liable to transportation for work in Germany until he was forty years old and was regarded as available for forced labour in Holland up to the age of sixty. The more fortunate citizens in the Province of Utrecht, just along the road (of whom I was now one), were free from any such demands after the age of forty-five. To bring my age up to forty-five it was necessary only to add eleven years to it on the paper. My present condition and appearance made that look just about right.

In the planning for our journey, with the papers in order, provisions came next. Bread, tinned bacon, butter and cheese were found out of the household's dwindling stocks, supplemented as necessary by levies upon the households of other members of the family. That of Uncle Ko, who was still locked up in his forced labour camp, was not exempt. Uncle Zwerus contributed handsomely. I knew that he wanted to include a couple of bottles of cognac in our stores, and that to get them he had been obliged to make up something out of something else from the paint factory store and barter the product for the cognac. He succeeded and sent the two bottles round.

John was to be in charge of the operation, however, and his mother was keeping a careful eye upon our preparations. Were not two bottles of cognac, she asked Aunt Mien, rather too much? We might be put to considerable exertion it was true, and even some privation and hardship in bitter weather, but surely in that event butter was better than brandy? John's mother took one of the bottles away and exchanged it in the town for a good slab of butter.

The next thing was a bicycle. Something more dependable was wanted, and with better tyres, than the decrepit machines which were, for the most part, all that had survived the attentions of the Germans.

Another uncle of the family, Uncle Wim from Oosterbeek, came to the rescue. From the paint factory, where he and his family now lived, he produced a real bicycle. Its tyres were thin and smooth but they were still sound. It was agreed that when

John had eventually seen me off on the last part of my journey, by water, he would somehow get Uncle Wim's bicycle back to him in Ede.

There were other little preparations and adjustments, too many to tell. The black silk cover for my luminous watch, which Mary had made for me for the night attempt by Wageningen with Menno that had not come off, would now be useful. Aunt Ann allowed me to take an English New Testament for the journey. Someone else produced a pair of thick British aircrew socks.

Then came the final visits and the last report from people whose work I had been following with such sympathy and admiration.

Dr. Krayenbrink came and had another look at my stomach. He said it would do and we had the last of our many long talks. He told me of what he was doing for the men from Rotterdam, who had been marched down ill clad and badly shod, underfed and often ill, to work in miserable conditions on the defences south of Ede. He had been ordered by the Germans to undertake their medical supervision but he had made it quite clear to the Todt Organization, with admirable courage, that he regarded it to be no part of his duties as a medical man, under any circumstances, to get the maximum amount of work out of the people in his care and that he would look after them on his own lines or not at all. The Germans were obliged to accept. The men from Rotterdam were falling sick all round. Some had died. There was little medical aid to be had and the Germans had to take Dr. Krayenbrink on his own terms.

From the time he took this task on he had grimly struggled to/get the men adequately housed, fed and clothed. But he had also evacuated scores of them, one at a time, to the hospital where he also worked and, once he had them there, he secured for them whatever papers he could to authorize their return to their homes. Out of four hundred he had already got away nearly a third.

I asked him had he considered what might happen if any of these cases were traced back to him.

He said he had.

He also told me of what he heard from Amsterdam, that lack of medical supplies and the weakness of nursing mothers were resulting in an infant mortality rate, in the first three weeks, of ninety per cent. Some maternity institutions could not even find cotton wool or lint.

We talked for a while longer and he got up to go. I tried to

153

thank him. He broke into the very young and infectious grin I knew so well.

'You thank me for absolutely nothing!' he said, 'It was all a great pleasure.'

It seemed a lifetime since he had come to the house on my first night in it, when he had admired Kessel's surgery and told me that I would either die or recover and there was very little he himself could do about it.

Dominee Blauw came. He looked worn and pinched but the eyes in his thin face blazed with the same unquenchable spirit.

He told me how hard it was, and getting harder daily, to keep his greatly augmented flock comforted and hopeful. There was so little to eat, their clothes were so poor in the bitter winter, fuel was so scarce, and there were few who did not live under the dark shadow of bereavement or danger.

He was a man of high spirit, but he was also a tranquil man. His power for good over his own people, I knew, was great.

We also spoke of the difficulty many of his people seemed to find at the present time in reconciling the injunction to forgive our enemies with what seemed to be their duty towards their nation's enemies—the enemies, indeed, it almost appeared, of all mankind, the Nazis. It was not as difficult, said Dominee Blauw, as some claimed. He had taught his people that they knew all the rules. Let them act on each occasion as, under the circumstances, their consciences dictated. They would not then, he was confident, go far wrong. They would probably find in general that they would fight tooth and nail against their oppressors, as a whole, but if individual Germans were in pain or distress they would help them.

Our last conversation was about spiritual things. Then he prayed with me and said goodbye.

I had a farewell visit from Uncle Zwerus and his wife, a solemn and kindly little interview, in which it was quite impossible for me to express my thanks. We made little speeches to each other, none the less sincere for being touched with ceremony, and to these marvellously kind people too I said goodbye.

There were other visits, from Uncle Ko's family, from Uncle Wim who owned the bicycle, from Menno and Bill, and from Blue Johnny whom I now knew better as young Zwerus de Nooij.

On the day before we were to leave, sometime about midday, Uncle Wim's bicycle arrived. It had to be tried out before nightfall, for tomorrow would be a full day and a strenuous one.

In the late afternoon of that day, 29th January 1945 and my last in Torenstraat, I set out from the house on a practice ride with John. It was not snowing just then but the snow lay thick on the ground, beaten and packed on the roads into a hard and treacherous surface, uneven and slippery. In a high state of elation I followed John out of the little garden gate. I then mounted Uncle Wim's bicycle and pedalled along Torenstraat, turning left-handed out by the church tower into the High Street. The road surface was slippery, the tyres on Uncle Wim's bicycle old and smooth. To lean much either way from the vertical on this icy surface would start a skid. The brakes did not work. I had not ridden a bicycle for some time and from the start could see disaster not far off. I only hoped it would not happen until we were out of the town, which was thronged with Dutch civilians and Germans, and in the country.

It was not to be. A small child, instead of continuing to cross the road as I had expected, stopped in my path. I swerved. The front wheel slid out sideways. It then turned round and locked and I took a spectacular fall on the hard ice in the very centre of the town. Passers by, including a German soldier or two, turned to look at me as I sprawled upon the ground. Several people came forward to help me up. John was still cycling on ahead, unaware of the catastrophe.

'Here, let me help you,' said a Dutchman, 'are you hurt?'

I did not dare speak.

'Are you all right?' said a woman with him. They looked at me curiously.

I opened my thin black overcoat, the Gestapo coat, and with a little helpless gesture showed the deaf button on my jacket.

'He's deaf,' said one, 'he can't understand what you say.'

I was picking myself up and dusting the snow off my coat, thinking how hard the ground was.

'He seems all right,' said the woman, smiling at me.

I smiled back rather helplessly. Then John turned up, cycling hastily back and looking worried, and together we wheeled our bicycles away.

On the outskirts of the town I mounted again and did a little better but was still not very good at it. John lent me his own machine, with a brake that worked and some remnant of tread on the tyres. I found that easier. We cycled along the snowy road towards Lunteren, between the pine trees. Men were going home from work and children were towing toboggans. Sometimes laborious little groups of people passed, dragging through the snow part of a tree.

We turned and cycled slowly back to Torenstraat in time for supper.

This was my last night. Tomorrow we were off. My kit came out of the hiding place and was again most carefully packed in the large pack and small haversack found for me so long ago in St. Elizabeth's Hospital by Danny McGowan.

John's plan for our cycling tour followed the common practice of Underground travellers who were being careful. We ourselves would carry nothing incriminating. Ahead of us someone would ride with all our 'dirty' luggage. This would be one of the usual couriers (most of whom were female) who knew the job and the route and had been doing this sort of work for some time. Women could pass much more freely than men. They were not liable to work, as the men were, and so were ignored by the Todt people. The Germans (was it that they were used, perhaps, to a system in which women were given little initiative and responsibility?) rarely seemed to regard women as dangerous. In consequence a woman stood a better chance of getting unchecked through a control post than a man. Even if stopped she could usually avoid being searched, if she knew her business and was intelligent and quick. If she happened to be unlucky, and what she was carrying was examined, she could often get off by pleading ignorance of the contents of her package. She could also use emotional aids, to which the Germans were often susceptible. Even in the last resort the penalties imposed on women for carrying 'Deutschfeindlich' matter were rarely severe. For men they were extreme.

We were to pick up our first courier next morning and ride a few hundred yards behind her. If there were a control post and we saw her pass through it we would carry straight on, expecting to be stopped and interrogated but knowing that the dangerous load was safely through. If she were stopped we should dismount where we were, a few hundred yards behind, look at our tyres and watch to see what happened.

Carrying nothing difficult to explain away, with reasonable papers and my deafness, we were sure we had a good chance. If I had to talk German I had enough of it to sound, to a German, as much like a Dutchman talking bad German as like an Englishman doing the same. Unless we had some unexpected disaster (there were such infinite possibilities here that it was a complete waste of time to think about them) and unless I was unlucky enough to fall in with Dutch Nazis instead of German (when I would soon be found out) we ought to be all right. Our story, to be put across by John where necessary, was that we were two cousins cycling west to visit aged parents separated from us by evacuation.

Out now came my airborne smock with the holes in it and the battle dress jacket, shirt and vest, with their fading bloodstains, my British identification papers (which I would need later) the papers from Piet and others for onward transmission at the other end and all the odds and ends which would be useful for the journey but were obviously of British origin. There was also the Delft plate I was given on my birthday and the de Nooij family's joint letter to the Queen of Holland. All this went into the 'dirty' luggage. A small fibre suitcase had been lent to me and was packed with what the British army called my 'small kit' — shaving things, comb, soap and so on — together with dressings and some very precious things on loan from John, a couple of handkerchiefs, a spare pair of socks, a hairbrush, a pair of pyjamas and a little pair of scissors. This suitcase was then strapped on the carrier of my bicycle, while the 'dirty' luggage was made ready to lash on to that of the courier.

On this my last evening in the house in Torenstraat we sat round the table in the Voorkamer in the usual family group, talking quietly and hopefully of the end of the war and of when we should meet again. Satisfaction lay upon us. An exacting task was nearing its end. The task, in which everyone there had shared, had been that of hiding, protecting and nursing a wounded British officer until he was ready to go home, under the very noses of the enemy and in danger, privation and difficulty. As a member of the family, I shared in the general satisfaction. I too had contributed what I could. I had been united with the others in a common effort towards a common end. The fact that I was myself this officer and, as a result of what had been done, might soon be restored to family and friends, was a matter for great personal joy and boundless private gratitude. What mattered most just now, however, was the deep and quiet contentment shared with the other members of the family. The end of the last furrow was in sight.

I promised first of all to let them know when I was safe in British hands. This would be done by a signal from the other side through Vandyck.

Just as important, and possibly more so, I would let them know in my own way when I was back in England, in my own drawing-room, by the fireside with my wife. Only when they heard that, they said, would they know that my journey was really over. I told them to listen to the Dutch broadcast from

157

the B.B.C. every night from 7th February onwards. When they heard the announcement that the Grey Goose was gone they would know that I had reached my journey's end.

We read our piece from the Bible and said good night. I took my lamp upstairs to the little northern room which opened off the landing. There, for what looked like being the last time, I went to sleep under the sampler of the Sleeping Beauty.

19

I AWOKE before sunrise, with that feeling a child has when it wakes on the morning of its birthday, that today is a good day, but just for the moment it is not easy to remember why. Then I knew. I jumped out of bed into the cold air, lit my candle and dressed.

It was not snowing now but snow had fallen again during the night, as it had for several nights past, and the little lean-to roof under my window, which I had as one of my tasks swept clear a few days before, was again heavily burdened.

Aunt Mien was already up preparing a good breakfast, which included an egg each for John and me, and soon Aunt Cor, Aunt Ann, Mary's mother and Mary were with us. We sat down and said grace before the last meal I was to have with them—for the time being at any rate.

Breakfast was not yet over when the courier arrived, a woman of about forty who spoke little or no English. We shook hands and after she had been given a cup of tea John handed over my large pack, to be lashed on her bicycle. Then she left to meet us later outside the town, while John strapped the General's stick onto my machine and I said goodbye to the family. The aunts and Mary made, one after another, tender and slightly formal little speeches of good wishes and farewell. I hugged and kissed each one and got on my bicycle, and John and I rode away.

The light was still dull. As it grew brighter we looked at the sky. It was unpromising. There was a hard cold wind blowing and the clouds were thick and heavy. We rode along Brouwer-straat past Menno's house and out through other streets where I had many a time walked in the dusk. It was strange to see these streets like this, in daylight, from a bicycle, and to be leaving them. To feel my muscles working smoothly and well as we cycled was a pleasure, and the sharp wind which cut through my woollen gloves and chilled the hands inside them stung my face into a glow and chased the blood around. I looked about me with mixed feelings, not without regret. It was like leaving school. There was the expectation of excitement and change, of freedom and a new life and the delight of setting out to go home. My spirits, borne upon thoughts like this, soared like a kite but at the other end of the string was a heavy little stone of sadness. I was leaving behind me a rare and beautiful thing. It was a structure of kindness and courage, of steadfast devotion and quiet selflessness, which it was a high privilege to have known. I had been witness to an act of faith, simple, unobtrusive and imperishable. I had often seen bravery in battle. I now also knew the unconquerable strength of the gentle.

As I look back now I can feel no surprise at the cheerful confidence with which John and I set out on this last journey. If those we had left behind had completed their self-appointed task in spite of all the difficulties, how could we fail in our part now? So we rode out, over the snowy roads in the growing light, in a mood of boundless optimism, past the mill, past where Aunt Ann and I had overtaken the Todt men, past the neat workmen's houses and the school where evacuees were housed, on to the corner where the great main road swept towards Utrecht, with the pine copses in the flat, open country standing up black against the snow.

The courier was waiting for us by her bicycle, on which I saw that my pack was strapped. John tightened up its fastenings, looked over all our tyres (which were none too sound) and pumped air into one of hers. We were ready.

'I'll go on ahead,' she said, 'you two boys follow.'

Presently we were bowling along the straight fast road and had left behind the row of pylons and the few houses which marked on that side the limit of my own acquaintance with the ground. We were in country new and strange to me now.

There was little traffic. A German military car passed us and a decrepit Dutch lorry of the food distribution organization rattled by. There were one or two people about on foot, plodding through the snow with the preoccupied look which was to be seen everywhere. Now and then there was a cyclist, usually a German soldier. The country spread out wide on either side, devoid of prominent features. Lines of pollarded willows showed where the ditches ran, clusters of farm buildings were scattered about in the apparently irrelevant way that seems special to flat countries, the frequent stumps among the trees along the roadside stood out blunt and forlorn. There was a drain and dyke on either side of the road and now and then the rusting wreck of an army vehicle, riddled and torn. The pine plantations were soon left behind. A pitiless wind swept across us: it would snow again soon.

John bicycled slowly, for my sake, but we made a fair pace. Twenty kilometres ahead was the village of Scherpenzeel, where a friend of his was in hiding and we would rest.

Presently, a hundred yards or so back from the road on the left, a burnt and blackened farmhouse came into view behind a thin belt of trees. A good farm it must have been once, with fine cow byres and outbuildings planned, as in so many Dutch farms, in one whole with the farm house. Now it was a grim, charred shell. This, I learned from John, was where poor Bat had lived and worked, where they had found him and taken him away with a bullet in his leg and had later burnt down the house in which he had hidden. I pictured the two lorry loads of German soldiers coming along the road we were now on, from opposite sides, on the tip the informer had given, and I could see the troops tumbling out and swiftly surrounding the house. Menno might have been there too, and this was the farm to which Colonel Boerei had so unwisely gone to ask for straw, before they burnt it down, and had been arrested. What had happened to Bat now we did not know. There had been no more news of him since we heard that he was lying in hospital with both legs in plaster and a guard beside him, under frequent interrogation.

It began to snow now in flakes which stung the left cheek. We passed through a village. Downcast men in poor clothes were marching dejectedly in line before German guards.

'Diggers,' muttered John.

We passed German soldiers and uniformed officials, in ones and twos or in larger groups. I said 'Good morning' to them in Dutch as we went by. Some ignored it sulkily, some grunted, some gave me a pleased and effusive greeting back. One had a purple face and blue nose and miserable watery eyes.

'Cold, isn't it?' I shouted cheerfully in my bad German.

He looked as though he would willingly have killed me.

It was snowing hard now and the road was more difficult. Twice we overtook the courier and had to wait until she got ahead of us again. I welcomed these pauses for I was already getting tired.

John said, 'Let's go on. We can wait for her at Scherpenzeel. Or I can come back for her.'

We pushed on through the wind and falling snow. I was pedalling mechanically now. It was even hard work, I think, for John. The exceptional severity of the weather did at least have the advantage, John explained, that German road blocks were not being manned where he expected them.

We approached a village.

'Scherpenzeel,' said John. 'Soon we can rest.'

He cycled on, while I fell back a length or two. He turned in at a gate and I followed him round the back of one of a row of houses. We dismounted stiffly and I swept the ice from my moustache.

John knocked and presently a farmer's woman came. He spoke to her and we were let inside, shutting the door hard against the blast and shaking off the snow, I from my thin Gestapo coat and John from his leather one.

We went into the cow byre, opening off the front hall of the farmhouse. A young man was in there, moodily forking down hay for several beasts. He was clearly not a farmer. This was John's friend and they greeted each other. John spoke to him a little, while I stood apart, and then he went out to go back along the road and look for the courier. I guessed that the young man knew about me.

This was the first time I had been alone with a stranger, in a strange place, with no member of the family close at hand. It made me restless and uncomfortable.

I watched the young man at work while the cattle, neck-yoked at intervals, grumbled until the hay came to them. They were what I knew as Friesians. I wondered what they were called in Dutch.

'What are these?' I asked, in Dutch, with the tell-tale accent I could not afford to let anyone hear but those who knew.

He looked at me in surprise and almost with a trace of annoyance.

'Cows!' he said. The conversation died.

John came in again at last. He had seen no sign of the courier and would have to cycle further back to look for her.

First he took me into the farm kitchen. There was a bright polished stove and a shining copper, a dresser filled with blue and white china and a table covered with a red cloth worked in white. I, who had until today been living for so long among familiar things, was now in a world completely foreign to me.

'I must leave my friend here,' said John. 'He is deaf I'm afraid. It is no use talking to him. I shall be back soon.'

The farm woman led me to a cane chair in the corner by the stove. The kitchen was unbearably hot after the snow and wind outside. I shifted the chair further from the stove and sat down to wait in silence. To be in a place I did not know, left among strange people, was most unwelcome. I began to feel more and more uneasy.

Another woman came in, an elderly person with a sharp bony face and a little peaked lace cap.

She spoke to me politely.

I answered with my practised greeting.

'It's no use talking to him,' said the farm woman, 'he's deaf, poor fellow.'

The other gave me a compassionate look and sat down at the table with some crochet work while she chattered with the farm woman, who was meanwhile cooking something on the stove.

Snow beat against the window panes. I looked around me, fretful and disoriented, longing to have John back.

A girl came in, a heavy fair creature, with a fading prettiness and a dull and disinterested look.

She looked at me curiously for a full half minute until the farm woman spoke to her sharply and she turned and went slowly out again.

The young man came in from the cow byre and sat down on the other side of the stove. He had put off his wooden shoes outside and was in his stockings. He spoke cheerfully with the two women but left me alone. I was grateful for that.

A grey cat came and climbed up on my knees. The woman in the lace cap smiled at me and went on with her crochet work.

The clock on the wall above me ticked loudly in the silence and in ever growing anxiety I wondered what could have become of John.

An hour after he had left the kitchen door opened and there he was at last, covered in snow. I rose in deep relief as he exchanged a polite word or two with the older women. Then I went out with him into the passage. I do not think I had ever been more pleased and grateful to see anyone.

He had found the courier quite a long way back struggling in the snow and unable, in his opinion, to go much further if she were to get back to Ede before dark. He had therefore, in spite of her protests, taken the pack on to his own bicycle, thanked her for her trouble and set her on the way back. The absence of road blocks on account of the storm would enable us to get on without her.

We ate our sandwiches in the kitchen. John then thanked them all and said goodbye and about midday we set off again. My relief at being alone with him again was very great.

It was not easy going. The snow lay thick on the road and, though it soon stopped snowing, the wind was still strong. We had to be at our rendezvous, thirty kilometres away, by four o'clock. It was dark and stormy and few people were about. We pedalled laboriously on, now carrying heavier loads.

Soon we swung left-handed, which brought the wind dead ahead. We were no longer on the main highway. The road was narrower now and there were fewer well beaten wheel tracks in which to ride. Occasionally, for a stretch, I would get off and walk beside my bicycle. Once or twice I rode clumsily into a patch of deep snow and fell off. It was then difficult to get going again. The bicycle was too big for me and I would have to struggle hard to get up enough speed in the loose soft snow to avoid falling off again. Sometimes I would make two or three false starts and then stand for a moment, my knees trembling with weakness and fatigue, before trying again. A man in blue overalls came to my help once and John came flying back to make sure that I need say no more than a gruff 'Thank you' and 'Good day'. He was like a mother bird with young.

There were no hills, fortunately. The going on the flat was hard enough without them: It was open farm country all the way, with trees along the roads and clumps of trees about the buildings. We passed through villages, where an odd German soldier or two stood about in front of the desolate shops and empty cafés. The paint peeling from brave signs, the little tables standing rusty and deserted in the snow and the forlornness of the winter scene added to the sadness brooding everywhere.

There were fewer Germans here. The front line was now much further to the south, beyond the Lower Rhine, or Lek, and along the banks of the River Waal.

It was not far now to Doorn, near which was our rendezvous.

Though it had been a struggle we were up to time—ahead of time in fact—but we did not know exactly where we were. It was better not to ask strangers for directions. Even carefully done this would draw attention to us. Soon, however, there was no alternative. John drew ahead, I hung back a few hundred yards. He stopped a man and I could see him talking in his polite and guileless way. The man spoke and pointed. John thanked him, raised his hat and rode on. Round the next corner he was waiting for me.

'This is Maarn,' he said, 'we are nearly there. All we want now is the railway bridge. We shall meet there the man who knows Dr. Hendrijksen.'

We rode on into the village of Maarn. I looked with interest at the blank and unresponsive faces of the houses. Would any one of the houses we saw be where we should spend the night?

Again John had to ask the way, this time to find the railway.

We soon came upon it and cycled along its high embankment. On our right lay open swampy fields now covered with ice. We were looking for the bridge.

Presently a main road came in from the right. There were trees about with a house or two in them and a little provision shop on the corner. The main road ran under the railway. Here was a bridge: this must be the rendezvous.

All we wanted now was the man whom we were to ask where Dr. Hendrijksen lived. There was no such person, we knew, but a man we should find at the bridge would offer to show us the way to the doctor's house. That was the man we were to follow.

Under the bridge, as we approached, in the double carriage-way separated by piers in the middle, there was no civilian to be seen. There was something rather less pleasing instead. A German army lorry stood there with its tail towards us, full of soldiers. The driver was sitting on the running board of the cab and a senior N.C.O. stood near by. There were waiting for something.

It was clear at once, to our great relief, that they were not waiting for us. We rode up boldly like men with clear consciences, dismounted and sat down a few feet from the lorry to rest.

Presently a civilian came.

John got to his feet.

'Can you tell me please,' he said, with his usual polite air of simplicity, 'where Dr. Hendrijksen lives?'

'Never heard of him,' said the man. 'Does he actually live here in Maarn?'

'Near Maarn,' said John.

'No doctor of that name round here,' said the man, looking doubtful.

'An evacuee,' said John, 'came over here from the Veluwe. Hasn't been here long.'

'Sorry,' said the man. 'Can't help you.'

The German soldiers listened dully, without interest, probably without comprehension.

Another civilian came: he too knew nothing about the doctor, nor did a third.

John said to me in Dutch, 'Let us go to the shop and ask.'

I answered him in Dutch.

We wheeled our bicycles out into the open again.

Once out of earshot of the Germans John turned to me and spoke in English. 'We can't ask much more,' he said, 'and we can't stay here much longer, either.'

Anyone who attracted attention to himself and whose business was not transparently obvious tended to be looked upon with suspicion. Two young men on the move, and strangers, were apt to be suspect anyway.

I waited under the trees with the snow over my ankles, while he went into the shop. I spent the time removing snow from my pockets, my hat, the turn-ups of my trousers and all the other crannies into which a driving wind and several tumbles had carried it. There was little to be heard except the occasional soft sound of snow, as it slid from overweighted branches onto snow beneath. The little shop looked threadbare and poverty-stricken, with a blackboard outside announcing in a chalk scrawl the ration for the day.

'Vandaag — pudding' — so many grammes.

It was nearly half past four.

John came back.

'No help for it,' he said, 'we must go on a little and ask for the house.'

He had had from Vandyck some specific directions in case of a breakdown like this, not be used except in an emergency, and then only by very cautious inquiry. I was glad of this evidence of Vandyck's trust in John.

We pushed our bicycles back under the bridge and out beyond it. The Germans were still there, waiting. More had got out of the lorry now and were standing or sitting about.

John went on ahead a little. There was a road fork. A tall thin brown man in knickerbockers, with a rucksack on his back, was walking towards us. John addressed him and asked for the road to a certain village. That was it, the man said, the road to the right. We took it and cycled off. We were not going to that village, but this was the right road. Now we wanted a gate with stone lions on it.

As we pedalled away from the bridge our spirits rose. It had been depressing there, with no news of Dr. Hendrijksen and all those Germans. It was better now.

Soon the road began to rise. Before long we had to get off and walk, pushing our bicycles through soft snow up a steep hill. It was hard work. They slid about and mocked us. There had long since ceased to be, as far as I could see, any way I could find of doing what we had to which was easy and without pain. It all seemed to be endless. The best way to keep going was to choose a tree a little way ahead and think as far as that and no further. When you got to that tree you started again with another.

Soon we found some stone lions and started trudging up a long country house drive, where deep and untouched snow lay between fir plantations. I have no clear recollection of that last stretch. To keep my bicycle from falling over while I pushed it through the snow, and to go on picking one foot out and putting it ahead of the other, needed all the concentrated attention and effort I could muster. It was desperately hard work and I was very tired.

Now we were approaching a clearing and a block of low buildings looking like cottages and stables, with hedges and paths. We seemed to be in the grounds of a fair-sized country house. John went on ahead again but there was no longer need for caution. A door opened and there was a familiar good-natured face with a smiling greeting: it was Vandyck, and behind him stood a little round Dutchman.

In a state of boundless relief, on my part at least, we went in and found ourselves in a large kitchen, warm and friendly. There were one or two people I did not know—Dutchmen. Coming forward to meet me, however, to my pleased surprise—for I had not realized he would be there—was none other than Lipmann Kessel! This almost banished tiredness. To meet old friends again—above all Kessel, whose outstanding skill had saved my life, and then to find with him Theo Redman, another airborne doctor, who had been in my brigade for two years and whom in Egypt, Palestine, Tunisia, Italy and England I had got to know well and greatly to like—this, I now realized, was something I had sorely missed these last four months. I sat down in their company and looked about me with great contentment.

The kitchen was very large. At a big table two or three young Dutchmen were busy with a typewriter and papers. I was introduced to these but could not really sort anyone out yet. From where I was sitting in a bow window I could see a great kitchen stove set back on the right with dressers and cupboards opposite, and on the left a big sink. Doors led out in the far left and right corners. We had just come in through the one on the right.

This was the sort of kitchen you might expect to find in a large cottage occupied by the upper outdoor servants of an opulent country house. That was just what it was. We were in the garage or coach-house compound of a large house, standing a few hundred yards away, which had been taken over as an institution for the infirm. The little round Dutchman, who sat so quietly and kindly, smoking (when there was tobacco) and saying little, had been the head chauffeur. His wife, clearly once beautiful and still most pleasant to look at, cooked and managed for a household (of which I was now one) of rarely less than six and sometimes nearer twenty. One son was here at home with them and another, a policeman, had come back on leave from his duty station and had been prevented from returning by the airborne landings. He had stayed here. He it was who was to be asked where Dr. Hendrijksen lived. He was even now still waiting by a railway bridge for two strangers. There were, it appeared, two such bridges a mile or so apart; we had waited at one, he was still waiting in the snow at the other. His brother set off to find him and bring him back. There was a shorter way than the one we had used and they were both back within the hour.

Theo, Lipmann Kessel and I sat round and talked with deep interest and pleasure. It was fascinating for each of us to find out what had been happening to the others. Theo I had not seen since before we took off in England for the battle. He had been wounded early and had later escaped.

Then Graeme Warrack arrived, the big man, and with him Derek Ridler from the 1st Brigade. Our pleasure deepened. We all had a tot of Uncle Zwerus's cognac and toasted each other and laughed a great deal. Then we had supper round the big kitchen table, and John played a game of chess with Lippy, and Theo and I played a gentler game afterwards, and then I went to bed in some blankets on a stretcher in one of the garages, quite content but almost too weary to sleep.

20

I HAD spent the night in a small boiler room which was also a store, shared with Lipmann Kessel, in a bed rather less comfortable, I must confess, than those I had known in Torenstraat. In the morning John and Vandyck both left early upon their separate missions and I settled down to await their return.

I had held a little conference the night before and summed up the position as it now stood. Vandyck still had nothing definite to offer about his eastern route. John was going down to South Holland, as we had agreed, and would try to bring back the answers to Vandyck's exacting questions. Vandyck was returning to his own location near Barneveld and in three days' time would be back here with whatever proposals he might then be able to make for his eastern plan. John would be back by then too, with his own information from the south. We sorted out between us exactly what Vandyck wanted to know to convince him that John's plan was feasible. I reserved the right to decide between the relative merits of the two schemes when they were finally presented. Vandyck and I briefed John together and I wondered, with misgiving, how far he would be successful. He was being asked a great deal. I hoped he would bring back enough to allow me to decide in favour of his plan, for my confidence in it, and in him, was undiminished.

It was now 30th January. John's friends south of the Lower Rhine expected us both to cross it together on 1st or 3rd February and a place was being kept for me in a canoe for the journey down the Waal on the 5th. If it had not been for the need to consider Vandyck's position and not add to his difficulties I should have gone straight on with John, after a day's rest, and tried to cross the Rhine on the 1st. This Vandyck knew. I now hoped at least to get over on the alternative date of the 3rd. It all depended now upon whether John could bring back enough of the information required by Vandyck to justify a decision by me to go on with the southern plan, even if Vandyck himself should continue to object.

As Vandyck got to know John better he was treating him with growing respect. He had already had sufficient confidence in him to entrust him with the exact location of the house we were living in, which was saying a great deal. What still worried Vandyck, however, was that this plan of John's depended on an escape route of which he was sure, if it were genuine, his control outside Holland would have told him.

Before John left I asked him for something more. Through the favour of his friends he had got me in as a single passenger on a route which its organizers had clearly tried to keep free from escaper traffic. But here were four friends of mine, living in or near this house, each of whom had made at least one attempt to get across the Rhine already. They could not be casually left behind, Graeme Warrack especially, with his invaluable experience of recent operations. All the others too were airborne doctors. They would be urgently wanted in England. To Lipmann Kessel I had in addition a deep and pressing personal obligation. I could not go and leave him.

I asked John, therefore, if he would try to persuade the people in the south to fit in at least two more on this trip and consider taking a few others afterwards. He said that he would do his best.

When John and Vandyck had left, cycling in the early morning out into the snow, I began to learn something of where I was. I also heard more of the recent history of the others.

This place — a large cottage with spacious garages, standing around a U-shaped courtyard — was the base for Resistance activities in the district. Set well back in the pine woods, secluded and innocent looking, it was little disturbed. Nonetheless, new arrivals like ourselves were shown a few safety precautions, how to slip out into the woods if unwelcome visitors came, for example, and where there was a snug little dug-out hidden in the trees.

This was a busy place. There was always movement, always something happening. It was apparently a kind of message centre. The daily news sheets were typed out here for distribution. I soon met the local N.B.S. chief and several of his assistants. There were people in and out all the time.

I kept a little apart from all this, for I had no place in what was going on. It was not as it had been in the household in Ede. I was a passenger here and kept out of the way of the crew.

The next few days passed quickly enough, though I was impatient for John's return. The company of Lipmann Kessel, Theo Redman and Derek Ridler was delightful. Theo was one of my own people, a very early member of the 4th Parachute Brigade and a charming, modest, friendly person whom I already knew pretty well and liked a great deal. Derek Ridler, who was a dentist, I got to know better. This was another good person.

With Lipmann Kessel, almost a stranger before, I had really only become acquainted in the hospital. We now played chess together, at which I usually lost, and we talked a great deal. He was a South African Jew, inclined to Marxism, an intelligent and sensitive person, who had settled into surgical practice in England in the thirties. Lipmann and I tramped around under the pine trees in the thick snow, which was now beginning to thaw, carefully obeying orders about where we could go. At other times we sat inside in a warm place opening off the kitchen and talked a great deal. This was a man well worth getting to know better. I wondered where his future would lie.

He lost little time in taking a look at my stomach in which he had, he said, a considerable technical interest. He was disappointed that the beautiful hairline of the scar was marred somewhat by festering. I now learnt that, in the effort to save weight wherever possible, airborne surgical teams carried, instead of bulky packages of absorbable surgical stitching, a roll of silk thread which would go much further. This was what had been used on me. Lippy said there had been a little trouble around the stitches and he would like to tidy me up, but he had no instruments or drugs.

The Underground people borrowed a set of instruments and other things that Lippy wanted and three airborne doctors set up a little operating theatre among the taps and tanks and pipes in the outhouse where my bed was. Lippy did what had to be done, which was no more painful than was to be expected, and bandaged me up again. Everything was going on perfectly well, he said.

In the afternoon of the third day Vandyck came back and in the evening John too. John was clearly very pleased. His friends in South Holland had led him, after much cautious discussion, to the wireless link and he had met a British operator whose code name was Foxtrot. This man had done his parachute training at Ringway and what John passed on of the conversation between them, with its reference to so much and to so many people personally well known to me, was entirely convincing.

Vandyck, on the other hand, had been disappointed. The best he could now offer was the possibility of a journey southwards up the east bank of the Rhine into Switzerland, either to stay there or, with luck, to get into France and join up somehow with the Americans. I weighed up both possibilities, with particular consideration to the responsibilities of Vandyck. To no one's surprise I elected to go with John. It was an added advantage in John's plan that his friends had told him that two others could be got out with me at the same time. I nominated Lipmann Kessel as the first of these and made arrangements to have Graeme Warrack brought in to join the party too. It was agreed that we should all start off from various points and travel in different ways. Vandyck would leave first, conducting the doctors. John and I would leave a little later, guided by a girl courier, who would join us in the morning.

21

I WAS awakened in my warm bed amongst the tanks and taps before it was light and got dressed in the parti-coloured woollen underpants, John's dark trousers and his shirt and tie, and the little black jacket found for me long ago by Blue Johnny, with Aunt Ann's deaf button on it.

In the light of a small oil lamp I saw once more around me the garden tools, the parts of machines, the old tyres, ropes, window-frames, glass jars and paint pots, the broken furniture, the shelves full of nondescript articles in wood and metal and the rest of the debris which crowded round the sleepers in this little dormitory. I took in the sum of things around me in a quick and forward looking farewell. Another chapter was beginning.

It was cold. I threaded my way through the coach house, with its shrouded vehicles and dim shapes of furniture stacked under dustsheets, to the glowing kitchen, where there was porridge and bread with a little piece of bacon for breakfast. A girl was there, a stranger, about nineteen years old with red hair (she had dyed it, I learnt, when the Germans got after her) and a pretty lively face. There was a slight appearance of constraint about her, almost of shyness. She was Elsa, I was told, the courier who was to guide John and me to and across the Rhine.

She was whispering with a member of the household. In a moment or two she came up to me and held out her hand.

'Are you the General?' she said. She gave a charming little bob, half a curtsey. 'I am going to take what you have to carry and show you the way.'

'It's extremely kind of you to take us,' I said, 'but I'm not really a General.'

'That's what they tell me you are,' said Elsa, smiling. She had a sweet and merry smile. 'What am I to carry?'

The old suitcase was produced, with the army pack holding my dirty and still bloodstained battle dress jacket, my identity card and the other few odd papers, and the haversack with all the other little possessions which might show, if they were found upon me, that I was a British soldier.

'That isn't very much,' said Elsa. She seemed, I thought, a little disappointed. 'I've been carrying explosives lately.'

'There's a letter for the Queen in that bundle,' said I. 'We can't lose that.'

Lipmann Kessel had gone off the night before to join up somewhere with Graeme Warrack and Theo and leave in the early morning guided by Vandyck. They were travelling cautiously and furtively, with weapons.

The warmer wind of the last few days had taken much of the snow away. There was even a hint of spring. We said goodbye to the calm and handsome woman and the silent little man, climbed on to our bicycles in the paved stableyard, surrounded by its low formal buildings with the dead clock, and cycled off down the drive through the fir trees. The deep drifts that had wearied us a few days before had now almost gone. The wind was soft with no bite in it and the grey clouds rode high in the early February morning.

Elsa rode ahead, John and I a few hundred yards behind. He and I made a cheerful and contented pair. We were out again and getting on with what had to be done to crown the endeavours of the devoted family in Ede. Again, as always, I was able to see myself a partner in the enterprise, as well as being the fugitive who was being helped.

What had been done, I reflected again as I rode along, had not been done for me at all. My dear friends in Ede had fought their part of the battle because they saw it as a charge laid upon them, and had won. Others now were also doing something to help because they too saw it as their duty. The person who by sheer accident was a focal point in all this high and single-minded endeavour, could admire, and be grateful, for what was being done. He could be thankful it was taking him towards what he wanted most. He could also be glad that he was allowed by providence to take a share in doing it.

John's bicycle, which I was riding, was in fine form but Uncle Wim's with its worn old tyres, ridden by John, soon got him into trouble. We had barely come to the main road, on the outskirts of a township, and were pedalling along the smooth surface with the wind singing in our ears when a sharp flapping sound followed by an ugly rhythmical thump announced disaster. John dismounted and looked sadly at a great rent in the outer cover with the pink flesh of the torn inner tube showing through.

Elsa had waited for us and came back. The tyre was past hope and the bicycle was useless. It looked to John and me as if we

174

must turn and plod back to the stable yard at the house in Maarn, there to plan again. What else could we do in this strange place? Bicycles were hard to come by anywhere and bicycle tyres were particularly rare and valuable. I could not believe that we had any hope of finding a replacement here.

This place was strange to us but not to Elsa. She thought she knew someone who would lend us a bicycle. She led us through the streets to a small neat house with a yard and a corrugated-iron shed in it, where a man in blue overalls with kind shrewd eyes was working at a carpenter's bench.

Else spoke to him quietly as he stood there with a plane in his hand. He responded briefly, giving a quick and not unfriendly look to where John and I were standing, inside the shed by the door. Then he went away and very soon came back wheeling a serviceable looking bicycle, which was handed over to John. It was left to Elsa to thank him and then we were off again, Elsa riding ahead. I remember a young German officer walking with a big Alsatian dog on a leather lead. He waved at the pretty girl on the bicycle and Elsa waved back. I remember our riding cheerfully down the main road in a flock of cyclists, past the noble church tower of Utrecht, and John coming alongside to whisper to me 'The city of Doctor Strabismus!' I remember taking a little rest by hanging on to a horse-drawn cart as it rumbled along, with a miserable looking elderly German soldier sitting on the edge of it, and shouting a cheerful farewell to him as it turned off our road, with no reply from the German except for a look of deep dislike. I remember eating our lunch — three slices of bread and four hard boiled eggs between the three of us — sitting under a railway culvert, with John and Elsa chatting happily together and laughing a good deal. I remember that we stopped to rest at a wayside tavern where nothing was being sold either to eat or drink. John and I went inside and saw a man there of the N.S.B., the Dutch Nazi organization, sitting at a table in the green uniform which was so widely feared and hated. Playing the game as we understood it we went and sat down at his table, John explaining our circumstances in answer to the N.S.B. man's casual questions.

What I remember chiefly of that day, however, was the journey that followed. It seemed to last almost for ever, along the road on top of the Rhine dyke towards Schoonhoven. We were cycling into the teeth of a strong head wind. I was now very tired. My whole being was concentrated into the grim effort to force one foot down upon its pedal after the other. Only the next thrust mattered; the future extended no further than

175

that. How long this went on I do not know but in the late afternoon we found ourselves in Schoonhoven, the town upon the Rhine bank where John told me Uncle Ko had earlier been hiding. We passed through that and cycled further on until we came to a house beside the river, outside a village. I was grateful to be allowed to stop and dismount.

There was a boat there, drawn up on the shore. Night was not far off. High spring cloud hung in a windswept sky. I waited by my bicycle, spent, while John found the boatman.

To take a boat out on the river without permission was, as we all well know, strictly forbidden under threat of the severest penalties. I wondered dully how John would manage. He came back soon to where Elsa and I stood by the boat with our bicycles. A man was with him, holding in his hand a pair of rowlocks. I hardly dared believe what I saw. The man began to make the boat ready.

Two pounds of darning wool, I later learnt, had been his price. With children to keep warm in a hard winter, the sixth winter of the war, and woollen clothes falling apart with no hope of replacement, the skein or two of darning wool that John had brought with him from what was left out of the shop in Renkum had been enough.

Only a few minutes before we had been quite alone on a considerable stretch of road. No sooner had the boatman put the rowlocks in, however, than another man appeared beside us. Then another materialized, with a woman and their two bicycles, and another woman, alone, wheeling hers. With urgency, with humility they begged to be taken across with us. The boatman looked at John.

'Why not?' said John.

The boat was dragged the few yards to the water's edge and we all climbed in, the bicycles in the bows. The boatman rowed from a thwart slightly forward of the centre. I sat facing him with Elsa beside me.

In a matchless, breath-taking moment the heavy boat slid gently off the mud and the boatman settled down to row her strongly upstream, obliquely towards the other bank.

The wind had blown pale, clear patches in the cloudy sky. Facing me where I sat in the boat the roofs of Schoonhoven, a mile or so upriver, shone in a sudden golden beam of evening sunlight, the sky behind them a cold blue. Spires, towers and steeply sloping tiles glowed in a rich haze like a setting for a fairy story. Everything looked serene, lovely and at rest. Nothing was hostile any longer.

The boatman glanced over his shoulder now and then but looked mostly straight ahead of him, at me. He was a friendly person.

'Better weather,' he said. 'Should be fine now.'

Elsa came in quickly to the rescue.

'Thank God the winter's nearly over now,' she said.

The boatman looked at her and back at me.

'What's that button you're wearing on your coat?' he asked.

Elsa spoke up again.

'He's deaf,' she said. 'That's what it says on the button. He can't hear what you say.'

He looked at me carefully for a long moment, then over his shoulder upstream again. He did not speak to me after that.

It took us about twenty minutes, I suppose, to cross the river. As we approached the far bank I saw with misgiving the heaps of broken ice piled up along the shore. Somehow the boatman got us through them. I remember two other passengers helping me out of the boat and handing up the bicycles as we clattered over the ice. Then we were coming up to the road that ran along the bank, climbing through a fence and getting on to our machines again.

After the brief rest I was awake and once more in the world. Spirits began to rise. The wind had dropped and the going was easy. We had not far to travel.

In half an hour or so we came to a scattered village. 'Groot Ammers,' said John. He knew his way here and guided us through the houses to a farm where we were clearly expected and the door was opened for us into a lamplit kitchen.

I had now almost fully recovered from the struggle of the afternoon, against the wind along the Rhine dyke, but was glad to sit and rest. This was the house of a farmer whose son, Klaas, was also there. The young man with whom our business mostly lay, Kars, chief Underground worker in the district, should also have been there and came soon after. He was a big fellow, robust and hearty. His greeting to me was most friendly, to John almost affectionate. It was clear that they were old friends and that their confidence in each other was high.

Kars was a student of mathematics and had already done a year at his university before he took up the livelier activities that now engaged him. He was a determined and energetic worker and an obvious leader. Everything he did was done with a rough gusto: he had a hearty laugh and the price the Germans put upon his head was to him a special source of pride and pleasure. He was also a cool planner, forceful and constructive, but prudent.

He was late because he had run into a little trouble. There were road blocks where they had not been expected and he had come across one of these quite suddenly. It had taken him time to get around it and across country back to the farm house.

There was a good deal of quiet talk in the kitchen. I sat apart from this in a deep chair by the stove. They had their own affairs to discuss and would come to mine in good time.

But apparently it was mine they were already discussing and John brought me into the circle. A party was expected from Sliedrecht that very evening to bring us their plan for the next move. It was not yet known to Kars and his friends when a boat would be going down the Waal but the weather forecast was far from good. We might have to wait a day or two.

Then we had supper, brought to the kitchen table by the silent farmer, brown bread and home-cured bacon, fresh butter and sweet warm milk, with slabs of soft yellow cheese, creamy and delicious.

Klaas, the farmer's son, told me of his own plans and how they had been upset. He already spoke English quite well: he was getting good practice in it these days, he said. Several British officers had recently been there. Klaas explained why it was important for him to know English. He intended to become a civil servant and the examinations required it, but he could not get on with these while the war lay like a great blanket over everything. There was nothing for him to do but wait, and help here and there with the activities of the Underground. Meanwhile, he had opportunities to improve his English. They must have my address in England, he said, and they would send me a cheese when the war was over. They made wonderful cheese in Groot Ammers, the best in Holland. They did a thriving trade in it in the good times.

He sat there spry and talkative, a slight young figure in a tweed suit and bow tie, grumbling a little. The old farmer, his father, was silently clearing the supper things away, looking at his son now and then with pride and pleasure. When the father had finished clearing away he came back with a huge hooked pipe, the bowl covered with a metal cap, and sat and puffed at it in his own arm-chair, looking at me now and then with good humour and friendliness, from eyes in which there was kindness and peace. He had taken off his wooden shoes now and his feet, in thick socks below blue canvas trousers, were thrust into big leather slippers.

I talked to him a little, as far as I could. It was not easy, for my command of Dutch was still limited. He used forms I did not recognize and pronounced words in a way unfamiliar to me. Young Klaas sometimes put in a quick word, 'My father means,' he would say. But I wanted to puzzle it out for myself. I would even rather not understand than have my contact with this direct and friendly man broken by an intermediary.

John and Kars meanwhile were chattering like schoolboys, indeed it was their schooldays that they were talking about. John's face was wrinkling up around his nose as he laughed. His eyes were shining with enjoyment and a mouth full of white teeth was opening wide to let out the high and merry laugh which was almost at times like a horse's whinny. Kars had lost the look of gravity and purpose which sat so well upon him as I saw him first, and was a boy again. His strong frame shook with mirth and gusts of laughter, like the baying of a huge and friendly dog, came welling up from deep within him.

'Mr. Hackett,' said John, 'Kars says they are all disappointed you would not be received with a guard of honour. They would not be very splendid, I can tell you, though Kars doesn't say so, but they all have Sten guns or other sorts of weapon and they think it was a pity not to show them to you.'

Klaas was listening to something else with an attentively cocked ear. He said a quick word to Kars, who stopped beaming upon us all and turned his head to listen too. Then he got up quickly and went out. The old farmer took out his pipe and waited and John and I sat silent.

In a moment there was a sound of cheerful voices outside and a young man and woman came in. The man looked like a student, dressed in loose grey clothes and a white sweater. The girl, good-looking, with a keen intelligent face, wore the uniform of a nurse. Both had curiosity written all over them: they looked quickly round the kitchen until their eyes came to rest upon me. The young man was talking to Kars, though his eyes never left me, and the young woman came forward.

'Good evening,' she said as she shook my hand. 'So here you are at last!'

She too was young but seemed more mature than her years. She was a trained nurse I learned later, and continued to work as one, chiefly because it gave her opportunities to move around. I found myself once more being taken in charge, being talked over and planned for. The talk was rapid, often in English but more often in Dutch. There was much I did not understand and did not ask to have explained.

The weather had not in fact been good. There was no boat that night, nor would there be one the next night, on Sunday. This did not surprise me. I had in fact expected quite a long wait at Groot Ammers. We were across the Rhine and that was already a great advance, probably enough to expect for the time being. It was therefore with something of a shock that I realized what they were telling me. There would probably be a boat on Monday, the day after tomorrow. By Tuesday, they said, I should be in British hands.

Foxtrot was in wireless contact with the other side. He would let them know I was coming.

'Now how about getting down to Sliedrecht?' John asked: 'how do we go, and when?'

There was no need for John himself to go any further, they said. They would look after everything from now on. John was free now to make his way back to Ede. The slightest trace of constraint crept over the conversation.

It was now my turn. I could not, I said, part from John until the last possible minute. It seemed to me privately far too untidy but I knew I had no hope of explaining that. What I did explain was that I should be wearing clothes of his and his family's which he would have to take back home again, and I was on his uncle's bicycle which would never get back to its owner unless John took it from me at the end of my land journey and led it home. Questions of bicycles and clothes usually commanded respectful attention in Holland at that time. My bicycle, however, was no longer important they said. They could not have me riding about on a bicycle. They had a car.

This was incredible, almost stupefying. How could they have got a car on the road, and how dare they drive it? It seemed that they could scarcely believe it themselves. They were all very young, which was apparent in the slightly incredulous look with which they turned to each other for confirmation of the stupendous fact that they had got hold of a car, and in the shy smiles with which they announced their firm intention to drive me down in it to Sliedrecht.

By what ingenuity this vehicle had been hidden from German soldiery starved of transport I never learnt, nor by what cunning it had been made to go and provided with fuel. I had another problem on my mind. It would be highly unwise for so many of us to go driving about the countryside together in an illicit motor car. The risk was quite unjustified and I was determined not to allow it. Moreover, John was coming with me as far as he could and we both hoped that this would mean to the very end of the journey by land. Neither of us was prepared to see the partnership broken up and new people in charge until this brought a clear advantage. John and I would have to part here if they took me on by car. Far from securing an advantage, however, it would simply be courting disaster to make use of the car.

Our new friends were not easy to persuade. They were very proud of their car. They were young and brave, with a high regard for panache. I was torn by anxiety not to hurt their feelings but I had to be firm.

In the end they agreed to abandon the project, but only with reluctance. There was a feeling, I suspected, that they were dealing with a spoilsport.

They promised, however, to provide guides. Three of them would come up next day to take us down. We demurred again. Three would be too many. It was clear that these young men and women attached high importance to the successful handling of this affair. There also seemed to be some competition to get in on it. But we did not want a crowd. In the end they agreed to send only one. It was very disappointing. We all parted good friends, but I could not help thinking that they felt a little let down.

I slept for the next two nights in a little bare room with rat holes round the edges of the floor boards. It was cold and far from cheerful. On my first night I was very tired and soon slept. I was wakeful during the second and listened to the secret scratchings of rats behind the wainscot and the occasional noise, surprisingly hard and loud, made by one of them scampering across the floor of the room itself.

Tomorrow the last stage of my journey would begin.

There was no light as I lay and brooded in the lumpy little bed: not positive aggressive darkness, but just no light. In that grey and cloudy night there must have been some light coming through the uncurtained window. To me, where I lay, there seemed no light anywhere.

It was a long night. Towards morning I slept a little, to wake again in a reluctant winter daybreak. It was too early to get up, too late to sleep any more. I lay there in a state between sleeping and waking, in what was neither day nor night. My own life seemed to be in a state of suspension too, hanging immobile between one state and another.

There was no noise. Even the rats were silent. The sparse furnishings of the little room could now be seen in outline, the table, the one chair, the chest, though the light was not yet sufficient to distinguish their details.

Everything about me was motionless and quiet. There was no colour except in tones of grey. In the distance, far behind me, stood the high citadel of Torenstraat, its outline already indistinct. John was still somewhere about, a last living link with a world of clarity and vivid life, but he was soon to leave me, dispirited and lonely, in a world of cold shadow.

I was in limbo again.

22

I⊤ was on a Monday morning, 5th February, that John and I,
after a good breakfast in the farmhouse at Groot Ammers, said
goodbye to Klaas and his parents, the friendly farmer and his
kind and quiet wife, and set off on our bicycles behind the guide
sent by Kars to show us the way down to Sliedrecht. Graeme
Warrack had also arrived at Groot Ammers and had now, we
heard, gone on ahead. He and I had briefly met the afternoon
before: I had been taken to see him in the house of the village
Dominee, where he was being lodged.

Elsa had already gone too. I had said goodbye to her, with a
kiss, on the night of our arrival and she had set out early the
next morning on her journey back. Now that we were on the
road again John and I felt her absence keenly. Friendships grow
quickly under pressure. Our journey to Groot Ammers from
Huis Maarn had been one that none of us would easily forget
and we both knew that we were going to miss this lively
charming girl.

The bicycle ride to Sliedrecht was short, no more than an
hour or two. I remember little now of what seemed to me, even
then, still only a restless dream. Only one incident in it comes
back to me at all clearly. I had been up to now most meticulous
in avoiding the use of English outside the house except when
there was no possibility of being overheard. For almost all the
time, indeed, I hid behind my deaf button and said nothing.
This way of life was now near its end, however, and I thought I
could safely indulge in one small and cheerful indiscretion.

We were riding in a loose group of cyclists, beside one of
whom, a German soldier, a very big dog was bounding along,
barking wildly.

'Is that your dog?' I shouted, pointing at it and then back at
him. My meaning would, I knew, be clear even if the words
were not.

'Ja! Ja!' he shouted in reply, nodding his head vigorously.

'Then keep the bloody thing quiet!' I bellowed, and rode on,
confident that the German soldier would make little of what
had been said but for some reason I felt cheered up a little by
having said it. John Snoek, riding alongside me, heard it all and

burst out laughing. He did not look at all disapproving and I had the feeling, not for the first time, that he sometimes understood me better than I understood myself.

We arrived in the afternoon at a house by the water and were met by friendly people. But everything for me was overshadowed by the fact that I had now to say goodbye to John.

It all happened, when the time came to part, in a matter-of-fact sort of way. I handed over what I was sending back with him. He shook my hand warmly with a wide grin.

'Goodbye, Mr. Hackett,' he said, 'and good luck!'

Then he wheeled Uncle Wim's bicycle out of the garden gate with his own and was gone. It was hard to believe.

An agreeable young woman who also seemed to be a nurse and lived there, or next door, gave me a bowl of pea soup with pieces of bacon in it which I remember was very good. Of the time I spent in the living-room of that comfortable suburban house overlooking the water in Sliedrecht, a doctor's house I think it was, I can recall little else. I was still in limbo. Something was over and something else was about to begin. I was a sleeper about to awake, not suddenly but slowly. It had not really begun to happen yet.

After a while they told me it was time to go. Someone had come to guide me on.

There was still some after-light in the sky as I walked out, some thirty paces behind my guide, through the winding streets of Sliedrecht towards the outskirts of the town. High cloud in the north-west held a suggestion of wind but with the approach of night the sky was growing clearer.

We were moving down a broad street with tram-lines, going away from water towards the north-east. There were few people about and no one was loitering. Those we passed were walking purposefully, with that air of minding their own business which, I suppose, is general in an occupied country after several years of war. It is more noticeable in the evenings. Most were by themselves, elderly men and tired-looking middle-aged women. Of couples there were few, of young women still fewer and of young men none at all.

I was a little more nearly awake now, walking along with a feeling of confidence and hope, even of pleasure. I could look at the occasional passer-by with sympathetic detachment, hugging my own secret to myself. The world was dying, almost dead, like the day whose tired grey fingers seemed no longer able to hold up the sky. But tomorrow was a new day. The world would be reborn, fresh and sparkling, a better and a brighter world.

I was a phoenix on its funeral pyre, soon to arise new fledged out of the dying embers. Already the transformation had begun. Under the sad black overcoat I no longer wore John's old suit. I had put on the battered remains of my own uniform, the torn battle dress blouse with its faded parachute wings and medal ribbons and its dull stains. In one breast pocket was my British army identity card — the little oblong piece of stout pinkish paper with my own name on it and the photograph of an officer in His Majesty's uniform. Beside it was that other identity document with its photograph of a sick-looking, older man in a black civilian jacket, bearing some resemblance to the first but called, it appeared, van Dalen. I was still both of these but felt myself growing hourly more and more the first, less and less the second.

In the other breast pocket was my silver pencil and the silver cigarette case, each with my own name on it, constant companions without which I had never made a parachute descent. These things, hidden away or carried by others from the time the family in Torenstraat had first taken me in, were now once more in my own possession and I was not far from being myself again. Only the walking stick in my hand with the 'U' carved on it and my marching boots, now soled with Uncle Zwerus's good leather, had been with me all the time, had come all the way in my keeping from the old life that had ended in the sad groves of Oosterbeek through another whole lifetime into the present, to go on with me into tomorrow.

Already, with the parting from John, Torenstraat had receded far into the distance. The outlines of the edifice those devoted hands had built stood out only the more clearly, bathed in a pure and steady light. There was no shadow of doubt in my mind that what they had begun would end as they intended. From this sprang the confidence, and even the private bubble of merriment, which attended my walk in the winter twilight through the silent streets of Sliedrecht.

The night was likely to be cold. There would be good reason to be grateful for Aunt Mien's thick blue and white underwear and the long white woollen jersey (I had been allowed to keep these for the journey) and perhaps for the rest of Uncle Zwerus's cognac as well.

My guide turned away from the tramlines in an easterly direction and waited for me to come up. Thereafter we walked together, not speaking. Another twenty minutes walking, through deserted streets of small houses and shops, brought us to more open spaces and the sight of water gleaming through gaps in the buildings. He stopped at the gate of a factory on the water's edge.

'Wait,' he said, 'I must get the keys to the boathouse. The night watchman has them.'

He made off into the darkness and I stood and waited, watching a red beacon light somewhere out in the river shining on the water. Soon he was back with another man who took no notice of me at all. The newcomer grunted a word or two to my companion and then led silently through the iron gates and round the factory buildings to where there was a clutter of jetties and sheds by the waterside, and the great grey expanse of the river stretched before us into the dusk with the single red beacon light far away in the middle of it.

I stood on a quay while a boathouse was unlocked. With a clatter of rowlocks that shattered the brooding silence a boat was brought alongside.

The night watchman settled me into the stern and handed in the haversack and rucksack. Then at a word from my companion at the oars he pushed out the boat's head and walked quickly away in silence, back in the direction of the factory.

Visibility was fifty yards or so and the night cold and clear with no more than a trace of mist. The water was smooth but there was clearly something of a current. In a silence broken only by the noise of rowlocks and the occasional splash of an oar, with the musical rustle of water along the side, he drove the boat on with short practised strokes. For nearly an hour he rowed, while the red beacon shone unwinking on the water from the same direction on the port bow and seemed always to move away from us. Then it swung to the beam and stayed there, aloof and baleful, while I drew my thin coat around me and shivered in the cold. We might have been alone on a boundless ocean except that now and then, as if to emphasize the trance-like quality of our progress, a stream of tracer bullets would shoot up like rhythmic sparks into the air, far out of earshot, or a distant parachute flare would appear from nowhere to hang brooding for a while and then vanish.

Suddenly I was aware of darker shapes. We came alongside a rough stone jetty. People appeared out of the dark and lifted me from the boat. My companion stood beside me for a moment.

'I have to go straight back,' he said, and shook me warmly by the hand. 'They will look after you now.'

He got back into the boat and rowed off at once into the gathering mist in the direction of the beacon.

A hand took my arm and helped me up over the slippery rocks of the jetty to a muddy shore. There seemed to be three or four people there. In silence we climbed a short rise to where the dim shape of a cottage grew out of the dark. Another hand restrained me while a man went forward. The calm and mystery of the journey on the water had now given place to drama. I imagined myself a child again, playing smugglers. I was sure that I knew, with an echo of certainty from a time when the nursery fire gleamed on the brass fender and we children were being read to after tea, just what the man was going to do and what would happen next. It happened as I had expected. He knocked three times deliberately on a door, paused and knocked quickly once or twice more. A crack of light appeared, a low word was spoken, and the door opened to let us in. Before me in a long room was a scene I looked at with relish. Men in blue jerseys and sea boots sat cleaning and oiling weapons, mostly revolvers, with a Sten gun or two. Brass cartridge cases glittered on the table in the lamplight. Other men were putting letters into a small canvas bag, while another bag was being sealed up with red sealing wax. A burly cheerful man seemed to be in charge. He shook my hand heartily and handed me over to his wife. The others were too busy to do more than look up and give a greeting before they turned once more to their work.

The woman put me in a deep chair and spoke kindly in Dutch. There were two very handsome young women in white jerseys who were presented as daughters, one of whom was sent away to return presently with a tray carrying steaming cups of cocoa. The men gave me whisky from an authentic-looking bottle of John Haig and cigarettes from a round tin of Players standing in a row with other tins. These were things I had not seen for a long time. I sat tired and passive, floating on the tide of activity around me.

'Are you really a General?' whispered one of the daughters, looking curiously at the red tabs on my battle dress and the pinched face above it.

'Sort of,' said I. She smiled at me happily.

'We haven't had one here before,' she said. She seemed to be enjoying her war, or at least this part of it.

I sat back in my comfortable chair, content to be carried along on the stream. It was like being a child again, led by the hand in a crowd. I had neither power to influence events nor curiosity to inquire into their nature. I waited only for what would happen next.

The girls hovered around me, under the kind eye of their mother, and brought little cakes and biscuits and chocolate.

'Eat what you can,' shouted the burly man. 'We have plenty. Our men go back and forth nearly every day.'

I ate a little and waited.

The big man looked at the clock. His hearty manner had an agreeable trace of the conspiratorial.

'We are nearly ready,' he said, 'soon we go out to the boat. You must be careful and make no noise. Sometimes there are German patrols not far away. We shall show you.'

I was offered a revolver but said I thought I was better without it.

'Never mind,' said the big man. I thought there was a shade of disappointment in his voice. 'We shall put one in the boat for you. Just in case.'

It was time to go. I exchanged farewells and warm handshakes with the ladies. They brushed aside my thanks and said the pleasure had been theirs. In a party of four all laden and led by the big man we went through a passage out of a back door and into the black night. I had my pack and haversack in my hand, as I came out in the party's rear, but at the last moment there was some flustered whispering behind me and the dim form of one of the girls appeared.   '

'Please give them to me,' said the voice of the younger and she took my bundles from me, leaving me only the stick.

In single file we made our silent progress, the figure of the man in front just visible to me where he walked four or five paces ahead. The way wound now and then by water splashing gently against stones or lying still in narrow channels. It took us across fields, through marshy places full of reeds and loud with bullfrogs, over fences and again into a maze of water channels. There was no moon and the sky was overcast. There was rather more wind now.

At length we came, slowly and with caution, to a tree. In front of it I could see the curve of another channel. The leader silently halted the party and went gently forward alone. The girl gave me back my bundle with a quick farewell and was gone.

Mystery and drama lay thick upon us. From a little distance there was what sounded like the cry of a marsh bird and then silence. In a minute or so the cry came again and again silence followed. I could almost hear my heart beating in the suspense. There was a third call, on a more urgent note, and silence again.

Then all at once the bright glass globe of mystery was shattered and lay in fragments all around us.

'Curse the fellow,' said the loud gruff voice of an impatient Dutchman, out of the darkness where the marsh bird had so lately cried. Our leader reappeared before us. 'He's late again,' said he in normal tones and sat down by the tree. 'Who's got a cigarette?'

'Is it safe to smoke?' I could not help asking.

'Of course,' said he with a slight trace of annoyance. 'There are no Germans for miles.'

So we all sat down and lit cigarettes, talking and presently laughing.

'They will use a canoe,' the leader told me, 'one with an electric engine and a battery. The Canadians brought them. They are wonderfully silent. But the battery does not last all the way and there is always some paddling to be done. Piet will do that. He's the best of them. He knows this route backwards now.'

Then he explained to me what I had been trying to piece together. This was the courier service through which the Dutch Government in London and its forward echelon in South Brabant communicated with the organizations in occupied Holland. The canoes carried mail mostly, with a few urgently required light stores and an occasional passenger. I gathered that these canoes did not constitute by any means the only traffic upon this route, along which something almost like a regular passenger service was being run by the boatmen of the Biesbosch marshes.

The Germans had posts along either bank of the Waal but they were widely separated and situated alternately upon the two banks, so that none was opposite another. They were also set back some distance from the river bank. Each might have observation over a considerable stretch of river but small craft could run along under the bank on which they stood with a good chance of escaping notice. With expert navigation, therefore, as well as exact knowledge of the location of these posts, using the dead ground under one before crossing the river and then proceeding out of sight of the next on the other side there was quite a good chance of getting a boat down in safety. The river was about a thousand yards wide in the main channel and wider lower down. Patrolling by the Germans was dilatory between posts at night, both on land and water. A few miles further on they ceased to control more than the right bank. With care, therefore, a skilful boatman could slip through these posts until he emerged beyond the last upon the left bank. It was then only a matter of river pilotage — a complicated enough task without lights at night, even in a shallow-draft canoe — over the broad expanse of the Lower Waal to reach some spot lower down in Allied hands. The boatman who was to take me had made a dozen or more safe passages already.

'I hope he will be here soon,' said the big man.

As we sat and listened there was presently to be heard an occasional splash, growing louder, and a slim shape slid into view upon the water.

The big man called and was answered. The dim shape came closer and became a canoe. It was brought into the bank and one of our party held it while a short thick figure got out and talked in low tones with our leader.

'Where are you, sir?' said the big man presently and I came forward. 'This is Piet. He couldn't start the engine. But he's here now and you ought to be off.'

My hand was almost paralysed by the grip of Piet's, huge and hard. I said a quick goodbye to the others and was settled into the canoe, my feet stretched out with the stick between them, a blanket and tarpaulin tucked round me and all the gear packed in. Then to the sound of cheerful 'Goodbyes' and 'Good lucks' we were off.

23

PIET was paddling carefully along the narrow cut in the direction of a dim mass which soon turned into a high wall of reeds. He found a small opening and swung the canoe's nose into it.

The night was darker now. Cloud had gathered. The wind had freshened but it was not uncomfortably cold. The canoe, moving strongly forward under Piet's paddle between banks of rustling reeds, was well trimmed and rode easily. There was little freeboard and it was just possible, from my own low sitting position, to trail a hand in the water without unduly disturbing the trim of the craft. I had always liked doing this and had quite forgotten how pleasant it could be.

I have found out since much more of what was happening there than I knew when I stepped out, a partly new-fledged phoenix, from the house in Sliedrecht and was taken by my guide across the water to the cottage on the shore. The river we had crossed was the Merwede. We were now travelling through a maze of swampy waterways to where a bar of land separated us from one of the broad main channels of the River Waal.

Piet had spoken once or twice in a deep and friendly voice soon after we had set out but he now paddled in silence. From time to time he turned with quick confidence from one narrow reed-lined waterway into another. Soon we came out on to a wider stretch, about the breadth of the Isis at Folly Bridge in Oxford, lined with high dim masses of bending reeds. After about an hour of travel along it Piet began to paddle more cautiously. We moved forward at a slower pace and now and then he stopped while the canoe drifted, swaying a little on more broken water. Piet seemed to be listening. Then, as though satisfied, he would paddle on. Gradually the channel broadened. As the reed banks receded the wind blew more strongly and the movement of the canoe grew more pronounced. Then a long, darker mass appeared before us and the canoe nosed its way into what appeared to be a recess in the irregular stone-faced side of a low bank.

Other hands pulled the canoe in and made it fast, while Piet climbed ashore and helped me out. I was stiff with cold and moved slowly.

A movement on my part to bring some of the kit out with me was checked by Piet.

'No, no,' he said. 'We wait.'

A number of people seemed to be standing about in scattered groups, though there was little enough to be seen in the darkness. From the occasional glimpse of some lighter or darker shape and the odd snatch of low talk blown about us by the wind, however, it was possible to sense the presence there of what was almost a small crowd. There seemed also to be some tension among them and a focussing of interest on our arrival.

Piet led me up the bank, stumbling in the dark. On the top the full strength of the wind met us with startling force. It was blowing really hard. I was conscious of apprehension and a dull disappointment. Would anybody be willing to take our little craft out in conditions like these?

I was led over to the other side where there was partial protection from a groyne. A few feet further down the slope waves slapped angrily on the rocks. White tops showed briefly here and there in the gloom.

'Bad wind,' said Piet. 'Some people wait for boats. Probably no boats come.'

'What shall we do?' I asked.

'We wait,' said Piet and went off again up the slope.

I had the impression that I had been put carefully on one side, away from the other travellers. These, I supposed, would be some of those of whom I had heard earlier, who for personal reasons of greater or less urgency were trying to get through into South Brabant. There would be disappointment for many that night — perhaps for me too, though that would only mean postponement. Who could say what tragedies might not result for others?

I was cramped and stood up to move about a little. The wind blew in great gusts. Stinging drops of water, whether of spray or driven rain, hit me in the face. A shape grew before me, hovered uncertainly and drew close. It was a woman.

'Good luck,' said a low voice in English.

A man appeared beside her.

'Good luck,' said he and a hand found mine and grasped it.

They turned and left me like wraiths as a third came up.

'Good luck, Englishman,' a voice murmured in Dutch.

Another woman's form materialized.

'Goodbye.' The voice was a whisper blown by the wind, barely heard.

Yet another stood beside me, and a hand felt for my arm.

'Look, here are biscuits,' and a little paper packet was thrust into my hand.

Then I was suddenly alone again, moved and uplifted as I had so often been before among the Dutch.

I was upon the groyne and drew the thin coat around me, waiting for what might happen. Was it my fancy, or was the wind now a little less rough?

Piet came.

'We are ready,' he said.

'What of the others?' I asked.

'There will be no boats. They must go back. Come.'

He led me down to the water's edge further along. The canoe had been carried across the dyke and now lay there, moving restlessly under the hands of the men who held her in the shifting waters of the Waal.

I was helped in.

'Goodbye, good luck,' I heard, and strong hands pushed us out while Piet's urgent paddle drove downward and the little craft bobbed crazily over the tops of rolling waves.

The world was now all plunging darkness, wild movement and crashing noise. I held on to what I could find, my face whipped with spray, and bent my mind to becoming one with the moving boat. Time went by, measured in a measureless gulf only by a rhythmic, rolling lurch from crest to trough of black water.

Then it became noticeably easier.

'I can paddle,' said I.

'You are sick' was Piet's gruff reply.

'No,' I insisted. 'I can paddle.'

Without another word Piet passed me up a paddle and I set to, as he seemed to wish, upon the starboard side.

Soon it was smoother and the wind less boisterous. A fleeting star appeared.

I was glad at first of the exertion but very soon the old dark enemy of weakness and fatigue was again upon me. The universe contracted with sickening familiarity into the single grim problem of the next stroke.

I was still paddling when I remembered that I had heard Piet's voice several strokes earlier on.

'Stop now,' it had said. I stopped and pulled in the dripping paddle.

A gentle, rhythmic whisper crept up from below and behind us and the canoe moved forward on its motor.

The night was a little lighter and the wind had dropped to a gusty breeze. Far away on the left hand a flare blossomed in the sky and then dropped slowly out of sight. Now and then a burst of tracer bullets, too far away to be heard, sped across the sky in a soundless curve of intermittent light, a parabola of sparks each in its turn suddenly put out. More and more stars appeared. Sirius was soon before us, calm and bright. It was cold. I loosened the lacing of my boots to help the circulation in feet which were getting numb and wriggled my toes. In my haversack, at hand, with the Delft plate and the letter to the Queen, was Uncle Zwerus's brandy. I took a pull, grateful for its tingling warmth, and passed it back to Piet. We ate a little chocolate and some of the biscuits the unknown well-wisher had given me on the dyke. All the while the soft whisper of the electric motor came up to us and the water rustled by.

The sky was clear in the south-west now. Orion had sunk out of sight but Sirius was still high. I sat in the boat and watched him, my old friend and favourite among the stars, shining strong and steadfast above his troubled reflection in the water. He was a link with many parts of a varied living past and a welcome companion in this twilit waiting time of the present. I remembered again how I used to look for his coming at night in winter as we rode over the cold Transjordan plain. He always lagged behind Orion and when he first appeared over the horizon was wan and pale, growing in glory as he rose. I remember him serene and high, riding in the gentle splendour of a winter night on Galilee, and again and again in deserts as I waited through the night for whatever was to happen, with the chill, creeping desert wind cold on my cheek. I remembered him as I had last seen him in Ede, hanging lambent above the vault of trees that lined the street, like a great lamp upon its chain in a cathedral. Here he was again, bright in light and pale in colour, cool and lovely. I was very glad to see him.

The motor was running more slowly. The accumulator might soon give out. I told Piet I was cold and asked if we could paddle.

'Soon,' said he. 'Don't talk now.'

In silence we ran on, rather more slowly, turning eastward. I realized then, knowing roughly what our course involved, that we must have made several turns in the hour since we left the bar behind us.

We straightened out now upon what the stars showed to be

194

our old course. I could see no more about me than I had seen before. We cruised this way for twenty minutes slowing down perceptibly, then turned out into the stream again. After a few minutes the motor came to a stop.

'It's all right now,' said Piet in a louder, more cheerful voice. 'We can paddle now.'

I remember little of what followed. We seemed to spend a long time paddling. From time to time Piet started the motor again. It would run feebly for about ten minutes and then stop. We would go on paddling.

It was getting lighter now. I could see, as we passed, poles driven into the river bed, while the canoe went in and out between small muddy islands crowned with reeds. I noticed, now that I could see more, a slight current running with us: this must have long been helpful. The appearance of the islands suggested that we were near the river bank. Soon we found ourselves in a kind of channel between a string of small islands on the right hand side with, on the other, a continuous line of what appeared to be land.

'Is that the river bank?' I asked.

'Yes,' said Piet.

Before us there appeared an opening a score or more yards wide. 'We must wait now,' said Piet. 'We have to wait for the other boat.'

This, I supposed, must be the canoe which was bringing Graeme Warrack. I had not realized before that our two journeys were to be made in concert. There had always been much in my time in occupied Holland that I did not know. There would always be much I was sure that I should never discover.

We waited in the cold, almost motionless in the slack water. The shore was no more than twenty paces off, low and swampy. In the growing light I could now distinguish stakes here and there, and one gnarled and wretched-looking tree. Piet kept the canoe steady with an occasional movement of his paddle.

A slight drizzle began to fall.

'Maybe they are there before us,' said Piet. 'But we must wait.'

I do not know how long we waited, while I gazed at the sad-looking tree. It may have been an hour: it could have been five minutes. I was very cold and my feet were numb.

'We'll go in,' said Piet and set to work with his paddle.

The canoe moved on up a channel, between banks now visible on either side, towards where a light showed. Soon we were among other craft and coming up alongside stone steps in what looked to be a small river port. People stood about, dimly seen on the quay. Piet shouted and a couple of them clambered down. I was helped out of the canoe and up the steps, very stiff and awkward. At the top in the dim but growing light, stood a tall figure with something under his arm. This could just have been a telescope but I saw it was a bottle.

'Hullo Shan!' said someone in a friendly, cheerful voice.

I knew this voice. In my confusion I struggled in vain to attach it to any person I could expect to meet here.

But whom could I expect to meet here anyway? What was I thinking of?

'Tony Crankshaw,' said the voice, almost indulgently. 'Eleventh Hussars.'

Of course, of course: this was an old friend, a marvellous big cheerful man. Like all his regiment he was a great operator in armoured cars. We had met last in the Western Desert two years before — or was it two thousand?

'We've been expecting you,' he said. 'Have a drop of brandy.'

I had arrived, after a journey by water from Sliedrecht of about twelve miles, all told, at the little river port of Lage Zwaluwe, where the main waters of the rivers Maas and Waal met to flow in a broad channel to the sea.

24

THE 11th Hussars with their armoured cars were holding lightly a long stretch of the south bank of the Lower Waal, where the river was very broad and there was little likelihood of German attack. This was a time of rest, for much of the regiment at any rate, between one period of high pressure and another. It was wonderfully comforting to know I was among them. There was perhaps no other regiment in the army which was better known and liked in mine than the 11th Hussars. If I could not step ashore into the hands of my own regiment — which would be too much to ask — it was at least for me a good second best, and a great enough and marvellous surprise at that, to be received by the 11th, Prince Albert's Own.

We crossed the quay to a house.

'Another canoe came in a little while back,' said Tony Crankshaw.

The door opened and there before me was the great bulk of Graeme Warrack, the big man, full of warmth and cheer.

'Hullo, hullo,' he roared, his face alight with pleasure, 'here he is! The little man at last! We wondered where you were, God bless you! Come in now and get warm. How is the old tum and all? Have some whisky! Plenty of medical comforts now. Wonderful stuff!'

He had my arm in a bear grip, leading me in. I blinked in bright hissing lamplight. There was a haze of tobacco smoke and a stove. Around the stove there were men sitting or standing in khaki battle dress. It was all hard to believe. Upon tables, walls and windowsills were maps, steel helmets, the woollen hats we called caps-comforter, army greatcoats and enamel plates. Rifles stood around and there was web equipment and bedding on the floor. I sat down upon a kitchen chair surrounded once more by the familiar and comfortable jumble of the British army in the field. I was amongst my own people again.

Piet came in and we looked at each other with interest, in the light, for the first time. He wore a blue fisherman's jersey and long sea boots and under a cloth cap his lined face looked brown and hard. It was a determined face but good and friendly.

We talked a little, with steaming mugs of tea before us, and I did what I could to thank him.

He was worried. A canoe with Lipmann Kessel in it was long overdue. He was going to take his own back alone to search for it. The weather looked like being wet now and he had no coat. I offered him my own sad gabardine Gestapo coat. He thanked me diffidently but thought a soldier's greatcoat might be better. They willingly gave him one. He buttoned himself into it, shook my hand, and was gone.

Graeme was tremendously at home, with his great laugh tumbling round him. Tony Crankshaw stood and looked on, asking a question now and then with interest and amusement on the long, humorous face with its bold nose, but he was also busy with other things. Soldiers came and went and a sergeant was telephoning in a corner.

I sat and talked a little, as far as I remember, but of what we talked I do not know. I only know that I was wondering, at times, if I were there at all and not just dreaming still. At other times I began to wonder if I had ever really been anywhere else.

Then Tony gathered me up, with my stick in my hand and my haversack and pack, and took me off in a jeep to the billet occupied by another old friend, Martin Grant-Thorold, who was now the Lieutenant Colonel commanding this regiment. Martin was away. I crawled like an automaton into his bed, and slept.

Next day brought me back a little further into a world I had known before, at once familiar and astonishingly strange. I was driven off in an army car. The officer who took me, urbane and friendly, a typical 11th Hussar, talked quite naturally of things he thought might be of interest to us both. There was good wild fowling to be had here he told me, and the pheasant shooting had been great. I heard from him of the whereabouts of many friends.

What struck me almost with awe, as we drove, was what I saw around me. There was military traffic everywhere. Where I had just come from, on the enemy's side, where I had been in fact only a few hours before, the roads by day were almost empty. Only in the dusk did the lines of ramshackle lorries appear, well spaced out, with foliage tied over them for better concealment. I remembered the nondescript carts drawn by thin horses, beside which morose Germans stumbled, dressed in a mixture of military and civilian clothes.

That was only yesterday. Here, today, on this side of the river, great groups of new and prosperous-looking motor trucks filled the roads in close convoy or stood about in the open, bold as brass. It was easy to see here who had mastery in the air. Those distant days were clearly now forgotten when we on our side had been vulnerable to air attack and had been driven to extreme precautions to avoid it.

From the apparently endless quantities of new equipment, the well-fed faces of the troops in their new-looking uniforms and the bounding air of confidence over everyone and everything it was easy to see where final victory would be. Victory was a plant which, whenever it might come into flower here, could never flourish at all in the grim and poverty-stricken atmosphere of the army I had just left on the other side. One telling sign of a completely different situation was that, whereas in occupied Holland the German soldiers eked out their own scant resources by preying on the populace, and the troops were everywhere to be seen with bits of civilian clothing or domestic equipment in their use, the exact opposite was the case here. It was the civilians now who were to be seen dressed in pieces of army uniform, in battle dress trousers or blouses, in army socks and boots, or khaki shirts and sweaters. All the while the children flocked around the soldiers like seagulls and were given chocolate by them, and biscuits, while the elders stood about and contentedly smoked the soldiers' cigarettes.

I was taken to a military unit concerned with the handling of escapers. Here they gave me clothing and anything else I needed and I began to put in hand all those things that I had been commissioned to do upon the other side. Here too I was visited by a Canadian surgeon. He turned over in his hand with a thoughtful look the field card from the Field Ambulance in St. Elizabeth's Hospital, which I still had. Having dressed the places round my middle he clapped on them a marvellous great piece of elastoplast, thick and wide. I thought of the endless winding and unwinding of the mass of grubby bandages he was now, almost in disgust, casting away, and how they always slipped down when I walked or sawed wood, and fell clear away when I bicycled. What would I not have given then for a great broad stretch of elastoplast like this, taken so casually now from a roll almost as big as if it were linoleum for a corridor. Nothing in the richness all around made a deeper impression on me than this.

Here too I was reached by a message from my old American

199

airman friend, Major Joel Crouch (or was he a lieutenant colonel then?) who had dropped me by parachute so often in the past. He had miraculously heard in England that I was out and was now offering to come with a C.47 to any airfield in Europe to bring me home.

Next day, on Monty's orders, I was brought to Headquarters 21st Army Group, there to be received with the sharp eye and the friendly welcome I knew so well. Monty gave me a dinner of a sort I had almost forgotten. There were oysters and other marvellous things to eat and a good bottle of wine. The ration ran to more than six hundred calories here.

'I suppose you wonder why I am in a house and not in a caravan,' said Monty as he greeted me before dinner in his mess.

I was indeed about to ask him that. He had become a caravan dweller in the desert, where tents were regarded as inefficient and time-consuming inducements to immobility. Even when 8th Army moved into places where there were houses, old habits persisted and we retained our inclination to live in caravans. Monty made rather a virtue of it.

'It's my doctor,' said Monty. 'He makes me. But come along. Have some of this cold tea stuff. Some of you chaps seem to like it.'

He pushed over a sherry decanter. The thin, high voice was just the same and he did not appear to have changed much in other respects either.

It was very pleasant to be in an agreeable room, with good food and wine, in good company. This was the first time I had been in a comfortably appointed house, except briefly in the middle of a battle or as a fugitive afterwards, since I had left my own in England.

The Army Group Commander was in capital form. He did, however, bring out again the outrageous old story of the two young officers who had argued with him in his caravan at Burg el Arab, where 8th Army Headquarters had been located before the battle of Alamein.

'What were you both at the time? Full Colonels?'

'Only bogus Lieutenant Colonels, I'm afraid.'

'Well, I was a rather junior officer too. I was only an Army Commander then.' Monty again!

'High words were exchanged,' he said. 'High words! You and young David Stirling were rude: you positively hammered the table at me.' He went on to say that he had asked for me to command an armoured brigade in 8th Army next day, possibly forgetting that at his own instance I was even then beginning to raise the 4th Parachute Brigade at Kabrit, in the Suel Canal zone.

'Well!' said a charming young member of the Field Marshal's personal staff, a captain in a very polished cavalry regiment, 'Let that be a lesson to us all: I for one am never going to be polite to anyone again!'

A familiar world was materializing around me again. The following morning, having done all I could at HQ. 21st Army Group to carry out the tasks given me by people in the Dutch resistance and having seen old friends there like Bill Williams, Monty's Intelligence Brigadier, I was flown in the Army Group Commander's aeroplane back to England.

On my arrival at Northolt airfield I got to a telephone and, as a result of previous inquiries, found Colin Harkess ninety miles away at the other end, again in that part of England from which we had all set out for Holland nearly six months before. I passed him a short message. In little more than an hour, as I stood waiting by the control tower, a C.47 with U.S.A.A.F. markings touched down and out of it when it came to rest bundled Joe Crouch with a bounding dog, together with another old American air force friend from those who had helped to take us across. I thought the three of them would pull me apart. Almost at once Joe took off again, with all of us aboard, and a well remembered countryside sloped quickly away below us as we talked and laughed around Joe at the controls until, in almost no time at all, we were at Cottesmore aerodrome and I was being met by the person with whom above all others I had most longed to be.

In a few minutes more I was in my own house in Rutland, by my own fireside, with a joy that was not in the slightest lessened by the memory of the sense of inevitability with which I had long looked forward to my homecoming. Soon mixed feelings settled into a steady awareness that I was really and truly now at home. I called a telephone number in London. It was arranged that the B.B.C. broadcast to occupied Holland that night, on 7th February 1945, should include the message 'The Grey Goose has gone'.

25

My wife, on the day of my return, was within a week or so of becoming a widow, at least from the official point of view, for I had been posted 'wounded and missing' long enough for the automatic sequel 'presumed dead' to be now not far away. The letter sent out by the hand of Gerald Lathbury had arrived but had come through channels so sensitive from a security point of view that its contents could not be made widely known. There had also been a hint or two since then to give added hope but nothing more. On the long drawn-out fear that had preyed upon my home, of which I had imagined much and now learned more, I will not dwell. It was something that has darkened many households and does so still, in many places, and there would not everywhere be a happy return, like mine, to draw the curtain aside.

A day or two after my arrival a telegram was delivered to the door. I opened it. I had in fact been waiting for it.

'You will be pleased to hear,' the telegram said, 'that your husband is in safe hands and will be with you soon.' I was grateful for this documentary evidence of official concern, glad that the aeroplanes of Monty and Joe Crouch had outstripped it.

Widowhood for a soldier's wife meant serious financial loss. When the husband is killed his pay stops. So also, in those days, did the marriage allowance to his wife. I recognized the unkind logic here but wondered whether I was still in time to prevent this from happening to us.

On my first visit to London, which for many reasons had to be soon, I went to the desk in Cox & King's branch of Lloyd's Bank where my pay was handled.

'Hackett?' said the man in the bank, who was a stranger to me, turning over the pages of a great book.

'Initials? Regiment? Number?'

I had to look the number up in a little book of my own, for I was still not used to having a personal number, introduced for officers only since the outbreak of war. I always forgot it.

'Acting Brigadier, commanding 4th Parachute Brigade?' he said.

The approach to final identification clearly gave him pleasure.

'That's it,' said I.

He looked up from the book and closed it.

'Wounded and missing,' he pronounced. The customer's query had it seemed been answered.

There was a pause.

'I came about several months' back pay,' I said, perhaps a little diffidently.

'I can't give you any pay,' he said. 'You're missing.'

'I thought we had just cleared that up,' I said.

'Of course you're here,' he said, 'and I'm very glad to see you naturally. But under the rules we can't pay anyone who's officially missing. I'm afraid that until we're told by the War Office that you're no longer missing we can't give you any pay.'

He assured me, however, that until they heard that I was dead my wife's marriage allowance would go on. Then with a friendly goodbye he turned elsewhere.

There were urgent things to attend to of a less personal nature and upon these I had begun to work without delay. I had much to pass on in the War Office and elsewhere about the work of the Resistance in Holland and of the activities of our own people in their manifold organizations (too many, in my opinion) among them. There were matters of organization and supply of personnel. I had seen it all at work at both ends and with very recent experience of what was going on in clandestine operations in the field was able, I hope, to help clear up some misunderstandings. Special operators in secret services are also people. They have problems about pay and promotion and allowances and things of that sort just like anyone else. Their special difficulty lies in their remoteness and the tenuous nature of their communications. For security reasons radio traffic must be confined to operational essentials. A grievance that could be cleared up in a short conversation can, with no chance to air it, fester on for months.

What I had to do in London took some days but it was urgent. Only when I could do no more would I agree to go into a hospital. I was allowed a choice of hospitals and chose the Radcliffe Infirmary in Oxford. It would be good, when the time came to emerge, to find myself in Oxford again.

At some time in the future, I was sure, there would be a resolution of the pattern of events in the past few months, a decisive drawing together of the threads. How this was to come about I did not know. Only time would show that. I would have to wait and could rest now. This was welcome, for I was very tired.

There was not much to be done for my injuries. The abdomen, after Lipmann Kessel's astonishing surgery, was doing well. The pierced thigh only needed slow and careful treatment. This would take time, though I was told that there was damage to nerve and muscle which might never be fully repaired. More than surgical treatment, however, what I really needed was a chance for overtaxed resources to restore themselves. How much I had overdrawn upon them and how far the tensions of my recent life had now relaxed I had no immediate means of knowing. A ludicrous little incident gave me something to go by.

Tired though I was I chafed at being kept in bed in the hospital and asked whether I might not get dressed and go out. A kind young house surgeon, who had been told as much of the story as security considerations allowed, and had asked many questions, looked at me quizzically.

'You might not like it much just yet,' he said, and added something about my having let my hair down. In the end permission was given and I was allowed out.

After no more than a week in bed my legs were strangely weak. I could only dress with difficulty. I left the little room and made my way, with some misgiving now, to the hospital gate, which opened on to a road not, in those days, a very busy one. Everything outside was huge, noisy and menacing. Great violent motor cars swept along their predatory path as though they longed to snatch me off the pavement. I began to cross the road but had taken no more than a step when an enormous red bus, which seemed to have been lying in wait just for that, came charging down like a roaring dragon, straight for me. I stood staring at this great red monster, rooted to the spot in horror, gripped with panic. I could not move while it bore down upon me, until with a prodigious effort of will I managed the backward step which took me to safety on the pavement, there to watch as the bus trundled sedately by. I was trembling in a cold sweat and suddenly convulsed with laughter. Then I walked weakly back to the little hospital bed and crawled gratefully in again, sharing the amusement of the young doctor when he heard of my adventure later.

Before long I was out again, better able to meet the outside world, living as an outpatient in my own college, which was New College, fortified with good port. Soon I was allowed home.

Now at last, for everything must as far as possible happen

at the right time and place, I was enlarged, like a horse put out to pasture, into *Paradise Lost*. My wife had given me for my homecoming the Oxford edition of Milton's poetry, in the wartime reprint of Beeching's careful text, with the poet's own spelling, the facsimile plates, the appendices and translations and Skeat's *Reader's Guide*. During my time in the Radcliffe I had put this carefully by. I had found a Homeric grammar and was learning by heart bits of the *Iliad*, which I had never known well and now saw a chance to know better. Milton was for me to read at home.

With *Paradise Lost*, when I was at home again, I roamed about at large in a very rich field, with the added pleasure that had come from putting it off, only wishing that this splendid book had been with me in Torenstraat. It had to be conceded to the 'Gems' that the editor had culled his passages from among Milton's very best. It is nonetheless frustrating to be confined to extracts. The important thing is to be able to stop reading Milton when you want to, not when you must. This I could now do. It was also important to me to discover, without surprise, that like other great poets (Wordsworth came quite naturally at once to mind) Milton could at times be very dull.

In my home General Roy Urquhart came to see me. I had long been looking forward to this. There could have been no one in the 1st Airborne Division without the highest regard for Roy Urquhart, both as an officer and as a man. I have never seen anyone show up better in a battle.

I remembered him in his divisional headquarters in the cellars below the Hartenstein Hotel late in the battle, when pressure on the bridgehead perimeter was high and it was now clear that 30 Corps would never reach us. He was bound, he said, to send a signal telling higher command exactly how things were. The outlook for the remnants of his division in its thinly held position was bad. It would not be going too far to call it hopeless. There was no food, little ammunition, a growing shortage of effective weapons, no armour and very few anti-tank weapons, while further casualties were adding rapidly to numbers already beyond the resources of his medical services.

He did not want, he said, to overstate the case and produced a draft signal for comment by Pip Hicks and me and by one or two officers on his staff. I remembered thinking, as I read it, that this was a model of what, in a situation so difficult, such a communication should be. It was short, calm and sensible, giving all the essential facts and suggesting that the withdrawal of what was left of the Division, if no early relief was in prospect, should now be seriously considered. That was all.

It is always hard, looking back on events in retrospect, to recall what it was like when you were there — the stresses, the noise, the weariness, the fear — and harder still to imagine what it was like if you were not. It is scarcely possible to put a message written then, and read or reread now, back into its proper context. I can only remember hoping, as I handed this one back to Urquhart and said that I thought it was just about right, that any one of the rest of us would have been able to send the same sort of signal and wondering how many of us could have done so. Pip could have, and Charles Mackenzie the chief general staff officer of the Division (who may have drafted this one, though it was very much Roy's signal), and also Robert Loder-Symonds commanding the Division's artillery and Eddie Myers its chief engineer and Graeme Warrack the doctor and perhaps a few more. There were men of high courage and great endurance still around, possibly even men as good as Urquhart, but there were none better.

It was very good to see this kind, stouthearted man again. Before he came to my home, however, an odd thing had happened. I had found a walking stick in the hall, the very brother of the one with the 'U' carved on it in my hand that had come home with me. The stick in the hall must be the new one I had bought in Oakham. I had left it here, not taken it as I had supposed to my brigade headquarters at Knossington. The unseemly suggestion I had made to General Roy, so roundly rejected by him, that he had taken it off by mistake and left me a worse one in its place, rested only on a foolish mistake.

I now gave him back his own. It had been with me since I first took it up in the room in the hospital in Arnhem, leaving poor Kenneth Smyth alone and going out with Piet to an uncertain future. It has been most useful, but it had also been a talisman and a token—almost like a staff or badge of office, to be returned now on the completion of a mission to the hand under which the office had been held.

'You keep it,' said Roy. 'It's yours now: keep it as a souvenir.'

It had served its purpose. It no longer held for me the same high significance it had had in the recent past. I carelessly left it later in a taxi-cab outside the Cavalry Club and never saw it again.

Time was going by. I had made certain preliminary arrangements and now awaited developments in Allied operations in Holland.

Meanwhile another pressing task arose. I had sent out from occupied Holland with Gerald Lathbury the recommendations, written in St. Elizabeth's Hospital in pencil on what paper the Dutch nurses could find me, for the awards for gallantry I thought had been earned in my brigade. There had been no one else to write these, either then or later.

The brigade had come out on the withdrawal a small remnant, not more than a hundred strong. Of the three battalion commanders two were dead and one a prisoner. Of the three seconds-in-command only one had come back, and one of the three adjutants. Out of the hundred-odd officers who dropped on the Ginkelsche Heide some thirty-five were dead and many more were prisoners. The casualties included almost all the company commanders.

Unit organization in 4th Parachute Brigade, therefore, could be said to have vanished. Even if it had not, impetus and guidance in this important matter was lacking where you would normally expect to find it — at brigade headquarter level. There had been in all these months no brigadier, and of Brigade Headquarters and the officers attached to it the Brigade Major, Bruce Dawson, was dead, his successor for a day, brave Tiny Madden was dead, George Blundell the Intelligence Officer was dead, Jimmy James was dead, and of the other members of that close-knit band of friends four were prisoners, two wounded and only one staff-officer, Jasper Booty, and Colin Harkess the Brigade R.A.S.C. officer, were at home and whole. Small wonder that nothing had happened.

Gerald had brought my recommendations carefully back as he had promised, and put them into the machine. Nothing more was heard. I learned later that as they had not been submitted on the proper form there was nothing that *could* happen! They could not go forward as they were and if they were transcribed onto the proper form there was no originator to sign them. They had been put on one side and then, I think, been lost. One or two awards had been recommended by others outside the brigade, by the General himself in some cases — but no one could originate those that had to come from me.

I set to, therefore, with General Roy's encouragement and gathered from wherever I could the material I needed for another set — entered on the right form this time. Much correspondence, many visits and a great deal of inquiry was needed before the work was done and it took a long time. In the end the outcome was for the most part fair enough, though I sorely missed the advice of some who were not there to give it.

Long before this necessary duty was discharged, however, I heard what I was waiting for.

26

A TELEPHONE message came from London. Canadian and British troops had advanced to Ede and beyond. The Germans had been driven from the town. My friends in Torenstraat were free and I could now go to them.

I quickly got together the bundles standing ready for my departure. There were packets of tea (real tea!), coffee and sugar—none of them plentiful in England then but gladly given in considerable quantity by kind friends in Rutland. There was a consignment of tinned goods from similar sources as large as could be handled. There were clothes and other presents and the precious letters from my family at home to that other family in Holland. I did not forget what I had borrowed and must now return, including the great white sweater and the parti-coloured underwear. An army car brought me to an airfield and soon I had taken off in an Oxford aircraft and was flying with my cargo back to Holland.

I was reading as we went the little I still had left to read of the twelfth and last book of *Paradise Lost*, where Michael was leading the first man and woman away from Paradise, one by either hand. Over the English Channel I read the last few lines:

> '*The world was all before them, where to choose*
> *Thir place of rest, and Providence thir guide:*
> *They hand in hand with wandering steps and slow,*
> *Through Eden took thir solitarie way.*'

I closed the book as we crossed into Belgium. Wisps of smoke were rising in the West from still beleaguered coastal towns in France. An hour or two later we were landing at an operational airfield in Holland, where another army car waited, and in the afternoon I came to Ede.

It was spring. The roadside trees, in full late leaf when first we had come here in September, soon to be stripped bare in the storms of a long dark winter, were alive and green again. April winds chased high cloud in a blue sky and there was warmth in the sun.

More than winter had gone. The transformation in the

scene around me was greater, more tumultuous, more joyous than any that could be brought about by the coming of spring alone.

The Germans, withdrawing westwards, were not far beyond the town. Allied guns were making a tremendous din as they battered the rearguard. But the Germans might have been on another planet for all that anyone seemed to care. The houses were open, up and down the streets, and there were flags everywhere. Gay bunting, long hidden, flaunted warm orange with the tricolour of Holland. Hand-painted Union Jacks sprouted in shop windows upon little sticks. The streets, so long nearly deserted, were now thronged. Where only a few sad elderly people could be seen before, moving with slow step and downcast eye, or young women hurrying along with anxious faces, there were now people of all ages everywhere, looking about them as though they had never seen the place before, smiling, laughing, shouting to each other. A leaden pall of mourning had lain over this town when last I saw it. Now everything was as gay as a village wedding.

There was a breathless excitement and astonishment every-where around to which I too fell a prey. This was indeed the Groote Straat, there was the church tower, there the post office where Aunt Ann and I had posted the leaflets, and there was the photographer's shop. But could all this really be true? Was I really driving along, dressed as a British officer, open and unafraid, looking about me as curiously and freely as I pleased? Where were the shabby uniforms of sombre grey, past which the girls had walked so proudly with averted head? There were none. Instead I saw a ruddy-faced sergeant in khaki, with a child's hand in each of his, and a laughing group at the tailboard of an army lorry.

Meanwhile tanks and guns were moving through, with an endless stream of military transport, head to tail. Occasionally a soldier would wave his hand from the turret of a tank and there would be a sudden little cheer from the roadside. Here and there were khaki-clad groups of soldiers walking in the street. Little Dutch boys and girls would come up to them with smiling faces.

'Hullo Tommy!' they would say, at once shy and friendly, drawling out the unfamiliar syllables.

'Hullo Tommy!'

It was like a greeting to a close relative from far away, someone you have heard about all your life and now saw for the first time.

With the certainty of a sleep-walker I directed the British army driver along the High Street, past the bookshop whose owner had lent the shoes for my birthday, where Mary and I had later spent the day in hiding, up the narrow opening of Torenstraat and out into the little open place in front of our house. There before me was the fence of white palings whose gate I had opened so often, the shape of whose latch I can still feel in my fingers. There was the little house, with the tidy curtains to the sitting-room below, and the room above out of whose window from my bed I had watched the last leaf on the tree. In the door stood Aunt Mien.

There was no surprise upon her serene face as she came to meet me, only shining happiness, but she was in tears and laughter at the same time as I embraced her. Then her sister Ann, my dear friend, and Mary's mother, and sweet Mary herself joined us, everybody laughing and crying and talking at once. Then Aunt Cor, summoned from the chemist's shop, rode up on her bicycle at a great pace, her face warm and beaming, and last of all John came. He was grinning with delight and looked a proud and happy man as he grasped my hand.

'Mr. Hackett,' he said, 'we are very pleased to see you again!'

Inside the house everything was exactly the same, neat and spotless, the chairs, the little mats, the brass ornaments, the stove.

'The wood has lasted since you left us,' said Aunt Cor, 'and we had some for our friends too.'

I went out and rummaged among my packages. We would divide these up later. All I wanted now was some coffee. Aunt Mien whisked it away from me at once and soon we were sitting around the big table again, with little cakes and biscuits and my very own mug, 'Mr. Hackett's mug' with the picture on it, before me.

The only difference I could see in the inner room was that the wireless set now stood boldly out upon a table.

'Did you get my message?' I said. 'Did you hear about the Grey Goose?'

'Three times,' said Aunt Ann. 'We were so pleased and thankful.'

Aunt Mien's merry laugh pealed out again.

'We danced a jig around the table,' said she 'every time! I do wish you could have seen us. Oh dear!'

And she laughed so heartily that she had to wipe her eyes again.

Then there was fine conversation, the gossip of a family in a troubled time when one of their number has been away and come back again. I heard how John had been caught and put into forced labour on the Rhine defences and had got away; of further narrow escapes for Menno; of all that was happening in the brothers' families: of how the hiding places under the earth were being opened up now and their household treasures brought out, and how Uncle Zwerus had at last been able to let his hair grow.

There was much for me to do. The presents were unpacked and little piles made for this family and that. There were visits to be paid and, as the result of messages sent around, other visits to be received. While John put the finishing touches, from his better knowledge, to the rough division of the things I had brought, I explored the house. Everything was the same. The upstairs landing was festooned with washing above the trapdoor to the hiding place. I lifted the carpet and the boards and got in again, remembering our practices when it had been more difficult for me to move than it was now. My own little room was the same, with the sampler over the bed, and there came back to me again the cold bite of dark winter mornings, when the thermometer which was still hanging on the wall showed ten or twelve degrees below freezing and I was dressing for a walk in the snow. In the barn outside the kitchen door, with its methodical rows of drawers, the nails here, the screws there, the axe and saws lay where I had used them. I felt again the sharp cold on my hands and smelt the fresh pine sawdust as I sawed away, doing a little more each day. I thought that I could almost see, through the little window, past Aunt Mien's curtains, the yellow uniform of the man of the Todt Organization at the end of the garden.

Aunt Cor came out on some errand as I was standing on the tiny grass plot before the summer house, in the spring sunshine. I was looking at the back of the house from which the Feldgendarmerie had moved only the other day.

'There is no butter on your head now, Mr. Hackett,' said Aunt Cor.

But there was little time for reverie. Dominee Blauw was there to see me, looking frail and pinched in the same worn suit with the frayed collar, but with an air of quiet happiness about him. We sat for a time in the Voorkamer, on either side of the window past which the German soldiers used to stroll, in comfortable talk.

Later when we made our quiet farewells and he had gone, I

knew what he wanted. It was the *Encyclopaedia of Ethics*, in English, together with some other books. He was proposing soon to start reading for his Doctorate of Divinity and needed them. When I was back in England again I enlisted Basil Blackwell's help. He could get most of the other books, though one had to come from India, but he pulled a grave face over the Encyclopaedia. It was not only an expensive work but it was also long out of print. It might be years before a set turned up. But I believe no one who has followed this story will be any more surprised than I was (though I was indeed delighted) when within a few days the library of a Divinity don, lately dead, was disposed of and a watchful eye spotted just such a set among his books. Basil Blackwell bought it. Having heard the story he insisted, in a manner characteristic of him, that it should be a gift from me to the Dominee with no payment on the part of anyone but himself. A day or two later, through the kindness of friends in London, a Mosquito bomber made its swift passage to Holland carrying nothing more lethal than a parcel of books, to be sent post haste, by special messenger, to Dominee Blauw in Ede.

I am digressing, for this was still to happen, and come back to my own visit.

After the meeting with the Pastor I paid a little call on Colonel Boerei and his wife, that kindly and indomitable pair, in the house I lived in on the Station Road with the holes in it which my own bombs had made. I called also on Dr. Krayenbrink and his new wife.

It was quicker now with a car. I remembered how long we had taken on the first short walk to the Boereis' house that night, when I was still sick, but had had to move from Toren-straat. I was back in Torenstraat from Stationsweg in a few minutes now, promising myself longer visits later to these other friends. The promises were to bear fruit but that is no part of my story now.

I went to see Menno's family in Brouwerstraat, to thank them and their gallant son. Back in our own house I met Bill Wildeboer again, robust and shrewd, in the same room where I had seen him last and we had laid our plans for the escape attempt I was never to make, the room in which I had before that tried to lessen the pain of failure over the second mass escape.

I met in that day more people than I can remember and in the evening was back once more in the peace of Torenstraat.

Then came the uncles. The entry of Zwerus de Nooij was a

triumph. We all stood up and in the courtly exchange of greetings that followed I found myself raised a rung or two towards the old gentleman's own dignity. We made little speeches to each other. There was warmth in his twinkling eye.

'Look at my head,' he said and bowed it. 'My hair grows again. The war is over,' and he laughed with us over a glass of the excellent wine I already knew so well.

Aunt Mien hovered round, all grace and merriment, Aunt Ann spoke with her kind and friendly gravity, Aunt Cor's wit flashed in and out. We sat down together to supper again as one family, and read the Bible again together after it, Aunt Mien reading aloud in Dutch and each following in his own Bible. Before me was the English Authorized Version, brought from the same place as ever, put in front of me as usual and restored to the cupboard again when the reading was over.

Everything was just as it had been before but somehow a hundred times better.

I found Aunt Mien looking at my uniform and smiling.

'What is it?' I asked her.

'My wish,' said she, 'it came out all right. I couldn't tell you of course. It wouldn't have come true then.'

'Oh Mien,' said Aunt Ann. 'How can you say such things!'

'I think I knew what it was,' said I, 'even then. It was to see me back here soon in uniform, with all that that would mean. Wasn't it?'

'Yes, that was it,' said Aunt Mien. 'And here you are.'

I went up to my little room and slept again under the embroidered sampler of the Sleeping Princess on the wall.

Next day we said our farewells at the garden gate, and as we stood together a sturdy little boy came up, fair haired and blue eyed. It was Pietje, from next door.

'Hallo Tommy,' he said cheerfully, in the same slow voice I had heard from the others the day before.

'Pietje!' said Aunt Ann. 'Look again. Don't you recognize Mijnheer Pietersen?'

Pietje approached us with a doubtful air and looked more closely. Dawning recognition chased disbelief from his round blue eye.

'So!' said Pietje at last. He looked around him with satisfaction, in all the solemnity of a five year old.

'So!' he said, 'Mijnheer Pietersen has become a Tommy!'

POSTSCRIPT

REAL people do not cease to exist when a story in which they figure comes to an end. The people in this story were all real and it may be thought appropriate to say a little more about them and perhaps to add some other observations as well.

Of the four ladies of No. 5 Torenstraat three are now at rest. Miss Cor still lives in Ede but not in Torenstraat. The house, where I was often able to visit them in the first few years after the war, has now disappeared, demolished to make way for what were considered necessary improvements in the town.

John Snoek took Holy Orders in the Reformed Church. He had had no intention, before the events I have described, of taking orders and was scarcely even a practising Christian. He has now told me that reflection on his experiences in the last winter of the war had much to do with his decision. He married not long afterwards; of his five children two are already of university age. His ministry caused him later on to spend some years in Tiberias, the town beside the Sea of Galilee where my wife and I first met. It brought him then to the World Council of Churches in Geneva. He last wrote to me from Holland, where he has now settled happily into a parish near Rotterdam.

John's sister Mary, active as a Christian missioner and social worker, largely in North Holland, has remained unmarried. She and her brother, with other members of their family (brother Wim for instance) and of mine have come together since those days whenever we could. We have always kept in touch. John and his dear wife came recently to visit us in England.

The de Nooij family business has prospered and Menno, as resourceful and engaging as ever, has prospered with it. He too is married, with a family like John's, now growing up.

Elsa Caspers, hampered by ill health, completed her medical studies after the war and entered on a career in practice, which was always her ambition. A friendship developed between Elsa and my own family (I have a daughter who qualified in medicine) which has given us all much pleasure. We too have often met, in Holland and in England. Elsa has had much to do in Holland since the war with the care of those who worked for

215

the Resistance. Once we met by chance, neither knowing the other would be there, on the lawn at a Buckingham Palace Garden Party. Elsa had been invited to England with others who had helped in the business of escape, by the Royal Air Force. Perhaps it should be added that she was not baptized 'Elsa' at all. This was her operational name. I got to know her as 'Elsa', however, and so did my family afterwards and that is what she has been between us all, in conversation and in correspondence, ever since.

I began to put this narrative on paper in the year the war ended, during which the first draft of it was almost finished. It seemed to me then on the whole best not to use the actual operational names by which under-cover agents had been known and certainly to avoid use of their real names, even when I knew them. In this final version I have left the names used in the first draft as they were. This is not intended as source material for the historian: that can be found else-where. Nevertheless, for the sake of tidiness, if for no other reason, some of those mentioned can now be more precisely identified.

'Bat' was an agent of MI9 known to them as 'Ham', working with a wireless operator who was called 'Bacon'. I do not know even now what their real names were. 'Sam' was a member of the Belgian S.A.S. Squadron. From September 1944 onwards, under the field name of 'King', he was engaged in an operation known as 'Fabian'. In some accounts of what took place (e.g. Graeme Warrack's *Travel by Dark* (Harvill Press), which is an excellent story) he is referred to as 'Fabian King'. His real name is G. S. Kirschen.

The person I call 'Vandyck' was then known operationally as 'Frans Hals'. His real name was Dignus (or Dick) Kragt. I was very much in Dick's debt and am glad to say that after the war it was possible to regain touch with him too.

The boatman who took me down the river to where my old friends the 11th Hussars were, to be met by a very real person in the shape of Tony Crankshaw, I called in the story as I first wrote it 'Piet' and have left him with that name in this its final version. His real name is Koos Meijer and he still lives by the Biesbosch. I shall not easily forget how much I owe to Koos Meijer.

Twenty years, and even a little more, after the events described in this book I found myself serving in Germany as Commander-in-Chief of the British Army of the Rhine and Commander of the Northern Army Group in NATO—under whose command, incidentally, for training and operations came the First Dutch Corps. This gave me another chance—like those I had made use of in earlier postings to BAOR in other capacities—to see more of my friends in Holland.

The Dutch were then making a film record of the Biesbosch escape route. I was brought in on this as a former client, largely through Elsa. Under Elsa's arrangements the two boatmen who had most to do with my own journey were brought over to see me in H.Q. BAOR, in Germany: Koos Meijer, who had taken me, and his colleague Jan Visser, who had brought down the other canoe that night, the one in which Graeme Warrack arrived. It gave me deep satisfaction to see these two again. Each of them produced a well-preserved empty cigarette packet (once of ten Players) upon which I had signed my own name— the first time I had done that for a good while!—and added the date. They had asked me to do this, as far as I could remember, on the wind-swept dyke that night by the Merwede.

Much has been written, from one point of view or another, on events in Holland after the airborne invasion—perhaps not all of it notable for its accuracy. Lipmann Kessel's *Surgeon at Arms* (Leo Cooper) is well worth reading. He wrote to me soon after the war to say that he was writing a book (for professional reasons under a *nom de plume*) about his experiences as an airborne surgeon and asked whether he could use my stomach. I wrote back: 'My dear fellow, it's *your* stomach. You must do with it what you please.' Kessel, who has been in successful and distinguished surgical practice since then and is now a Professor of Orthopaedic Surgery, wrote a very good account in which he understandably says little of his own achievements. I have mentioned *Travel by Dark* by another 'medicus dilectus', Graeme Warrack. Leo Heaps, the Canadian, has also recently published a book on these events and his own share in them. There are a good many more.

On the battle itself much has also been written, possibly even too much, and I have little doubt that there is more to come. What has appeared so far ranges from sober military analysis through personal reminiscence to highly publicized group-journalism put forward as instant history. I offer no more of a bibliography here about the battle than for the books about the aftermath and would only mention now, in the category of personal reminiscence, a book called *Men at Arnhem* (Corgi), whose author (also using a *nom de plume* for professional reasons) calls himself 'Tom Angus'. In spite of all the changed names I would say, speaking as the anonymous 'Brigadier' in the narrative, that this book gives the best and most truthful account of the fighting in defence of the Oosterbeek perimeter of any that I know. I cannot help wondering how long the author's identity will remain concealed.

In this story of my own I had originally included a good deal of personal reflection and some account of developments in the Dutch Resistance. My publisher advised me that the first was unlikely to interest anyone but me while the second, as I could see for myself, was written too soon after the event to be complete or even reliable. Both have been removed. The second of these topics has now been well covered in M. R. D. Foot's recent book *Resistance* (Eyre Methuen).

Danny McGowan was awarded the Military Cross for his brave work in Holland, which did not cease when we parted in the hospital. He came home with a problem which seemed to him possible in the end to resolve only in one way. He left the priesthood. I recall helping him, as far as I could, to a post caring for young people in Westmorland, from which he later moved on to other useful work for others. He married and — though stricken with polio, which he bore with his usual fortitude — was happy in his family. A deep debt is owed by many people to a good and courageous man in Danny McGowan.

I have in my possession in England the one-volume Shakespeare from which I used to read in Ede and the edition of Scott's verse, both sent to me by John, with de Nooij signatures in them and his own greeting. A kind friend has found for me the 1867 edition of the 'Gems' — quite a rare book now — from which the one I had in Torenstraat was a reprint. I still keep Mijnheer van Dalen's identify card and the deaf button.

*　　*　　*

At the beginning of this book there is a quotation from a passage in St. Matthew's Gospel which seems to me to throw the clearest possible light on what was done by the people into whose care I came in Holland and why they did it. To end by recalling the words that follow, in what was said on Olivet not long before the crucifixion, may also be appropriate.

Then shall the righteous answer him, saying, Lord, when saw we thee an hungred, and fed thee? Or thirsty, and gave thee drink? When saw we thee a stranger and took thee in? or naked, and clothed thee?
Or when saw we thee sick, or in prison, and came unto thee?

And the King shall answer and say unto them, Verily I say unto you, Inasmuch as ye have done it unto one of the least of these my brethren, ye have done it unto me.'